Sabine Fischer, Heiko Pleines, Hans-Henning Schröder (Eds.)

Movements, Migrants, Marginalisation

Challenges of societal and political participation
in Eastern Europe and the enlarged EU

CHANGING EUROPE

Edited by Dr. Sabine Fischer, Dr. Heiko Pleines and
Prof. Dr. Hans-Henning Schröder

ISSN 1863-8716

1   Sabine Fischer, Heiko Pleines, Hans-Henning Schröder (Eds.)
     Movements, Migrants, Marginalisation
     Challenges of societal and political participation in Eastern Europe and the
     enlarged EU
     ISBN 978-3-89821-733-0

FORTHCOMING (MANUSCRIPT WORKING TITLES):

Heiko Pleines, Daniela Obradovic (Eds.)
Civil society groups from the new post-socialist member states in EU governance
ISBN 978-3-89821-750-7

Jochen Tholen, David Lane, Gyorgy Lengyel (Eds.)
Restructuring of the Economic Elites after State Socialism
Recruitment, Institutions and Attitudes
ISBN 978-3-89821-754-5

Sabine Fischer, Heiko Pleines, Hans-Henning Schröder

(Eds.)

MOVEMENTS, MIGRANTS, MARGINALISATION

Challenges of societal and political participation
in Eastern Europe and the enlarged EU

ibidem-Verlag
Stuttgart

Bibliografische Information der Deutschen Nationalbibliothek
Die Deutsche Nationalbibliothek verzeichnet diese Publikation in der
Deutschen Nationalbibliografie; detaillierte bibliografische Daten sind im
Internet über http://dnb.d-nb.de abrufbar.

Bibliographic information published by the Deutsche Nationalbibliothek
Die Deutsche Nationalbibliothek lists this publication in the Deutsche Nationalbibliografie;
detailed bibliographic data are available in the Internet at http://dnb.d-nb.de.

∞

Gedruckt auf alterungsbeständigem, säurefreien Papier
Printed on acid-free paper

ISSN: 1863-8716

ISBN-10: 3-89821-733-7
ISBN-13: 978-3-89821-733-0

© *ibidem*-Verlag
Stuttgart 2007

Printed in Germany

Contents

Foreword

This book presents the results of the Changing Europe Summer School on 'Justice as a societal and political matter. Equality, social and legal security as conditions for democracy and the market' that took place in Berlin in July 2006. The Summer School, organised by the Research Centre for East European Studies at the University of Bremen, brought together more than 30 young scientists from all over the world who work on issues related to Central and Eastern European nations and the enlarged EU. Summer School participants were selected with the help of international referees.

The participants in the Summer School, mostly doctoral students from the disciplines of political science, sociology, economics and law, all presented their current research work. Some of the best Summer School contributions were selected for publication in this edited volume.

The 2006 Summer School held in Berlin represents the first in a series. In the years to come, the Changing Europe Summer School will become a regular event, taking place in a different European capital every year. The best contributions will be published in an annual edited volume. This first collection ushers in the Changing Europe book series.

This book would not have been possible without ample support. First of all, our thanks go to the participants in the Summer School, who, with their enthusiasm and knowledge, made it an unforgettable event. We would also like to thank all the referees who supported us in the selection of appropriate participants. We are additionally grateful to all those who helped to organise the Summer School and the book production, namely Hilary Abuhove (language editing), Christopher Gilley (language editing), Julia Kusznir (organisational support), Matthias Neumann (technical editing), Susanne Schaller (Summer School organisation) and Tobias Schulz (final editing).

Last but not least, we want to express our gratitude to the Volkswagen Foundation, which generously supports the Changing Europe Summer Schools.

Bremen and Berlin, January 2007
The editors

Sabine Fischer, Heiko Pleines, Hans-Henning Schröder

Introduction

The end of socialism posed a historical challenge to European societies. The former socialist Central and East European countries were faced with what has been called a 'triple transformation': mutually dependent changes in the political, economic and social spheres. At the same time, the old EU member states had to develop strategies to react to these developments and integrate former socialist societies. This post-socialist transformation of Europe coincided with a number of broader trends in the political, economic and social spheres, which are often collectively referred to as globalisation. Success or failure to adapt to these changes creates winners and losers. The focus of this edited volume is on various groups of 'losers' and the challenges they face as a result of their marginalisation.

By looking through the prisms of political and social movements, migrants, property restitution and social marginalisation, the contributions in this book analyse societal and political participation in various European contexts. The first part deals with political participation. The chapters by Elke Fein and Alla Samoletova revolve around the Russian party system. Together they describe the constraints that limit political participation in the post-Soviet regime.

The second part presents a comparative perspective on strategies for representing societal interests in different countries. The contribution by Susanne Schatral and the chapter by Noémi Kakucs and Róbert Sata look at efforts to combat violence against women in Russia, Hungary and Great Britain. The following chapter by Diana Schmidt examines civic initiatives against corruption in Russia with regard to overlapping international, national and local contexts.

The third part turns the readers' attention to the old EU member states. The integration of migrants in a climate of globalisation and post-socialist transformation is one of the main challenges confronting the EU today. Oksana Morgunova interviewed Latvian migrant workers in Scotland to analyse the cultural conflicts occurring between immigrants and their new social environment. David Duncan goes on to assess the concept of multiculturalism based upon the Dutch example. These two researchers present migrants' forays into societal participation from a bottom-up and a top-down perspective. Aleksandra Wyrozumska broadens the spectrum to include the issue of citizenship within the EU. She presents the stakeholder model of citizenship, which aims to reconcile different loyalties in a multi-national and multi-ethnic context.

The fourth part of the volume returns to a familiar challenge for post-socialist societies. The issue of restitution of property expropriated under communist rule provokes serious debate about societal justice and equal rights for those seeking redress. The three contributions by Csongor Kuti, Katerina Koleva and Damiana Otoiu provide an overview of the different approaches adopted by the post-socialist countries that joined the EU in the first and second waves of Eastern enlargement. They also investigate the role of different actors, politicians, interest groups and national as well as international courts in shaping specific regulations and addressing the balance between individual and societal interests.

The final part of the book presents three very different cases of classic social marginalisation. The chapters by Aisalkyn Botoeva, Carina Keskitalo and Anastasiya Ryabchuk unfold in disparate geographies: Kyrgyzstan, northern Scandinavia and Ukraine. The contributions also investigate different societal groups from rural and urban populations as well as various traditional communities. The authors find that all of these groups exhibit feelings of powerlessness and despair. They are perceived – and, for the most part, also perceive themselves – to be in a state of social marginalisation.

Taken together, the contributions in this volume reflect the wide variety of challenges and conflicts linked to political and societal participation in European societies. Although nearly every country is confronted with these problems, the broad spectrum of cases investigated in the book serves to illustrate the significant differences in degree, nature and political reactions shown by societal and governmental actors all over Europe.

1. Defining the Right to Political Participation.
The Case of the Russian Party System

Elke Fein[1]

Re-Defining Justice and Legitimacy in the Post-Soviet Space. The Case of the First Russian Constitutional Court

Introduction

> The functioning of a legal system is decided outside of this system. (…) How laws are being applied is determined by external forces. We can thus speak about a strategic situation which marks the frame of how courts are being used and how laws are *de facto* being applied (Volkov, 2005, 76).

The idea of law and the quest for political legitimacy have been among the central motivating forces of Eastern Europe's transition processes. However, differentiating, let alone separating the spheres of law and politics still poses a considerable challenge for countries which have known their almost complete fusion for decades. In post-Soviet Russia where no social memory of impartial, politically unbiased justice was available after the collapse of the Soviet Union, the question of how 'law', 'justice' and 'legitimacy' are perceived and/or constructed by social actors is of crucial interest with regard to the functioning and development not only of the judicial system but, thereby, of the political system altogether.

While today's Russia is witnessing a new rapprochement of law and politics, the two spheres, formally separated during the Yeltsin era, have never been fully independent. Although serious efforts have been made to establish an independent judiciary based on the rule of law, it is obvious that notions such as 'justice' and 'legitimacy', which had been defined in a partial, Marxist-Leninist way for the past decades, were not likely to and probably could not easily be re-defined through a simple adoption of their western liberal connotations in the process of transition. How then, were they re-defined and which consequences did this entail?

By focusing on the first Russian Constitutional Court (RCC or CC, 1991–1993), this article highlights the double dilemma typically faced by Courts and judges in changing and instable transitional contexts: the necessity to obtain judicial and political legitimacy at the same time, as well as the strategies put forward by them to deal with these challenges. It is argued that the shaping of new institutions and the actual functioning of legal systems is not only decided by institutional arrangements themselves, but to a large extent by and through discursive struggles over the definition of basic rules. This is true especially in transitional societies. Thus, by adopting a constructivist perspective, i.e. by looking at the way basic rules and principles are

---

1   The author is grateful to the editors for helpful comments, as well as to Andrew Larrew for linguistic advice.

(re-) constructed in the transitional context of post-Soviet Russia[2], two theoretical aims are pursued: first, problematising some of the typical challenges faced by newly established or transitional Courts in need of self-definition and legitimacy, and second, discussing the competing powers of institutional and discursive resources in the process of building and shaping new institutions on a more general level.

In order to do this I will first outline the genesis and institutional design of the first Russian Constitutional Court. In a second step, the discursive 'coming into being' of the Court, i.e. the shaping of its 'corporate identity' is discerned as a central 'variable' of its operation in the period preceding the adoption of a new constitution: how did the judges themselves perceive their task(s) and how did they try to accomplish them? The Court's 'politics of justice' is then, thirdly, illustrated at the example of several cases, above all the so-called CPSU trial. The Russian evidence used here is largely taken from a study on the CPSU trial based on an intensive document analysis and interviews with participants (Fein, forthcoming).

The Making of a New Institution

With regard to the relation of law and politics in transitional Russia and the question of the RCC's political independence, two aspects need to be addressed: first the legal-institutional setting and second the Court's personnel, i.e. the human resource factor.

New Court and Old Constitution

The first Russian Constitutional Court operated from 1991 to 1993 and was an element as well as a symptom of Russia's ambivalent transition process. It was created by the Russian Congress of People's Deputies (CPD) in May 1991 after long and painful debates about the design of the institution itself, as well as about the principles it should be based on.[3] While the establishment of constitutional courts in transitional societies usually is a consequence of the adoption of new democratic constitutions, based on the rule of law and the separation of powers (Bos, 2004), this was not the case in Russia. Even though the ideas of judicial review and constitutionalism had become more and more popular here already during perestroika, when Russia experienced a dynamic, yet steady and peaceful evolution towards the rule of law[4], political

---

2 While the Soviet Union was about to dissolve when the RCC was created, Russia's political system still continued to be 'Soviet' insofar as the Soviet parliament and constitution were still in power until October/December 1993.

3 Vedomosti Verkhovnogo Soveta RSFSR, Nr. 13-28a/1991, Pos. 1017.

4 Robert Sharlet primarily credits Gorbachev for this development: 'In the last years of the Soviet Union and the first year of newly independent Russia change moved at lightning speed and was often expressed in legal forms. This represented a sharp break from even the near-

elites were not able to agree on a new constitution even after the attempted coup of August 1991. As a result, the Russian Constitutional Court was established almost two years before a new constitution had been adopted. So by 1991/92, paradoxically, independent Russia had a Constitutional Court based on modern and liberal constitutional principles but still lacked as of yet a democratic constitution based on these same principles. The constitution which was still valid then dated back to the times of Brezhnev (1978) and had been amended many times during perestroika. As a result, it was highly contradictory even with respect to central principles defining the structure and functioning of the state. However, the parallel existence of old Soviet-type rules and newly introduced liberal and democratic principles[5] which was to become a stumbling stone to the Court later on, was not the only major difficulty determining the work of the first RCC.

As indicated above, the Court itself was constructed according to the ideas of the rule of law and the separation and balance of powers even before the underlying principles themselves had legally come into being. It was declared to be the highest organ of judicial control of the constitution and awarded wide ranging powers and competences, including the right to impeach the president.[6] Also, it had the right to produce expert opinions on any problem of norm control on its own initiative, as well as the right to propose new laws. This gave it the possibility to actively intervene in the political process, which it did extensively during its first term, the Zor'kin era.

The law on the CC (LCC) declared the RCC to be the 'most impassionate and independent' of the three powers. A further guarantee of its independence and imparti-

---

term Soviet past, when change was rare, moved glacially at best, and was invariably defined politically by the ruling Communist Party. Gorbachev, whatever his shortcomings, must be given credit for this "change to change" and the tendency to institutionalize that change in law and constitutional writ. Despite his ultimate inability to manage the social forces he had unleashed, Gorbachev's legacy to Russia has been an emphasis on constitutionalism' (Sharlet 1993, 1). The growing importance of constitutionalism manifested itself even during the attempted coup of August 1991, since the plotters themselves made reference to the Soviet constitution (see 'Zayavlenie sovetskogo rukovodstva' (18.8.1991), published in: Pravda 20.8.1991). Richard Sakwa therefore notes: 'However paradoxical it might appear, this was in a sense a "constitutional coup". The plotters tried to present their actions as being in conformity with the constitution and thus sought to draw legitimicy from their formal legality' (Sakwa 1996, 15).

5   The most difficult contradiction was probably the introduction of a new article 3 declaring the 'separation of legislative, executive and judicial powers' to be the basis of the state order, while the old article 104.2.1 entitling the Congress of People's Deputies to decide any given issue, still remained in force. Also, the introduction of liberal pluralism contradicted the values of socialism which continued to possess constitutional status.

6   The most important of them were the right to verify the constitutionality of laws adopted by the CPD and parliament, as well as of acts of the president and all executive organs, of international treaties signed by the RF, and to examine the constitutionality of political parties and legal practice in general (article 1.1 LCC; article 165 of the constitution; amendment of April 21st 1992. Frenzke 1975, 220).

ality was the fact that it had its own budget and that all public and private institutions were obliged to institutional support, as well as, above all, the irremovability and life term office of the judges and its incompatibility with party or other state offices or economic activity.[7] Their material equipment and privileges were defined by law.[8] Articles 4–6 of the LCC declared the RCC's judges to be independent of instructions and obliged exclusively to the constitution. How was this institutionally guaranteed independence realised in practice?

This article argues that the shaping of (new) institutions and thus, the actual functioning of transitional legal systems is not only decided by institutional arrangements but to a large extent by and through discursive struggles over the definition of basic rules. This is why, in order to analyse the actual operation of the Court, we have to look at other, non-institutional factors as well. The following sections therefore inquire into the question who the judges were, how they defined their task and what this meant in the circumstances described.

New Personnel with (High Ideals and Some) Old habits

The Court started work after the CPD had elected candidates to 13 of the 15 positions on October 30th 1991. The judges who, according to the Law on the CC, had to be 'independent and impartial' and dispose of 'particular moral qualities', mostly had either top-level academic backgrounds (10), and/or held government (3) or (unimportant) political posts (1) in the past (Spravochnik Konstitutsionnogo Suda 1997 and Fein, forthcoming, chapter I.3.2). With one exception, all of them had been members of the Communist Party which, given the fact that CPSU membership was common in the Soviet Union for all holders of higher positions, must not be overestimated as a factor compromising the judges' independence in advance. Instead, it seems more interesting to look at their subjective relationship towards the former regime and the CPSU, which can either be detected through respective utterances of the judges themselves, and/or by the point in time at which they left the party.

While some of the judges quit the CPSU as early as 1986, most of them left the party after the August Coup, whereas a few others, among them chief justice Valeriĭ Zor'kin, officially did not make such a move at all, but rather left the party 'automatically' at the moment of their being appointed judges of the CC.[9] So while all of them had been socialised inside the Soviet system and its totalitarian idea of law, their

---

7   This was only true for the first composition of the Court. The new LCC adopted in 1995 introduced a limited period of office instead.
8   See article 25 LCC and the President's decree of 14.12.1991, VVS RSFSR 1991, Nr. 51, Pos. 1841. Luchterhand 1993, 258.
9   Interviews with seven of the judges of the RCC in June/July 2001 (Ebzeev, Gadzhiev, Kononov, Luchin, Morshchakova, Vedernikov, Zor'kin). Morshchakova was the only one who was not a member of the CPSU.

attitudes towards the regime differed according to their age and personal experiences.[10] However, given the judges' collective experience of a judicial system completely subservient to the Communist Party, all of them strongly supported democratisation, marketisation and, most of all, the development of a fully fledged state of law. So even if the Court presented itself as a politically heterogeneous body, all of its members undoubtedly were among the critically engaged progressive elite of the country.

Between Law and Politics – the Discursive 'Coming into Being' of the CC and its First Trials

The fact that for Russia, an independent CC was a completely new type of institution lead to both high expectations of the public and ambitious goals of the judges themselves, accompanied by a considerable ambition of the latter to meet the expectations of the former. So how did the judges frame their 'mission' and how did they put it into practice?

Besides the ambivalent and partly contradictory constitution, the work of the first RCC was largely determined by the experience of Soviet totalitarianism and the lessons the judges drew from them. The experience of lawlessness was a central motivating force with respect to their professional self-definition and the construction of the new Court's *corporate identity*. Therefore, one of the central aims articulated by the judges was their willingness to strengthen the principle of legality. This endeavour was, of course, based on their wish – as well as public expectations towards them – to distance themselves from and to break with the totalitarian judicial legacies in order to foster the establishment of an independent and impartial judiciary based on the rule of law. This is why the judges demonstrated high interest not only in contributing to Russia's transition to democracy based on a full-scale separation of powers, but also in establishing a reputation as an independent, impartial and just judicial body. This self-declared mission was both articulated discursively and demonstrated practically in the course of various important proceedings during its first term (1991–1993).

The Discursive Self-Construction of the Russian CC

The basic principles articulated by the judges on multiple occasions in and outside the broad media as being fundamental to their work can be summarised by three somewhat contradictory ideas which therefore demonstrated a partly productive, partly conflicting relationship during the Court's first term.

---

10   The families of Ebzeev and Vedernikov, for example, were repressed for various reasons during the Stalin period and after (Fein, forthcoming, chapter I.3.2).

Fostering Constitutionalism – the Legal Mission

> We have had a punitive state for a long time. (...) It is the duty of the CC of the RF to in-
> troduce legal methods and legal thinking into the consciousness of society.[11]

The first element of the *corporate identity* as articulated by the judges was the Court's
legal mission as a supplier of justice and an outpost of constitutionalism and the rule
of law in transitional Russia. When chief justice Zor'kin declared:

> We must and we will live according to the law. (...) My twelve colleagues and I are like
> watchdogs. And the executive and legislative branches of power are the herd which I as
> chairman of the CC will safeguard. I will not allow that the president or parliament leave
> the path of law and to fall into an abyss. Therefore, the Court has all powers including
> that of impeachment[12],

he claimed a certain moral 'surplus' for the Court as a guardian of law, justice and
civil peace which gave the Court's task an almost missionary character. Even though
in the context of the contradictory and transitional legal system of the time, this was
a political mission as well, insofar as it implied a progressive, liberal and democratic
interpretation of the existing, ambivalent constitution, the Court's quest for law and
constitutionalism, ironically, largely resulted in its legalist submission to the contradictory but valid constitution.

'Bad, but Valid' – Submission to an Imperfect but Valid Constitution

The contradictory nature of the late (post-) Soviet constitution was not ignored, but
actively acknowledged by the judges. Zor'kin himself said the country needed a new
constitution as soon as possible[13] and called the existing one a 'strange hybrid with
one sleeve cut from a medieval caftan, the other from a modern business suit', invit-
ing lawyers to 'article-shopping' whereby they could pick what they wanted. However, he and his colleagues also stressed over and over again that it was better to apply
a bad constitution than none.[14] So even if the judges themselves called the constitution an obstacle to democratisation, they presented their emphasis on formal legal-
ism as a demonstration of judicial professionalism in an incomplete and fragmented
legal environment. The Court therefore faced the dilemma that, in order to foster an
independent judicial review and, thereby, the rule of law, it had to make reference to
a constitution that did not consistently promote these principles.

---

11   'U nas, kazhetsya, poyavlyaetsya tret'ya vlast", Interview with E. Ametistov, in: Literaturnaya
     Gazeta, 22.1.1992.
12   'Valerii Zor'kin talking to Vladimir Orlov', in: Moskovskie Novosti, 26.1.1992.
13   Moskovskie Novosti, 26.1.1992.
14   Komsomol'skaya Pravda, 15.1.1992.

Political Independence, Mediation and Neutrality

The third element of the Court's legal discourse was connected to the first one and can also be explained by the Soviet experience, or more precisely the judges' wish to break with the ideas and practices underlying Soviet legal reality. Therefore, they put particular emphasis on a clear demarcation of their field of competence against that of the government in order to demonstrate their political independence of the latter. This aspect of their *corporate identity* was often verbalised by the formula that the Court did not want to 'become a servant of the powerful'. This, however, turned out to be the source of a second dilemma, as it made the Court privilege a position of political-legal neutrality which, in the context of the as yet unsolved constitutional conflict, resulted in its self-imposed obligation to mediate between the conflicting political groups and their political and legal claims. Mediation, however, seemed to be understood in the sense of 'finding the vector in the centre', as Zor'kin put it, i.e. of taking equal distances to both sides instead of taking sides for a progressive interpretation of the constitution. Indeed, Valeriï Zor'kin called the law a means of harmonising interests[15], thereby constructing the Court's role primarily as that of an allegedly politically neutral moderator and mediator who, in the ambivalent legal environment of late (post-) Soviet Russia, simply *could not* be politically neutral. So by trying to make a political virtue out of the dilemma of the conflictual political and the contradictory legal situation, the RCC in some sense became a political actor itself.

The Court's Political-Legal Mission Put into Practice: the Most Important Cases of the First Term

The extent to which the first RCC was a transitional phenomenon with one leg marching towards a democratic constitution and the other one still remaining in the Soviet past is illustrated by the example of some of its most important cases which demonstrate different aspects of the Court's corporate identity, but also of its identity crisis.

The First Case: Independence and Separation of Powers

The CC's first case was widely appreciated as a huge success which not only fostered democratisation and the establishment of an independent judiciary, but thereby also strengthened the Court's reputation as an independent and professional judicial body. In its first ruling pronounced on January 14th 1992, the Court struck down as unconstitutional Yeltsin's decree which had tried to merge the ministry of the interior with the secret services (Sharlet, 1993, 14). When the president accepted the CC's ruling after a few days of hesitation, this entailed a double message: first, as a clear

---

15 'Pravo, éto est' opredelennoe soglasovanie interesov', author's Interview with V. Zor'kin.

signal against a return to past Soviet traditions of the concentration of power and a strong influence of secret services on politics, and in favour of a system of 'checks and balances' granting citizens' rights instead, and second, as a powerful practical demonstration of independence of the Court with respect to the government, and thus in favour of the separation of powers. Both elements helped to shape and strengthen the Court's profile and reputation as a politically independent body and a promoter of Russia's democratic transition to a modern state of law.

However, it can be assumed that, given the three major elements of the Court's *CI*, this success was possible only because two of the principles presented above (political independence and promoting the rule of law) were not conflicting here. This was different in the second big case, the CPSU trial.

The CPSU Case: Impartiality as Political Neutrality

The so-called CPSU trial took place between May and November 1992 and was about the constitutionality of Yeltsin's ban of the Communist party decreed in August/November 1991. In this case, which was commonly regarded as a severe test of the Court's independence as well as of the functioning of the separation of powers in transitional Russia[16], the demarcation line between advocates and opponents of democratisation and the rule of law was less clearly cut than in the RCC's first case considered above. Even though Yeltsin's ban of the CPSU seemed somewhat problematic from a legal point of view, it was much more difficult here to rule against the president and thus, in favour of the Communist Party (which, after all, symbolised not only the old political system but also the Soviet legal system which everyone wanted to overcome) without putting into question the Court's mission of fostering Russia's democratic transition. The fact that the CPSU-ruling pronounced on November 30th 1992 nevertheless turned out to be rather pro-communist raises interesting questions with respect to the (re-)definition of procedural as well as substantive legal notions, which shall therefore be examined in some more detail.

Justice as a Trade-Off Between Legal, Political and Institutional Interests

The CPSU trial is probably less interesting for its ambivalent (see below) outcome as such than for the way this was achieved, i.e. the re-definition and shaping of central signifiers such as 'procedural fairness', 'justice', 'legitimacy' and 'democracy' which took place during the process. In order to illustrate the mechanisms and strategies by which this happened, three levels can be distinguished. On each of them, a certain

---

16   Robert Sharlet even called it the 'most dramatic case to date' (Sharlet 1993, 5).

element of the Court's identity was challenged and, often enough, undermined, and thus reshaped through discursive struggles over the interpretation of the notions in question.

Procedural Justice

The first and most basic level on which the power relations between the participants of the trial were negotiated was that of procedural justice. Given the fact that the CC was a new institution, no rules of court had been passed as yet. This is why a large number of procedural questions, for example how many and which speakers, witnesses and experts were allowed and which documents should be accepted as an exhibit (official evidence), were decided *in actu*. Obviously, this gave the participants wide-ranging possibilities to try and influence this process, i.e. to make their respective definitions of what was to be considered a just procedure, hegemonic. This was especially the case since the Court lacked a corresponding tradition, just like the judges lacked institutional judicial experience of the rule of law. Given also the contextual factor of the Court's wish to gain reputation and to distance itself from the government, it was rather easy for the Communists to at least partially 'impose' their notions (and thereby: demands) onto the Court. This basically happened through a trade-off between certain procedural concessions to the Communists which were exchanged against their cooperation with and acceptance of the Court. As a result, procedural justice was re-defined in a way that obliged the Court to intervene in favour of the (supposedly) weaker party (here: the Communists), i.e. on a substantive basis and outside of procedural legal rules strictly speaking.

Substantive Justice and Legitimacy

Similar discursive mechanisms could be observed on the second level, where the definition of historical truth and democratic legitimacy was negotiated. With regard to the question of how to do justice to the forbidden Communist Party, an interesting, largely implicit struggle took place about the criteria according to which this was to be decided. Here too, formal-legal criteria (the violation of laws and/or the constitution) ended up by proving to be less important than a number of political and moral arguments put forward by the Communists, for example:

- the historical achievements of socialism
- the self-critique of and democratisation brought about by the party during perestroika and
- the absence of a moral right of Russian 'democrats' (the majority of whom were former Communists themselves) to 'judge' the Communists.

In the course of extensive debates about the CPSU's history and the Soviet past in general, the Communist's discourse again developed a number of criteria (in other words: conditions) of a just decision, thereby indicating to the Court that certain other versions of decision were going to be considered as illegitimate by the Communists. Again, this discursive strategy gained its power from the fact that the judges had demonstrated great interest in the Communists' cooperation with and acceptance of the Court. So here again, legitimacy and (substantial) justice were largely defined by the dominant (Communist) discourse and not by the institution(s) formally entitled to interpret the constitution and to take 'independent' decisions. In other words, in order to demonstrate its independence of 'the powerful' (the government), the Court, to a large extent, made itself dependent of other, more subtle powers, namely of the power of Communist discourse.

Political Mediation and Substantive Indifference as Sources of Legitimacy

The Court's quest for consensus resulted, thirdly, in a ruling which 'gave each side something' by partly confirming Yeltsin's ban of the CP but also partly re-legalising and re-legitimating the party. This entailed a conception of justice, legitimacy and democracy, which was largely defined on formal grounds, not in the sense of the observation of formal legal or democratic procedures, but of proclaiming equal rights of the inferior party, irrespective of the material (legal and/or democratic) substance of their claims. When chief justice Zor'kin called the existence of the CP an essential element of a democratic society and its ban therefore an injustice, democratic legitimacy was primarily attributed to a formal, substantially indifferent understanding of justice, which in this case, equalled a rather blind, pseudo-pluralistic, yet *de facto* dogmatic everything-is-possible approach (pluralism without boundaries). Moreover, the Court in this way not only reproduced the meanings attributed to justice, democracy and legitimacy by Communist discourse during the trial, but also institutionally fixed them as hegemonic.[17]

The result of this redefinition of central signifiers was a strange confusion of formal and substantive elements of law and democracy in the (post-) Soviet Russian discursive realm. Whereas, as shown above, with regard to procedural questions, a material definition paradoxically dominated a formal definition of legitimacy, it was the other way round with regard to the material outcome of the process, where a substantively indifferent notion of democracy was made hegemonic, granting full democratic rights to a party that had not overcome and did not plan to change its

---

17 The explanations given by the Court's chairman cited here were not the words of the verdict, but nevertheless publicly made statements.

basic undemocratic (or: democratic only in a traditionally Communist sense) ideo-logical goals and principles.

To sum up, the discursive trade-off between legal, political and institutional in-terests had two major results. First, it was shown that political mediation between conflicting and even principally irreconcilable political claims proved to be a central source of political and judicial legitimacy during the Court's first term. This 'politics of justice', as practised during the CPSU trial in realisation of the RCC's self-image as a political-legal mediator continued to shape the Court's behaviour during the last months of its activity. In the course of 1993, it actively intervened into the political process several times, so that political ambitions even seemed to overrule judicial ones. It is therefore not surprising that the Court's repeated efforts to reconcile ir-reconcilable political positions not only resulted in a political stalemate, but that this deadlocked situation also threatened the position of the Court itself. This is why the Court's mediating ambitions finally lead to its dissolution by the Russian president, due to insurmountable conflicts over the 'rules of the game'.

However, and this is the second major result of the redefinition of basic notions described here, their modified meanings kept their power even after the RCC was shut down in autumn and the new constitution was passed in December 1993. This is probably one of the reasons why the political stalemate between opposing forces (*'coincidentia oppositorum'*) became a kind of 'balance of powers *à la russe*' in the 1990s. Russia's transition process thus continued to be characterised by the utopian effort to combine elements of the non-democratic Soviet past with those of pluralist western democracy both in institutional and cultural terms.

Conclusion: Institutional Versus Discursive Resources of Power

The analysis of the operation of Russia's first CC has shown the competing and of-ten conflicting powers of institutional (formal-legal) and discursive factors, which is crucial especially in transitional social and political contexts. It was shown that the genesis and operation of transitional legal systems is to a large extent determined by discursive struggles over the definition of basic rules, through which the actual op-eration of new or transitional institutional arrangements is shaped and which, often enough, overthrows supposedly clear borders between the legal/institutional and the political. Moreover, it was argued here that a constitution receives its meaning not primarily by its formal-institutional construction but as a result of discursive at-tributions of meaning to the notions it is based on, in other words: that discursive power is to a large extent able to shape, to (re-)define and even to undermine insti-tutional power, thereby rendering unofficial rules decisive for the factual function-ing of laws and institutions, or, as Vadim Volkov basically put it: The functioning of a legal system is decided not only by the look of this system itself. How laws are being applied is also determined by forces external to, as well as by their interpretations of those laws. We thus have to speak about strategic power relations (in a Foucauldian sense) which mark the frame of how courts are being used and how laws are *de facto* being applied (see introductory quotation).

This, in the Russian case, unfortunately led to *de facto* opposition between the notions of democracy and that of the rule of law as such.

References

Bos, E. (2004), *Verfassungsgebung und Systemwechsel. Die Institutionalisierung von Demokratie im postsozialistischen Osteuropa* (Wiesbaden: VS-Verlag).

Fein, E. (forthcoming), *Rußlands langsamer Abschied von der Vergangenheit. Der KPdSU-Prozeß vor dem Russischen Verfassungsgericht (1992) als geschichtspolitische Weichenstellung. Ein diskursanalytischer Beitrag zur politischen Soziologie der Transformation.*

Frenzke, D. (1975), Die Rechtsstellung der kommunistischen Parteien als Testfall der Ostrechtsmethodik, *Recht in Ost und West*, 190–203.

Luchterhand, O. (1993), Vom Verfassungskomitee der UdSSR zum Verfassungsgericht Rußlands, *Archiv des öffentlichen Rechts* 118, 237–288.

Sakwa, R. (1996), *Russian Politics and Society* (London/New York: Routledge).

Sharlet, R. (1993): The Russian Constitutional Court: The First Term, Post Soviet Affairs 9:1, 1–31/1993.

Volkov, V. (2005), Jenseits der Gerichte. Warum die Gesetze nicht so funktionieren, wie sie sollen, *Schattenspiele. Informelle Politik im Osten Europas*, Osteuropa 10, 75–84.

Alla M. Samoletova

Different Paths of Party System Consolidation: Which Factors Matter for Political Justice?

Characteristics of Party Systems in Central and Eastern Europe

Central and Eastern European political parties have been developing in transition, as a result they are unstable and fragile. Without delving too deeply into national peculiarities (procedural and structural factors influencing the path of transition), it is still possible to identify a number of features typical of the party systems of the region.

Firstly, compared to most countries of Western Europe and the United States, the party systems of Central and Eastern Europe might be seen as emerging entities (Lipset and Rokkan, 1967; Rose and Urwin, 1970; Bartolini and Mair, 1990). While the party systems of contemporary mature democracies are based on sustainable social cleavage structures and issues of public concern that more or less stabilise electoral volatility, post-communist countries are facing a political identity crisis: The former social cleavage structures have either ceased to be relevant or have been totally changed (Römmele, 1999). On the one hand, this has allowed post-communist voters to freely perceive new political solutions. On the other hand, however, it has become impossible to use the former mobilisation channels that bridged the gap between supply and demand on the Central and Eastern European political market. Under such circumstances, it is no wonder that post-communist party systems have been based on personal ambitions rather than social cleavages.

This argument is supported by party building data in post-communist countries. Herbert Kitschelt (Kitschelt, 1995) ideal-typically distinguishes three possible outcomes of party formation: clientelist, charismatic and programmatic parties. Needless to say, major efforts are needed to establish programmatic parties, since these demand substantial investments in procedures of consensus building in order to build strong politician-constituency linkages. Central and Eastern Europe is generally lacking either strong partisanship or administrative infrastructure. Thus, clientelist and charismatic parties have been more closely examined in the region so far. However, for a party system to be consolidated, programmatic parties seem to be crucial.

Secondly, in evaluating the institutional development of post-communist political parties, one might have noticed that many post-communist parties still resemble proto-parties typical for 19th century Europe and America – weakly structured and split (Pridham and Lewis, 1996). Judy Batt calls them 'movement parties' (Batt, 1991), but the fact remains that post-communist political parties are experiencing institutional difficulties despite being substantially active. The movement parties of Hungary, Poland and the Czech Republic have managed to establish multi-party systems, but have failed to maintain political efficiency (Ägh, 1998, 204).

Thirdly, post-communist parties have to contend with floating voters, which is not only related to post-communist political culture (assuming depolitisation and passive political positions) but also to the characteristics of the post-communist political parties themselves. Despite low entrance barriers to the political market, post-communist parties are faced with survival problems resulting from organisational weakness and a lack of resources for permanent voter mobilisation. The only exception applies to communist successor parties, which, having lost their dominating position, still have the capacity for the electoral resource pooling of their predecessors (Dellenbrant, 1993; Grzymała-Busse, 2002). In general, however, the number of political actors is constantly changing. Moreover, these actors can be quite diversified (all the post-communist emerging party systems display features of Sartori's model of polarised pluralism). As a result, partisan identification has remained unsteady, with a high degree of electoral volatility.

Fourthly, Central and Eastern European political parties, while interacting with their respective states, often employ the practices of special interest groups, consisting of back-door bargaining, exploiting personal contacts and political apparatus games (Golosov and Meleshkina 2001). Unofficial communication channels, which prevail over official ones, do not encourage political competition (Gel'man, 2001).

Fifthly and finally, post-communist political parties are ineffectual in the decision-making process at the administrative level, even if there are no institutional barriers preventing them from achieving high quality results in this field (for instance a strong presidency). According to Anna Grzymala-Busse, the reason for this is that the post-communist state has not been depoliticised, even though the communist monopoly on state structures has faded (Grzymała-Busse, 2003, 1124). Parties continue to seek private benefits from the public domain by leeching material resources from the state and favouring their allies in state appointments and contracts (Ganev, 2000).

Party System Consolidation and Political Party Competition in Central and Eastern Europe

Despite all the above-mentioned challenges for post-communist party systems occasioned by the transformation process, party system consolidation in Central and Eastern Europe has been being shaped since the middle of the 1990s (Ägh, 1998; Ersson and Lane, 1998), engendering a shift from polarised to moderate pluralism (a process described by Giovanni Sartori (Sartori, 1998, 133)). Moderate pluralism implies decreasing the level of party system fragmentation so that party systems have at least 3 to 4 effective parties (Laakso and Taagepera, 1979) as well as decreasing the level of electoral volatility as measured using Pedersen's index (Pedersen, 1983).

However, as Albert Hirschman suggests, paths of political development basically follow a cyclical pattern: a period of stability followed by a period of instability (Hirschman, 1982). Voters might express disappointment with any kind of political solution, thus, even consolidated party systems are susceptible to increased fragmentation and electoral volatility. That is why in addition to two party system consolidation characteristics, a third may be developed in order to facilitate party system consolidation even during periods of instability. One such indicator of consolidation is the effectiveness of political party competition. Elections should be transparent and fair, so that even small parties can compete for seats in parliament. At the same time, political parties which overcome the election threshold should be awarded the number of seats to which they are duly entitled to according to the election results. Thus, a party winning 30% of votes should gain about (depending on whether overhang seats are taken into account) 30% of the seats. To put it in quantitative terms, the effective number of electoral parties must be more or less equal to the effective number of parliamentary parties. This balance is thought to constitute political justice and is actually expected by the voters. Dividing their votes between parties, they expect the seats in the parliament to be divided in the same proportion. Not only is the actual social cleavage structure then represented, but the balance of interests is also maintained in the policy-making process.

Nevertheless, such political justice has ceased to be an unquestioned outcome of political party competition when theory meets practice. To provide an example, I will analyse the latest parliamentary election results in Russia and the New Europe in a comparative perspective. A useful starting point for analysis here is the third free election in each country of the region, since according to transformation theory, they introduce party system consolidation. Under the working hypothesis, despite similar conditions in post-communist party system development, party system consolidation is taking different paths in Russia and the New Europe. While the party systems of the New Europe might be seen to represent moderate pluralism, political party competition in Russia in 2003 led to single party domination and a lack of political justice. In order to shed light on why this happened, I will examine the factors that might have had an impact on political justice in Central and Eastern Europe. Before I continue with these factors, however, the following key empirical data on post-communist party systems should be taken into consideration (Herron 2002, plus author's database). (Cf. Table 1 on the following page.)

Table 1

Country	Elec-tions	ENEP	ENLP	DISP	EV	Elec-tions	ENEP	ENLP	DISP	EV
Czech Republic	1996	5.26	4	-1.26	27	1998	3.67	3.65	-0.02	16
Estonia	1999	5.18	5.5	0.32	24	2003	5.4	5.48	0.08	34
Hungary	1998	3.33	4.1	0.77	32	2002	2.2	2.21	0.01	38
Latvia	1998	5.79	5.49	-0.3	45	2002	6.5	6.6	0.1	43
Lithuania	2000	3.84	4.04	0.2	49	2004	5.6	5.6	0	41
Poland	1997	4.6	3	-1.6	21	2001	4.5	3.57	-0.93	66
Russia	1999	6.8	4.55	-1.25	56	2003	5.34	1.97	-3.37	48
Slovakia	1994	5.88	4.35	-1.53	14	1998	4.45	4.75	0.3	20
Slovenia	1996	6.25	5.56	-0.69	24	2000	5.13	4.65	-0.48	19

Abbreviations: ENEP = effective number of electoral parties, ENLP = effective number of legislative parties, DISP = disproportionality, EV = electoral volatility.

As the table shows, the majority of the post-communist countries have held parliamentary elections at least two times since the third free elections, though there are several countries (Czech Republic, Hungary, Poland, Slovakia and Slovenia) that have elected their parliaments for the third time since the middle of the 1990s:

Table 2

Country	Elections	ENEP	ENLP	DISP	EV
Czech Republic	2002	3.6	3.67	0.07	12
Hungary	2006	2.5	2.38	-0.12	28
Poland	2005	5.9	4.2	-1.7	34
Slovakia	2002	7.8	7.3	-0.5	37
Slovenia	2004	5.88	4.9	-0.98	22

The empirical data prove Hirschman's theory on the path of party system consolidation. Political development in Central and Eastern Europe is indeed following a cyclical pattern. A decrease in the level of electoral volatility and party system fragmentation is followed by an increase, and vice versa. As far as political party competition is concerned, the countries of the New Europe have managed to maintain a fairly low level of disproportionality between the effective number of electoral parties and the effective number of legislative parties. Thus, it might be stated that the New Europe enjoys political justice, even if the data for Poland in 2005 present a borderline case (the level of disproportionality turned out to be -1.7). On the other hand, the 2003 data for Russia provide cause for concern. Out of five effective electoral parties, only one proved to be effective in the parliament. The level of disproportionality is -3.37, which is irreconcilable with political justice.

Which Factors Matter for Political Justice?

In political science, electoral laws are thought to shape party systems by virtue of their direct impact on the level of party system fragmentation. The effects of electoral systems were described by Maurice Duverger (Duverger, 1954), who suggested that proportional representation tends to lead to the formation of many independent parties, the two-ballot majority system favours the formation of many parties that are allied with each other, and the plurality single-ballot rule produces a two-party system. Duverger's assumptions are better known as Duverger's Law, which he supplemented with claims about mechanical and psychological effects that work in tandem to reduce the number of political parties in all electoral systems. The mechanical effect consists of the pure mathematical effects of the application of the electoral rule. This tendency is especially strong in the plurality single-ballot rule assuming that 'first past the post.' In proportional representation, the mechanical effect weakens, since the only restraint is the threshold (usually not more than 5% for individual parties). The mechanical effect is further enhanced by the psychological effect that creates incentives for strategic voting. Voters cast their ballots for those parties that have a better chance of winning elections and therefore of putting voters' policy preferences into practice. Strategic voting thus favours larger parties and forces small parties to act rationally. As Giovanni Sartori claims, small political parties are encouraged to coalesce into the largest possible blocs in order to increase the likelihood of being elected (Sartori, 1968), even if there are several mandates at stake simultaneously; voters will then not be so worried about wasting their votes on small parties.

Table 3 on the following page presents the electoral systems of the New Europe and Russia.

The majority of observed countries have introduced proportional representation (Czech Republic, Estonia, Latvia, Poland, Slovakia and Slovenia). Hungary can also be added to this category, because mixed electoral systems assuming compensatory seats are usually called semi-proportional systems. In such systems, seats in the parliament are distributed according to a proportional tier so as to correct the distortions in proportionality caused by the plurality formula.

Table 3: Electoral systems of the New Europe and Russia

Country	Electoral System	Threshold
Czech Republic	Proportional representation	5%
Estonia	Proportional representation	5%
Hungary	Mixed-member system with a two-ballot majority and compensatory seats	5%
Latvia	Proportional representation	5%
Lithuania	Mixed-member system with a two-ballot majority (in 2000 the plurality single-ballot rule was introduced)	5%
Poland	Proportional representation	5%
Russia	Mixed-member system with the plurality single-ballot rule	5%*
Slovakia	Proportional representation	5%
Slovenia	Proportional representation	4%

*The option to vote 'against all candidates'.

Robert Moser admits that the post-communist countries using proportional systems are especially susceptible to the effects of Duverger's Law. Pointing out Hungary and Poland, he claims that the 5% legal threshold introduced in the early 1990s, apart from reducing the number of political parties, encouraged the elites of these countries to act strategically. Small parties, having learnt from the devastating effects of the threshold upon them, consolidated into broad electoral blocs, cutting the effective number of electoral parties in half (Moser, 1999).

How then does Duverge's Law work in mixed electoral systems with an independent plurality tier?

At this juncture, a comparison of the effects of the electoral systems in Russia and Lithuania, which introduced the same mixed electoral formula in 2000, is instructive. The Lithuanian parties in the ruling coalition, the Homeland Union (Conservatives of Lithuania) and the Christian Democrats mustered 86 mandates (61%) in the Seimas (parliament), allowing them to override a presidential veto and affording them reasonably better chances of winning the forthcoming elections. According to Duverger's Law, small parties are supposed to group around the leading parties; however, the former preferred to stay apart from the latter, having formed coalitions against both the Homeland and the Christian Democrats (Clark and Prekevičius 2001). The new coalitions – the Social-Democratic Coalition and the Liberal Union – managed to gain enough votes to win the parliamentary majority. Thus, plurality tier not only failed to stimulate coalition-building, but also produced extra party proliferation (Moser, 1997). However, the effectiveness of political party competition was still reached, since both coalitions presented a single nominee in the single mandate plurality district contest, and, as coalitions of negative consensus, they were unlikely to split (Gel'man, 2001).

As for Russia, until 2003 the same deviation from Duverger's Law was relevant. While plurality tier produced extra party proliferation, small parties limited its effects in the single mandate plurality district contest by interacting with regional/local elites via clientelist or patronage interconnections (Fish, 1995; Yargomskaya, 1999). The formation of a territorial basis served them as an alternative to coalitional politics. However, this opportunity was undermined by the adoption of a new federal law on political parties that prohibited the formation of regional political organisations. All seats became swept into the bin of a single party, exercising equal support across all districts (Weaver, 1984; Golosov, 2005). Thus, United Russia, winning 23.42% of the popular vote, converted them into 46.4% of the seats (103 out of 225 mandates) according to the Single-Mandate-District (SMD) formula.

The party's success in the SMD component was also strengthened by excellent results in the proportional representation (PR) part of the electoral system. Upon receiving 37.57% of votes, United Russia successfully converted them into 53.17% of the seats (120 out of 225 mandates). Extra party proliferation was avoided due to the significant decrease in the level of fragmentation. In the case of Russia, besides the effect of the threshold preventing the liberal opposition from entering the State Duma, there was an additional suppressing factor in the 2003 elections: a vote 'against all.' The 'against all' candidate won 4.7% of the popular vote, thus occupying the fifth niche. During the parliamentary elections of 2003, the large number of invalid ballots was registered as well (1.56%) (Galkin, 2004). As a result, the 'lost votes' were proportionally distributed among the winners.

Hence, as Grigorii Golosov concludes (Golosov, 2005), the problem at hand is a so-called 'fabricated majority,' i.e. when a party for which less than half the electorate votes receives the majority of seats in the parliament.

However, the results of the conversion of votes into seats in the State Duma derived due to the peculiarities of the Russian electoral system do not necessarily promise the creation of a party system with a single dominating party. Having received 223 mandates in the 2003 elections, United Russia fared worse in comparison with the 1999 elections, when a party coalition consisting of four parties (Unity, People's Deputy, Regions of Russia and OVR [*Otechestvo-Vsya Rossiya, Fatherland-All Russia*]) won 234 seats. It turned out that the next transformation originated from the level of fractional distribution within the parliament. The replenishment of the United Russia fraction occurred due to the nomination of 24 deputies by other parties (primarily NPRF [*Narodnaya Partiya Rossiĭskoĭ Federatsii, People's Party of the Russian Federation*] and SPS [*Soyuz Pravikh Sil, Union of Right Forces*]), as well as independents. Of 67 candidates identified as independents, 56 joined the fraction of the leading party. Thus,

United Russia controls 301 rather than 223 seats in the State Duma, thereby exercis-ing an absolute (constitutional) majority.

On the one hand, this phenomenon can be explained by turning to Duverger's Law. Independents and small party candidates act rationally when they group around the party exercising the absolute majority in the State Duma. However, under closer examination it turns out that of 447 deputies, 67 were independents and 32 repre-sented parties which failed to pass the threshold. As the Lithuanian experience dem-onstrates, the optimal strategy is the formation of a deputy group (99 mandates), pos-sessing a huge coalition's potential. It is evident that the behaviour of independents and NPRF candidates is motivated by the latent coalitional agreements with United Russia at the SMD level of elections. Among the deputies who positioned themselves as independents in the districts having no candidates from United Russia, the share of candidates that joined the party in power reached 90.57%, and the number of deputies leaving the candidates of the leading party behind was 57.14% (Golosov, 2005).

The stake on non-transparent coalitional agreements can be explained by the peculiarities of Russian institutional design.

First, let us consider the institutional design of the countries of Eastern Europe and Russia from the perspective of the office of the presidency (Raina, 1995; Baylis, 1996; Easter, 1997; Frye, 1997; Woldendorp, Bugde and Keman, 2000) – cf. Table 4 on the facing page.

Although there are different interpretations of the data presented in the table in academic literature, let us consider that the majority of Central and East European countries are parliamentary republics (the index of the presidency does not exceed 3 (Krouwel 2000)). Both Lithuania and Poland can be ascribed to the semi-presiden-tial form of government (the index of the presidency does not exceed 4). Thus, the presidential system is detected only in Russia (the index of the presidency reaches 6.5). Despite the substantial powers of their presidents, the semi-presidential system category was chosen for both Lithuania and Poland because political parties in these countries serve as active political agents that participate in cabinet formation.

Let us delve more deeply into the case of Russia. The 1993 Russian constitution was written 'for' president Boris Yeltsin, who turned out to be the winner in the con-flict with the Congress of People's Deputies. Within the system of 'forced consen-sus,' the document initially contained an asymmetry in the relationship between the president and the parliament. The president was granted large powers in three cru-cial fields. The president possesses the right to dissolve the State Duma if: the latter rejects the candidate for the position of prime minister (proposed by the president) three times in a row, if the Duma votes to censure the government twice within two months or if it does not support the government after the cabinet initiates voting on

Table 4: Institutional design of the countries of Eastern Europe and of Russia

Country	Presidential elections	Parliament dissolution	Government formation	Legislative initiative
Czech Republic	Indirect	President + Parliament	President + Prime Minister	No
Estonia	Indirect	President + Prime minister	President + Parliament	No (amendments to Constitution only)
Hungary	Indirect	President (+Parliament)	President + Prime Minister	Yes
Latvia	Indirect	President + Referendum	President + Parliament	Yes
Lithuania	Direct	President + Prime Minister	President + Prime Minister + Parliament	Yes
Poland	Direct	Parliament (+President)	President + Prime Minister + Parliament	Yes
Russia	Direct	President	President (+Parliament)	Yes (veto power)
Slovakia	Direct (since 1999)	President	President + Prime Minister	Yes
Slovenia	Direct	President + Parliament	President + Parliament	No

the support of its policy. Thus, the State Duma has no control over the cabinet, while the right to vote to censure the government is contained by the right of the president to dissolve the State Duma. This curtailment constitutes yet another instrument with which the executive power can exert pressure on the parliament. Moreover, besides the State Duma's lack of supervisory powers, it is not enabled to form the government or influence its policy. Finally, according to the Constitution of the Russian Federation, the president is the guarantor of the constitution. This status broadens his/her rights significantly, insofar as in the event of a political crisis, it is the president who determines the future of both the government and the parliament (Chaisty, 2001, 105). It is worth noting that even the legislative authority of the State Duma (as Robert Moser points out in his article (Moser, 2001)) may be contested by the president, who, according to the Article 90 of the constitution, possesses the right to introduce decrees (which assume force of law as long as they do not contradict the constitution or related federal laws).

The 1993 Russian constitution created a political model perhaps fitting within the conceptual framework of delegated democracy. According to Guillermo O'Donell (O'Donell, 1996, 98), this paradigm presupposes that presidential power is limited only by the political context and fixed presidential term, while the rest of the political entities (parliament, Constitutional Court) play secondary roles and are ignored by the executive power. Actually, proceeding from what was mentioned above, it could be said that the power of the President of the Russian Federation is in fact absolute, especially since the procedures of impeachment and amending the constitution are ultimately difficult to realise. Many scholars stress the negative effects that the institution of a strong presidency has had on the party system (Lijphart 1994; Shugart and Carey 1995). For instance, Juan Linz mentions that the presidential form of republic is in principle incompatible with a disciplined and responsible party system (Linz, 1994), while Scott Mainwaring insists that a strong presidency in fact eliminates incentives towards coalitional governments (Mainwaring and Shugart, 1997). However, the conclusion that seems most suitable for this thesis, that the level of party fragmentation in the presidential systems should be high due to the organisational weakness of party systems, does not explain why the executive power in Russia has deliberately created a strong party of power and used the resources of its own legitimacy in order to provide this party with electoral success (recall that in 1999, Putin publicly endorsed the Unity party – established prior to the elections – thus ensuring a confident second place for the party in the State Duma (Moser, 2001)). The explanation is that in spite of the fact that the State Duma has been conferred the status of a totally subordinate legislature (Hague, Harrop and Breslin, 1998) during the presidency of Vladimir Putin, the Russian parliament is still the main legislative body. The presence of a loyal majority in the parliament tends to result in the adoption of the 'demanded' laws after the first reading (formerly requiring three readings, except for the budget, which demanded four readings) without the proposal of alternative drafts, a situation which undoubtedly serves the interests of the executive branch of power.

Conclusion

I started this paper by illustrating different paths that party system consolidation can take with respect to the effectiveness of political party competition. As the discussion made evident, Russia appears to be the deviant case. Initially I intended to explain the lack of political justice by referring to the peculiarities of the Russian electoral system and institutional design. Although these factors obviously matter for political justice, the research points to the mode of interaction between major political agents being a primary force in making the case of Russia different from other Central and Eastern European countries. Political injustice seems to exist due to non-transparent coalitional agreements concluded between United Russia and other political parties/candidates, on the one hand, and the executive branch of power, on the other hand.

References

Ägh, A. (1998), 'The End of the Beginning: the Partial Consolidation of East Central European Parties and Party Systems', in Pennings, P. and Lane, J-E (eds.), *Comparing Party System Change* (London: Routledge).

Bartolini, S. and Mair, P. (1990), *Identity, Competition, and Electoral Availability: The Stabilization of European Electorate 1885–1985* (Cambridge: Cambridge University Press).

Batt, J. (1991), *East Central Europe from Reform to Transformation* (London: Pinter).

Baylis, T. (1996). 'Presidents versus Prime Ministers. Shaping Executive Authority in Eastern Europe', *World Politics* Vol. 48.

Chaisty, P. (2001), 'Legislative Politics in Russia', in Brown, A. (ed.), *Contemporary Russian Politics: A Reader* (Oxford: Oxford University Press).

Clark, T.D. and Prekevičius, N. (2001), 'The Effect of Changes to the Electoral Law in Premier-Presidential Systems: the Lithuanian Case', in Jankauskas, A. (ed.), *Lithuanian Political Science Yearbook 2000* (Vilnius: Institute of International Relations and Political Science).

Dellenbrant, J.A. (1993), 'Parties and Party Systems in Eastern Europe', in White, S.; Batt, J. and Lewis, P.G. (eds.), *Developments in East European Politics* (London: The MacMillan Press Ltd.).

Duverger, M. (1954), *Political Parties: Their Organization and Activity in the Modern State* (London: Methuen).

Easter, G. (1997), 'Preference for Presidentialism. Postcommunist Regime Change in Russia and the NIS', *World Politics* Vol. 49.

Ersson, S. and Lane, J-E. (1998), 'Electoral Instability and Party System Change in Western Europe', in Pennings, P. and Lane, J.-E. (eds.), *Comparing Party System Change* (London: Routledge).

Fish, S. (1995), 'New Advent of Multipartism in Russia 1993–1995', *Post-Soviet Affairs* Vol. 11, No. 4.

Frye, T. (1997), 'A Politics of Institutional choice. Post Communist Presidencies', *Comparative Political Studies* Vol. 30, No. 5.

Galkin, A. (2004), 'O sensatsii, kotoraya ne sostoyalas", *Polis* No. 1.

Ganev, V. (2000), 'Postcommunism as a historical episode of state building, or explaining the weakness of the postcommunist state' (paper presented at the 12th International Conference of Europeanists, Chicago).

Gel'man, V. (2001), 'Postsovetskie politicheskie transformatsii: nabroski k teorii', *Polis* No. 1.

Golosov, G. and Meleshkina, E. (2001), *Politicheskie partii i vybory: Uchebnoe posobie* (St. Petersburg: Borey-Art).

Golosov, G. (2005), 'Sfabrikovannoe bolshinstvo: konversiya golosov v mesta na dumskikh vyborakh 2003 goda', *Polis* No. 1.

Grzymała-Busse, A. M. (2002), *Redeeming the Communist Past: the Regeneration of Communist Parties in East Central Europe* (Cambridge: Cambridge University Press).

Grzymała-Busse, A. M. (2003), 'Political Competition and the Politicization of the State in East Central Europe', *Comparative Political Studies* Vol. 36, No. 10 (December).

Hague R., Harrop, M. and Breslin, S. (1998), *Comparative Government and Politics* (Basingstoke: Maximillian Press).

Herron, E.S. (2002), 'Too Few or Too Many Parties? The Implication of Electoral Engineering in Post-Communist States' <http://www.isp.msu.edu/cers/Herron%2002.htm>.

Hirschman, A. (1982), *Shifting Involvements: Private Interest and Public Action* (Oxford: Martin Robertson).

Kitschelt, H. (1995), 'Formation of Party Cleavages in Post-Communist Democracies: Theoretical Propositions', *Party Politics* 1:4.

Krouwel, A. (2000), 'The Presidentialisation of East-Central European Countries' (paper prepared for presentation at the ECPR Joint Sessions Workshop on the Presidentialisation of Parliamentary democracies, Copenhagen, Denmark).

Laakso, M. and Taagepera, R. (1979), 'Effective Number of parties: A measure with applications to West Europe', *Comparative Political Studies* 12.

Lijphart, A. (1994), *Electoral Systems and Party Systems: A Study of Twenty-Seven Democracies, 1945–1990* (Oxford: Oxford University Press).

Linz, J. (1994), 'Presidential or Parliamentary Democracy: Does it Make Difference', in Linz, J. and Valenruela, A. (eds.), *The Failure of Presidential Democracy* (Baltimore and London: The John Hopkins University Press).

Lipset, S.M. and Rokkan, S. (1967), 'Cleavages Structure, Party Systems, and Voter Alignments: An Introduction', in Lipset, S.M. and Rokkan, S.: *Party Systems and Voter Alignments: Cross-National Perspectives* (New York: The Free Press).

Moser, R. (1997), 'Testing "Duverger's Law" in a Post-Communist Context: The Impact of Electoral Systems in Russia', *Post-Soviet Affairs* Vol. 13, No. 3.

Moser, R. (1999), 'Electoral Systems and the Number of Parties in Post-Communist States', *World Politics* Vol. 51, No. 3.

Moser, R. (2001), 'Executive-Legislation Relations in Russia, 1991–1999', in Barany, Z. and Moser, R. (eds.), *Russian Politics. Challenges of Democratization* (Cambridge: Cambridge University Press).

O'Donell, G. (1996), 'Delegative Democracy', in Diamond, L. and Plattner, M. F. (eds.), *The Global Resurgence of Democracy,* 2nd ed (Baltimore: John Hopkins University Press).

Pedersen, M.N. (1983), 'Changing Patterns of Electoral Volatility in European Party Systems, 1948–1977: Explorations in Explanation', in Daalder, H. and Mair, P. (eds.), *Western European Party Systems: Continuity and Change* (London: SAGE Publications Ltd.).

Pridham, G. and Lewis, P. (1996), 'Introduction: Stabilising fragile democracies and party system development', in Pridham, G. and Lewis, P. (eds.), *Stabilising fragile democracies: comparing new party systems in Southern and Eastern Europe* (London and New-York: Routledge).

Raina, P. (1995), The Constitutions of New Democracies in Europe (Cambridge: Merlin Books).

Römmele, A. (1999), 'Cleavages structure and party systems in East and Central Europe', in Lawson K., et. al. (eds.), *Cleavages, parties, and voters: Studies from Bulgaria, the Czech Republic, Hungary, Poland, and Romania* (Westport: Praeger).

Rose, R. and Urwin, D.W. (1970), 'Persistence and Change in Western Party Systems Since 1945', *Political Studies* 18.

Sartori, G. (1968), 'Political Development and Political Engineering', in Montgomery, J. D. and Hirschman, A. O. (eds.), *Public Policy* (Cambridge: Cambridge University Press).

Sartori, G. (1998), 'European Political Parties: The case of Polarized Pluralism', in Wolinetz, S.B. (ed.), *Party Systems* (Dartmouth Publishing Company Ltd.).

Shugart, M. and Carey, J. (1995), *Presidents and Assemblies: Constitutional design and electoral dynamics* (Cambridge: Cambridge University Press).

Weaver, L.N. (1984), 'Semi-Proportional and Proportional Representation Systems in the United States', in Lijphart, A. and Grofman B. (eds.), *Choosing an Electoral System: Issues and Alternatives* (New York).

Woldendorp, J.; Bugde, I. and Keman, H. (2000), *Party Government in 48 Democracies (1945–1998)* (Dordrecht, Kluwer Academic Publishers).

Yargomskaya, N. (1999), 'Izbiratel'naya sistema i uroven' partiĭnoĭ fragmentatsii v Rossii', *Polis* No. 4.

2. Defending Societal Interests. NGOs' Attempts to Frame Public Debates

Susanne Schatral

Stop Violence. Framing Strategies of Russian Women's NGOs

Introduction

Anti-trafficking activities in the Russian Federation started in the middle of the 1990s, when, as a result of the first conference on the problem, the term 'human trafficking' was introduced into the professional sphere (state officials, NGOs) and into public political discussion (Tyurukanova, 2006). Crisis centres for women, which formerly focused primarily on domestic violence, revised their targets in 1994 and continue to stand at the forefront of organisations assisting survivors of trafficking.[1] They can therefore be identified as 'key actors' in Russia's anti-trafficking system.

As a result of transnational networking and participation in international movements, campaigns and conferences, many of these NGOs frame their anti-trafficking demands and objectives as a women's human rights matter. But does doing so help to further NGOs' counter-trafficking projects and politics?

In order to answer this question, I take a close look at how the RACCW[2] network uses the women's human rights frame to voice its claims and concerns. As a first step, I explain the concepts of frames and master frames. Next, I clarify the paradigm of women's/human rights, and explore its significance for the international women's movement and counter-trafficking measures. On the basis of empirical material, I depict how RACCW effectively uses the women's/human rights frame in the Russian context. In closing, I will assess community outreach, capacity building and advocacy in order to discuss the success or failure of the network's framing strategies.

Frames and Framing Tasks

The concept of frames is mostly applied in studies about social movements. Besides *resource mobilisation* – formal and informal modes of organisation, which can rationally be used to activate a movement – and *opportunity structures* – the institutional contexts in which movements agitate and meet political changes or restraints – framing is one of the central tools for furthering the establishment and advancement of a movement.

---

1 The official term for persons who have suffered trafficking is 'victims.' I prefer the terms used by NGOs, such as 'survivor' or 'affected person,' in order to stress the victim's right to self-determination.

2 The Russian Association of Crisis Centres for Women is a network of about 47 centres in 38 Russian cities. These organisations address issues of violence prevention and render support to women and children suffering from different types of gendered violence.

Framing concerns the contentious construction of definitions to mobilise supporters and public opinion. According to Kai-Uwe Hellmann, framing is the staging of a protest theme (Hellmann, 1999, 91–113). By means of collective action frames, movement adherents negotiate a shared understanding of some situation or condition they define as problematic. The need for political change is then promoted; problem solutions are proposed, justified, and explained to the state and society, which are urged to act in concert to effect change. According to Benford and Snow, a social movement has to meet three core framing tasks in order to set up mobilising meaning constructions: *diagnostic, prognostic* and *motivational* framing (Benford/ Snow, 2000, 615). They are subjected to 'overlapping processes' described as *discursive, strategic* and *contested,* which are essential for the generation of frames and their potential impact (Benford/Snow, 2000, 623). In these processes, experiences and incidences are accented or highlighted in order to suit best the movement's purposes. Frames are amplified and intensified while slogans are developed, and link various issues and events together. Moreover, the frames must be able to withstand challenges from within and without the movement, and meaning constructions should incorporate opponents' counterarguments. The literature refers to strategic processes as *frame alignment* when ideologically congruent but structurally unconnected frames are linked, existing values are clarified or idealised and when frames are extended beyond the primary sphere of interest.

Successfully mobilising frames should also have variable features in common, such as:

- *centrality*: The frame should have a connection to the common cultural value system.
- *range*: The frame should be sufficiently broad in order to avoid addressing only narrow topics.
- *interrelatedness*: Components of the frame should be sufficiently linked to ensure that its arguments are firm and can withstand the burden of proof.
- *credibility*: A resonant frame should be backed by empirical evidence.
- *experiential commensurability*: The interpretation of issues and events should correspond with the experiences of the target audience.
- *narrative fidelity*: The frame should serve as a tool for capturing attention.

Frames with a broader range and more influence than frames that are structurally and thematically restricted to a single movement are classified as *master frames.* These frames are 'sufficiently broad in interpretative scope, inclusivity, and cultural resonance' (Benford/Snow, 2000, 619). The criteria for master frames are met by *rights frames, choice frames, injustice frames* or the so-called *'return to democracy'* frames. Master frames build on successful framing and enhance the prospect of success.

From Human Rights to Women's/Human Rights

For a global women's movement, one of the most important master frames is the human rights frame and its amplification of women's/human rights, whereby it becomes an effective discursive tool to claim women's social, cultural and political rights. During the 1993 Vienna Conference on Human Rights, women's rights were emphatically placed in the international public eye under the paradigm of human rights (Ruppert, 2001, 213). Since then, discrimination against women has been defined as a violation of human rights. Moreover, in 1993, the Declaration on the Elimination of Discrimination Against Women (DEVAW) was passed by the UN General Assembly. Two years later, the Beijing Platform for Action obliged a number of states to take measures to improve the situation of women.[3] While none of these schemes is legally binding to states, they might at least contribute to strengthening the norm of women's rights. But up to now the Convention on the Elimination of All Forms of Discrimination against Women (CEDAW), adopted in 1979 by the UN General Assembly, is the only instrument to explicitly protect women's rights at the global level. CEDAW is not a very strong norm according to international law, but it exemplifies the changing understanding of state sovereignty (Zwingel, 2002, 183). The most striking change is the rejection of the public/private divide; from this follows that states are held responsible for discrimination against women in both spheres (Brown Thompson, 2002). According to the convention, states commit themselves not only 'to ensure that public authorities and institutions' (Article 2d) comply with the treaty, but also to take action to 'eliminate discrimination against women by any person, organisation or enterprise' (Article 2e).[4]

Furthermore, the short phrase 'women's rights are human rights' reflects the prosperity of the international women's movement in gender politics. At the end of the Cold War, the revaluation of the UN and of human rights in general, the institutional spaces the United Nations provided opened up new windows of opportunity for asserting objectives like equal opportunity and the elimination of violence. During this period, women's rights activists also applied new strategies: Political demands based on local and national experiences were conveyed to the international sphere and, given the content, formed a strategic base from which to intervene in international politics. Conversely, international norms, institutions and policy outcomes

---

3   The twelve critical areas of concern are: violence against women, education and training of women, women and poverty, women and armed conflict, women and health, women and the economy, women in power and decision-making, institutional mechanisms for the advancement of women, women's human rights, women and the media, women and the environment and female children. URL: http://www.un.org/womenwatch/daw, downloaded on 12/14/2004.

4   See full text: http//:www.un.org/womenwatch/daw/cedaw/cedaw.htm. Downloaded on 15.06.2006.

were used as manifold links for women's politics on the local, regional and national levels (Wölte, 2002, 221).

The transnational feminist campaigns and lobbying strategies tended to highlight the topic of violence against women, whereas social and economical rights played a secondary role. Presenting violence against women as a violation of human dignity seemed the easiest way to achieve international concern and solidarity among women. But it was difficult to build consensus within a transnational women's movement on issues like poverty (Schmidt-Häuer, 2000, 286). Thus Julie Hemment argues: 'The very success of the framing can also be regarded as its weakness. Although the framing yields cross-cultural clarity, it does so at a cost. At the transnational level it works insofar as it is a catchall. However, this catchall quality screens out crucial nuances in the ways people define violence against women in different local contexts' (Hemment, 2004, 820). As a result – mainly in post-socialist circumstances – the women's/human rights frame deflects issues like redistributive and social justice.

Human Rights and Trafficking

However, the amplification of the human rights frame and violence against women as a violation of human rights, respectively, opened up new perspectives for combating the trafficking of women. With the emergence of the UN trafficking protocol in the late 1990s, civil society activists and especially women's right activists saw a unique opportunity to influence the first definition of trafficking in international law and to ensure that counter-trafficking instruments complied with human rights norms. Although the protocol shows weaknesses in considering the protection of the human rights of the trafficked person, it virtually guarantees that anti-trafficking strategies incorporate the '3 P's': prevention, protection (of human rights) and prosecution (law enforcement and international co-operation) (Pearson, 2005, 20–26).

Whereas the EU Framework Decision on Combating Trafficking (2000) still remains focused on law and law enforcement, experts agree that programmes like *Daphne*[5] and *Stop*[6] mirror the fact that as of the mid-1990s, EU policy began to perceive trafficking not only as a matter of irregular migration or organised crime, but as a severe crime against human dignity and as violence mostly geared towards women (Locher, 2002; Uçarer, 1999, 230–244). Also, the recommendations from the European Commission's Package of Measures from 1998 consider (regular) migration and social relief for victims as important tools in counter-trafficking strategies (Topan, 2000).

---

5   The *Daphne* programme aims at supporting organisations that develop measures and actions to prevent or to combat all types of violence against children, young people and women and to protect the victims and groups at risk.

6   *Stop* is an incentive and exchange programme for persons responsible for combating trade in human beings and the sexual exploitation of children.

In 2005, the Council of Europe's Convention Against the Trafficking in Human Beings specified concrete measures for victim protection and a group of experts will be monitoring states' compliance with the convention guidelines.

Despite embedding human rights in trafficking conventions and laws on the international level, NGO advocates globally and explicitly ask for anti-trafficking strategies that are broadly geared towards women's human rights. Ann Jordan from the Human Rights Law Group proposes a number of measures that advocates might encourage their governments to incorporate into national trafficking laws and policy responses, including: equality, access to justice, the protection of trafficked persons, the provision of basic services and changes in immigration law (Jordan, 2002, 28–37). To the German KOK e.V.[7], which as a member of the Human Rights Caucus[8] has become involved in the UN Trafficking Protocol's orientation on women's human rights, this means that all political concepts and practical approaches need to be oriented towards survivors of trafficking. In detail, this stipulates that:

- the legal claims of the survivors have to be guaranteed;
- states are responsible when human rights are violated, even if individuals committed these crimes;
- the socioeconomic rights of women can be demanded;
- matters pertaining to the new-world economic order and structural violence in conditions of exploitation have to be discussed and tackled;
- women's human rights must also be incorporated into the so-called 'hard law' domains, especially defence policy (Uhl, 2000, 94–102)

This understanding of a human-rights-oriented anti-trafficking effort implies that survivors are not passive victims who have to be rehabilitated but people who bear rights that they can claim. For the practical work of information dissemination and support, the human rights framework stands for empowering approaches to assist persons 'in retaking control over their lives and ensuring that women are treated as adults, not as children' (Jordan, 2002, 30).

Framing Tasks in Practice

But how do women's NGOs in the Russian Federation use the human rights paradigm in order to fight violence and discrimination against women? On the basis of teaching and training material for campaigns as well as profile leaflets[9], I examined RAC-

---

7   Bundesweiter Koordinierungskreis gegen Frauenhandel und Gewalt gegen Frauen im Migrationsprozess e.V (German Nationwide Coordinating Circle against Trafficking in Women and Violence against Women Who Migrate)

8   A group to co-ordinate NGOs that lobbied at the sessions of the UN Crime Commission (from January 1999 until October 2000).

9   Examples of profile leaflets: 'Peace on Earth begins at Home' and 'Protivodeistvie Torgovle Lyud'mi.' Information brochure: Crisis centre 'Sestry' (Ed.): Kak éto byvaet? Kto vinovat? Chto

CW's framing strategies. These sources show that the network uses the human rights frame, which runs through the material like a thread, to voice its political aims.

Following the pattern of Benford and Snow, an obligatory task for the generation of a working mobilising frame is *diagnostic framing*. This technique suggests what is at issue in a debate, assigns who is to blame and turns a situation into a problem demanding action. Therefore, it is essential to create a formulation of the problem that will be convincing.

RACCW publicly denounces gender-specific violence as a violation of women's equal, inalienable and indivisible human rights. It stresses that gender-specific violence happens in both the private and public spheres. In other words, violence against women has a structural dimension, but it can also be perpetrated by individuals. RACCW is convinced that gender-specific violence is a result of power abuse and is rooted in the historical status of women in family and society.

The figures and statistics presented illustrate that violence against women is an international problem with a huge scope, and it has to be tackled with urgency. Hence, the network is also committed to eradicating domestic violence as well as xenophobic discrimination against women and trafficking. The secrecy surrounding the issues involved greatly perpetuates the violence and discrimination. According to the network, this is a widespread phenomenon in Russian society: Violence against women is played down as a private matter and the affected persons seldom know their rights or how to claim them.

Consequently, the network encourages women and girls to talk about their experiences. Benford and Snow's scheme classifies these actions as prognostic framing: Reasonable solutions to the problem are articulated, a plan is proposed and ways for carrying out the plan are explained.

The self-defined role of the NGO is to uncover the problem, make it public and create a base where the problem can adequately and comprehensively be analysed, which is a prerequisite for following up on the issue both socially and legally. Or, to put it in a nutshell: 'One can fight violence only if one recognises it is a serious problem.'[10] The public is informed that the network diligently complies with its monitoring duties by means of the presentation of evidence, data, numbers and statistics of affected persons, preconditions, forms and consequences of gender-specific violence[11]. Besides demonstrating a great deal of illustrative material, this tactic aims at strengthening the frame's credibility and experiential incommensurability.

---

delat'?. Moskva: Terevinf, 2003. Books: (Sinitsyn, 2002a; Sinitsyn, 2002b, Sinitsyn, 2003; Abubikirova, 2004; Traïnerskiĭ Portfel, 2004.

10   Profile leaflet 'Peace on Earth begins at Home.'

11   Birgit Locher refers to this scheme as the 'human rights method,' a strategy that gained importance during the UN conference in 1993 (Locher, Fall 2002, 74).

Framing gender-specific violence as an infringement of women's human rights significantly contributes to the frame's interrelatedness. RACCW can rely on many international and national laws and documents, not only to demand the survivors' legal claims but also to hold the culprits liable – ultimately, not just individual perpetrators but single states as well as the international community. NGO advocates compiled manifold national and international legal documents to illustrate the importance of knowing one's rights in order to secure treatment as a legal person.

RACCW (re-) formulates this legal claim in gender-neutral language that stresses the human right – regardless of sex or gender – to a life free of violence. The phrase 'Peace on earth begins at home' neatly communicates that the violence-free home is prerequisite for universal peace; it is a notion that perfectly resonates with Russian cultural accepted values.

This basic formulation leads to another framing task: frame extension. Problematic questions and issues are raised that may be beyond the movement's primary scope of interest but are presumed to be of importance to potential adherents/clients. After all, the lives of women and girls in transition processes are not necessarily only affected by physical violence perpetrated by individual men but also by manifold structural injustices, gender stereotypes and patriarchy in general – threats to peace in the private as well as public spheres.

The network invigorates the extended frame and simultaneously broaches the issue of structural reasons for discrimination and violence against women. It presents in detail the forms of exploitation on the national and global levels that women face as a rule when they migrate.[12] Writings by scholars[13] on behalf of the organisation are convincing not only because their writing is scientific and authoritative, but also due to their profound knowledge of the Russian context of female migration (Traĭnerskiĭ Portfel, 2004). Their studies mainly centre upon NGO activists and the scientific community, who, in their role as advocates, are supposed to know the background issues in order to facilitate practical work and come up with theoretical solutions. As a practical community-oriented solution, the network runs hotlines all over Russia, where women can become informed about irregular migration issues and learn about psychological help and legal support at home and abroad. In this way, the frame wins credibility. The abstract phrase of 'protecting women's human rights' is translated into immediate, tangible support.

---

12 RACCW points out that Russian authorities behave almost indifferently to matters of female migration. This is accompanied by the extensive marginalisation of the women who migrate: Legal possibilities for labour migration are lacking, and women have to find precarious work in the sex industry or low labour markets (Malysheva / Tyurukanova, 2001).

13 A lot of mostly female scholars are attached to the work and ideas of RACCW and contribute to the network's publications. Feminist scholars were also significantly involved in the founding of crisis centres for women. For more on the history of crisis centres, see: Rimashevskaya, 2005.

Another aspect of RACCW's multifaceted practical work is the network's lobbying activities in the State Duma. A couple of NGO advocates took also part in the working group under the State Duma's Legislation Committee to draft anti-trafficking legislation and build formal and informal networks with all types of international and national state or non-governmental organisations. This is exactly the kind of work Ann Jordan suggests that human rights advocates ought to do: monitor and urge their governments to enforce (women's) human rights.[14] The network consistently documents and describes its multilayered advocacy and community work in detail. One can grasp a 'plan of action' with a mission, activities and services that (at least on paper) correspond.

Finally, the frame is presented in shorthand via the use of metaphors, catchphrases, and symbols to stimulate action. Such devices operate in a similar way to stimuli in a cognitive scheme. They immediately activate the whole frame, and suggest what is at issue without elaborating on it at length. The succinct questions written on the front side of an informational brochure ask: 'Such a thing happens? Whose fault? What has to be done?' This title not only unites the three core framing tasks, but is culturally highly resonant: It refers to prominent works of Russian literature that deal with culprits and structures[15] as well as with solutions to problems.[16] Another short, simple phrase, 'together we make it happen', reflects RACCW's perception of itself as part of a bigger national or transnational network of organisations and institutions that combat trafficking. The slogan suggests that networking is a prerequisite for an effective anti-trafficking policy and that RACCW is willing (but also has to) co-operate in order to reach this goal. Successful networking also strengthens public persuasion; inside the network's structures, RACCW might open new windows of opportunity and various channels for circulating its ideas and practices. Conversely, RACCW benefits from the flow of information provided by this kind of cooperation.

---

14 See page 5.
15 In 1846 Aleksander Herzen wrote his first novel, 'Kto vinovat?' (Whose fault?). It tells of a *ménage à trois* in an aristocratic milieu that destroys a happy marriage. To the question 'Whose fault?', Herzen responds that societal constraints may result in picking the wrong partner.
16 The question 'What has to be done?' recurs in Lenin's 1902 treatise when, in cooperation with Nadezhda Krupskaya, he drafted the main features of socialism: an army of professional revolutionaries acting as the vanguard of the working classes. 'What has to be done?' is also the title of a novel written by Chernyshevskiĭ in 1863. It describes the life of 'new men' inspired by Fourier's utopia and airs the ideas of collective life and co-operative work. The novel's central themes are education and women's liberation.

Women's Human Rights in the Russian Context

In order to assess the frame's resonance and to locate it in the Russian context, I will now draw on the findings of numerous studies on the topics of NGOs, social movements, western assistance and democratisation. I will adopt a taxonomy put forward by MacMahon and Ballentine, who distinguish among three sectors (which, however, are strongly bounded and depend on each other reciprocally), in which NGOs have to do well in order to survive: community outreach, advocacy and infrastructure (organisational capacity and networking) (McMahon, 29–53; Ballentine, 91–125). Subsequently, the impact the frame makes on the three sectors provides information about its resonance.

Community Outreach

Scholars frequently justify the NGOs' decision to frame violence against women as a violation of human rights by claiming that the concept of human rights fills the vacuum regarding cultural meanings left by Soviet ideology, which degraded the notions of equality and equal rights. Concepts like feminism or discrimination were perceived as foreign, bourgeois or irrelevant in terms of living conditions in post-Soviet Russia (Posadskaya-Vanderbeck, 1997, 380; Sperling, 1999, 87ff.). To this day, numerous activists refuse to call themselves 'feminists' because the term connotes a specifically western concept of emancipation (Feree Marx/Risman/Sperling, 2001, 1168; McIntosh Sundstrom, 2000, 207–229). Hence, is framing violence against women as a violation of human rights the most straightforward normative measure to sensitise public awareness to women's demands? As Lisa McIntosh Sundstrom argues, NGOs that promote universal norms, like the norm against bodily harm, are more likely to attract public support. NGO mobilisation will most likely succeed when discrimination and violence against women is not framed in terms of equal treatment but in terms of human rights (McIntosh Sundstrom, 2005, 419–449).

Advocacy

To align the women's/human rights frame's benefits with the network's infrastructure, activists must be able to perform as advocates – or, as James Richter puts it: 'Donors (…) identify women's rights as a priority within larger contexts of human rights and civil society. Because Russian feminists have based their movement on Western ideas, their mission and priorities were recognised and understood among Western donors' (Richter, 2002, 54–90). At the regional and local levels, government bodies and the mass media have argued with NGOs on the subject of 'elimination of all forms of discrimination against women.' The voice of NGOs can no longer be ignored, however, because they are speaking the language of international organisations and UN resolutions. They use this tactic as a strategy for making their demands more concrete, exerting pressure on policy-makers and insisting upon compliance with international rules (Sperling, 1999, 220ff.). RACCW has a long list of positive achievements that includes obtaining subsidies for printing costs, organising expert conferences, arranging round tables and seminars with journalists, cooperation with local police forces, and participation in the State Duma's inter-agency working group on anti-trafficking legislation. According to James Richter, focusing on international norms has 'enabled women activists to gain symbolic victories that may shape outcomes sometime in the future; in the short term, the focus on international norms may divert activists from the more fundamental work of mobilizing support from below.' (Richter, 2002, 54–90)

Networking and Capacity Building

Framing processes not only influence national policies and publics, but also further the exchange and circulation of ideas and practices across different movements and different cultures. They also aid in the instigation of a united, global movement. Bilingual publications as well as an international index of authors and descriptions of 'best practices' by foreign NGOs lay testimony to the advances made in this field. The fact that imported ideas and practices transfer positively to local contexts while also being subjected to significant changes serves as a further indicator that transnational processes of organisation are taking place amongst feminists. Nevertheless, scholars question if the constant lobbying of policy-makers and transnational advocacy work might come at the price of 'local belonging' (Hemment, 2004, 815–840).

Attaching to (women's) human rights matters especially in the search for potential allies, such as bigger transnational human rights NGOs, like Amnesty International[17], or well-known, nationally active NGOs, like the Moscow Helsinki Committee. Such co-operation not only ensures that women's rights will be accepted by 'classic' human rights NGOs, but also strengthens the legitimacy of women's rights as a part of the human rights advocacy work (Wedel, 2002, 106).

Conclusions

To conclude, I will assess to what extent 'women's human rights' constitutes an appealing mobilising frame in the Russian context. One of the most important findings is that in order to be successful, the framing strategies have to be adapted to the Rus-

---

17 In 2003 Amnesty International and RACCW launched a campaign aimed at raising public awareness of violence against women as a human rights abuse, encouraging dialogue with the authorities on implementing necessary measures, strengthening co-operation between Amnesty International's groups and crisis centres in the Russian Federation and organising joint actions between Amnesty International's membership and RACCW.

sian cultural and political context. By adopting this frame, RACCW avoids potentially offensive anti-discrimination language and stresses values and norms like non-violence and peace which appeal to the society as a whole. Nevertheless, public awareness about trafficking is very low; it is not considered to be a problem affecting the general public. Due to sensational mass media coverage, people frequently believe that trafficking in women is the result of the risky behaviour undertaken by young women who voluntarily engage in prostitution (Tyurukanova, 2006).

Promoting women's human rights seems to be a much more useful discursive tool when it comes to collaboration with state and international organisations. At this point the frame contributes to strengthening the advocacy position of the women's NGOs, be it in trials, when supported survivors appear as bearers of rights instead of victim-applicants, or in projects where women's human rights form a basis for negotiation and co-operation. But in order to avoid unrealistic enthusiasm about the norm's impact, it is worth mentioning that the ratification of an international convention[18] does not necessarily entail financial stability for anti-trafficking-projects or NGOs. Another relevant impediment for successfully advocating human rights is that for the most part, donor or state organisations hold sway over discourses and definitions, thereby leading to the reframing of counter-trafficking strategies as the control of irregular migration or the combating of organised crime at the expense of human rights approaches.

As a modest success for promoting women's human rights, one might consider an amendment to the Penal Code of the Russian Federation in December 2003. The amendment consisted of two new articles: 'Trafficking in Human Beings' and 'Exploitation of Slave Labour.' In January 2005, a law on the protection of victims and witnesses during investigations and court proceedings came into force as well. Compared with the holistic character of the draft law[19], important aspects like survivor rehabilitation and the prevention of trafficking in human beings were neglected, but it nevertheless was a small step towards the gearing of legal regulations towards the protection of women's human rights.

In conclusion, it is evident that successful frames depend on 'living resources' such as activists, experts, and scholars, who not only secure access to opportunity structures but also significantly influence the structure and the strength of the mobilising frame. The work of Marina Pisklakova (director of the ANNA crisis centre) might be seen as an example of the extent to which the success of frames depends on the abilities and efforts of an individual norm entrepreneur (Keck /Sikkink, 1995, 14). In various speeches, she has stated that violence against women is also a matter of

---

18   The Soviet Union ratified CEDAW in 1981. In its role as successor state, the Russian Federation assumed the obligations arising from CEDAW without reservations.
19   The draft law working group brought together several anti-trafficking advocates from different organisational backgrounds, such as NGO-activists, scientists and politicians.

reproductive health, which governments should be willing to protect by supplying NGOs with the necessary material assistance for the protection and support of survivors of violence. In the EU, linking new and old norms (such as the anti-violence norm, the norm of women's human rights, the norm of equality and the anti-slavery norm) turned out to be a successful strategy for norm entrepreneurs to reactivate and promote the anti-trafficking norm (Locher, 2002, 59–80). These positive experiences justify these frame-alignment strategies and nourish the hope for similarly positive outcomes in Russia.

References

Abubikirova, H. I. (ed.) (2004), Protivodeistvie Torgovle Lyud'mi. Sbornik normativnykh pravovnykh dokumentov, Moskva: EKSlit.

Ballentine, K., International Assistance and the Development of Independent Mass Media in the Czech and Slovak Republics, in: Mendelson, Sarah E. / Glenn, John K. (eds.): The power and limits of NGOs. A critical look at building democracy in Eastern Europe and Eurasia. New York: Columbia University Press, 91–125.

Benford, R. D. / Snow, D. A .(2000), Framing Processes and Social Movements: an Overview and Assessment, in: Annual Review of Sociology, (vol. 26), 611–639.

Brown Thompson, K. (2002), Women's Rights Are Human Rights, in: Khagram, Sanjeev (Ed.): Restructuring World Politics: Transnational Social Movements, Networks, and Norms, Minneapolis [u.a.], University of Minnesota Press.

Feree Marx, M. / Risman, B. / Sperling, V. (2001), Constructing Global Feminism: Transnational Advocacy Networks and Russian Women's Activism. In: Signs, (vol. 26), No. 4, 1155–1186.

Hellmann, K.-U. (1999), Paradigmen der Bewegungsforschung. Eine Fachdisziplin auf dem Weg zur normalen Wissenschaft, in: Klein, Ansgar / Legrand, Hans-Josef / Leif, Thomas (Eds.): Neue soziale Bewegungen. Impulse, Bilanzen, Perspektiven. Opladen: Westdeutscher Verlag, 91–113.

Hemment, Julie (2004), Global Civil Society and the Local Costs of Belonging: Defining Violence against Women in Russia, in: Signs: Journal of Women in Culture and Society, (vol. 29), 815–840.

Jordan, Ann D. (2002), Human rights or wrongs? The struggle for a rights-based response to trafficking in human beings, in: Gender and Development, (vol. 10), No. 1, 28–37.

Keck, M. E. / Sikkink, K. (1995), Activists beyond Borders: Advocacy Networks in International Politics. Ithaca: Cornell University Press.

Locher, B. (Fall 2002), Internationale Normen und regionaler Policy-Wandel: Frauen-handel in der Europäischen Union, in: WeltTrends, No. 36, 59–80.

―――― (2002), Trafficking in Women in the European Union. A Norm-Based Constructiv-ist Approach. Dissertation, Institut für Politikwissenschaften, Universität Bremen.

Malysheva, M. / Tyurukanova, E. (2001): Zhenshchina, migratsiia, gosudarstvo. Mosk-va: Academia.

McIntosh Sundstrom, L. (Spring 2005), Foreign Assistance, International Norms, and NGO Development: Lessons from the Russian Campaign, in: International Organ-ization, (vol. 59), 419–449.

―――― (Spring 2000), Women's NGOs in Russia: Struggling from the Margins, in: Demok-ratisiya, 207–229.

McMahon, P.: International Actors and Women's NGOs in Poland and Hungary, in: Mendelson, Sarah E. / Glenn, John K. (Eds.): The power and limits of NGOs. A criti-cal look at building democracy in Eastern Europe and Eurasia. New York: Colum-bia University Press

Posadskaya-Vanderbeck, A. (1997), On the Threshold of the Classroom: Dilemmas for Post-soviet Russian Feminism, in: Kaplan, Cora / Keates, Debra / Scott, Joan W. (Eds.): Transitions, Environments, Translations: Feminisms in International Poli-tics. London: Routledge, 373–382.

Pearson, E. (2005), Historical Development of Trafficking – The Legal Framework for Anti-Trafficking Interventions, in: Sector Project against Trafficking in Women (Ed.): Challenging Trafficking in Persons. Theoretical Debate & Practical Ap-proaches, Baden-Baden: Nomos, 20–26.

Richter, J.(2002), Evaluating Western Assistance to Russian Women's Organizations, in: Mendelson, Sarah E. / Glenn, John K. (Eds.): The Power and Limits of NGOs. New York: Columbia University Press, 54–90.

Rimashevskaya, N.M. (ed.) (2005), Razorvat' krug molchaniya. O nasilii v otnoshenii zhenshchin. Moskva: KomKniga.

Ruppert, U. (2001), Von Frauenbewegungen zu Frauenorganisationen, von Empo-werment zu FrauenMenschenrechten. Über das Globalwerden internationaler Frauenbewegungspolitik, in: Österreichische Zeitschrift für Politikwissenschaft, (vol. 30), 203–219.

Schmidt-Häuer, J. (2000), Menschenrechte – Männerrechte – Frauenrechte: Gewalt gegen Frauen als Menschenrechtsproblem. Hamburg, 286.

Sinitsyn, F. L. (ed.) (2002), Prevention of Human Trafficking / Predotvrashchenie Tor-govli Lyud'mi. Perm: Tipografiya Kuptsa Tarasova.

———— (2002b), Prava Cheloveka i Torgovlya Lyud'mi: Spravochnik, Perm: Tipografiya Kuptsa Tarasova.

————(2003), Pravo na zashchitu ot vsekh form nasiliia, Perm: Tipografiya Kuptsa Tarasova.

Sperling, V. (1999), Organizing Women in Contemporary Russia. Engendering Transition. Cambridge: Cambridge University Press, 220ff.

Tiurukanova, E.V. (2006), Human Trafficking in the Russian Federation Inventory and Analysis of the Current Situation and Responses. Report conducted by E.V. Tiurukanova and the Institute for Urban Economics for the UN/IOM Working Group on Trafficking in Human Beings, Moscow.

Topan, A. (2000), Transformationsprozess in Osteuropa und Organisierte Kriminalität am Beispiel des Frauen- und Mädchenhandels. Hamburg: Verlag Trevi.

Traĭnerskiĭ Portfel (2004), Protivodeistvie Torgovlya Lyud'mi, Moskva.

Uçarer, Emek M. (1999), Trafficking in Women. Alternate Migration or Modern Slave Trade, in: Meyer, Mary K./ Prügl, Elisabeth (Eds.): Gender Politics in Global Governance. Lanham: Rowman & Littlefield Publishers, 230–244.

Uhl, B. (2000), Internationale Lobbyarbeit für FrauenMenschenrechte, in: KOK (Ed.): Frauenhandel(n) in Deutschland. Frauenprojekte in Deutschland zur Problematik Frauenhandel. Eine Dokumentation. Berlin: Oktoberdruck, 94–102.

Wedel, H. (Fall 2002), Strategische Allianzen gegen sexuelle Gewalt, in: WeltTrends, No. 36, 102–122.

Wölte, S. (2002), Von Lokal nach International und zurück: Gewalt gegen Frauen und internationale Frauenmenschenrechtspolitik, in: Dackweiler, Regina / Schäfer, Reinhild (Eds.): Gewalt-Verhältnisse. Feministische Perspektiven auf Geschlecht und Gewalt. Frankfurt am Main: Campus-Verlag, 221–248.

Zwingel, S. (2002), Was trennt Krieg und Frieden? Gewalt gegen Frauen aus feministischer und völkerrechtlicher Perspektive, in: Harders, Cilja / Roß, Bettina (Eds.): Geschlechterverhältnisse in Krieg und Frieden. Perspektiven der feministischen Analyse internationaler Beziehungen, Opladen: Leske+Budrich, 175–188.

Noémi Kakucs and Róbert Sata

Violence against Women in European Societies: East and West

Introduction

The shift towards the internationalisation of social policy regulations marks not only the advancement of globalisation, but also the extension of responsibility to the global level. Since the late 1970s, violence against women has ceased to be considered a private issue to be treated in the domestic national arena; it has been upgraded to a public issue to be regulated globally. Violence against women has become a global social issue to be regulated primarily by the United Nations and other international organisations. Several international documents indicate a global commitment to protect women from discrimination and violence; one could therefore easily conclude that violence against women is a thing of the past. Nothing could be further from the truth, however. Due to the politically charged nature of the issue, the need for a global concerted effort to combat domestic violence received insufficient attention until the second half of the 1990s. Furthermore, the twofold private character of domestic violence (regarded first as a private issue and secondly as one that should be regulated by individual states) has served and continues to be used as grounds for non-intervention on behalf of numerous states.

This paper addresses the effect of global regulation on national policy developments on domestic violence against women. It also highlights the importance of country-specific social and political contexts in determining the impact of these international norms. The authors aim to identify how global regulations are implemented into specific national contexts. This is done through a brief review of the relevant international documents, followed by a careful analysis of specific policies aimed at protecting women undertaken in Hungary and the United Kingdom. We pay special attention to how international norms were incorporated into official policy in order to identify some of the relevant factors responsible for the dramatic discrepancy between the position of women in British and Hungarian societies.

The selection of the two case studies was motivated by the underlying similarities between the two nations: both are signatories of the relevant UN documents as well as EU-initiated statements on women's rights. At the same time, important differences between the two countries exist, most importantly in their political cultures; Hungary is a democratising post-socialist country with a young democratic culture, whereas the United Kingdom is considered a classical liberal state. Their positions within the EU differ as well. Hungary became a member only in 2004; the United Kingdom is an established and powerful member, joining the Union in 1973. This imbalance in status had important implications for the character of international pressure that the two countries faced in the decade before 2004. Hungary tended to put up little resistance, eager to become a member of the European Union (according to the popular rhetoric of 'return to Europe'). The United Kingdom, having one of the strongest Eurosceptic societies in Europe and a permanent seat on the UN Security Council, had a much stronger position against the tide of international pressures to change its domestic policy. What is important for this study is that while both Hungary and Britain are subject to the same international norms regarding the protection of women, they exhibit very different development in terms of their domestic policies aimed at combating the abuse of and violence against women. This observation highlights the importance of domestic factors as well as the role of international pressure in determining policy change due to supranational demands.

The Internationalisation of Women's Rights

Women's rights have been on the international agenda for a long time, but it was only the mid-1990s that saw a rapid development of internationally endorsed women's rights. The United Nations World Conference on Human Rights, held in 1993 in Vienna, recognised women's human rights as an integral part of universal human rights, calling for joint action to eliminate gender-based violence. In so doing, the UN compensated for the shortcomings of the *Convention on the Elimination of Discrimination Against Women* 1979 (CEDAW), which originally did not address violence against women at all. Furthermore, as of 1992, CEDAW includes violence against women, including domestic violence, in its definition of discrimination (clarified by *General Recommendation* number 19, adopted in 1992).

The UN *Declaration on the Elimination of Violence against Women* (DEVAW) was also adopted in 1993, the first specific international act to deal with violence against women. The Declaration clearly asserts that violence perpetrated in the private sphere constitutes a violation of human rights. By proclaiming that women's human rights must be protected not only in the public sphere but also in the home, the Declaration dismantled the public/private divide that had previously served to legitimate the lack of state intervention. The Declaration also reaffirms that violence against women is a manifestation of the historically unequal power relations between the sexes. Article 2 of the DEVAW (1993) prohibits violence against women, defining it to encompass battering, sexual abuse of female children in the household, marital rape and violence relating to exploitation (UN 1993).

The *Beijing Declaration and Platform for Action,* adopted at the Fourth World Conference on Women in 1995, is viewed by feminist scholars as a landmark of the transnational regulation of gender equality policy. The *Beijing Declaration* encourages states to take measures to prevent, punish and eliminate acts of violence against women, be they perpetrated by the state or by private persons. In 1999 the General Assembly adopted a protocol to the Women's Rights Convention, providing victims of sexual discrimination with a direct complaint mechanism. By ratifying the optional protocol, states recognise the authority of the Committee on the Elimination of Discrimination Against Women to receive and consider complaints from individuals or groups under its jurisdiction. However, the Committee only considers complaints after the complainant has already exhausted all available domestic avenues for redress.

The final report of the Beijing +5 Conference (UN 2000), held in June 2000 in New York, calls for additional measures to eliminate obstacles to the implementation of the Beijing Platform for Action. The Report of the Ad Hoc Committee highlights governments' responsibility to revise legislation and introduce effective legislation on violence against women 'to ensure that all women and girls are protected against all forms of physical, psychological and sexual violence, and are provided recourse of justice' (UN 2000). Furthermore, it recommended the prosecution and sentencing of perpetrators as well as the introduction of preventive measures.

However, governments have been slow to act upon these recommendations. It comes as little surprise that five years later, the Beijing +10 Conference resolution again concluded with recommendations underscoring the importance of governmental responsibility not only in introducing but also enforcing comprehensive legislation by allocating necessary resources for the prevention of violence as well as assistance and legal aid for victims (CSW 2005). This responsibility also entails monitoring the effectiveness of implementation via the compilation of sex-disaggregated data.

Within Europe, the main transnational organisations promoting the protection of human rights are the Council of Europe and the European Union. One of the major objectives of the Council of Europe is the protection of human rights and equal dignity and integrity for both women and men. Violence is viewed as an obstacle to achieving gender equality. Originally, the European Union (which is concerned primarily with economic issues) addressed gender inequality only within the frame of employment and labour market discrimination. However, since 1997, the European Commission has tried to include the issue of domestic violence on the highest political agenda by fostering co-operation and co-ordination between member states as well as by helping NGOs specialised in the field to improve statistics and information on violence against women. The same year, the European Parliament urged the Commission to launch a campaign to promote a zero-tolerance approach towards violence against women. Meanwhile, the European Women's Lobby created the European Policy Action Centre on Violence Against Women and its Observatory on Violence. Furthermore, there are several community programs funded by the European

Union that facilitate networking between organisations as well as the spread of information, like the successful Daphne I-III program running since 1997.

To conclude, recent international documents issued by the United Nations, the Council of Europe, and the European Union show consensus in that they regard domestic violence as both a gender crime and a serious welfare issue. Although these international regulations are often without legal binding power, one can still argue that they wield a strong normative power, because they define intolerable state behaviour as well as encourage countries to adopt a zero-tolerance attitude towards violence against women. Nevertheless, the promotion of international norms of protection of women has had mixed results, and the implementation of international recommendations by domestic governments is far from perfect.

Social Constructivist Theory and the Spread of International Norms

In order to assess the impact of global regulation on national policy developments, this paper relies on social constructivist theory of international relations that highlights the role of various types of non-state actors (including not only inter-governmental organisations but also epistemic and professional communities). According to this theory, the diffusion of international norms in the human rights area depends primarily on the existence and activity of transnational networks, which are capable of linking together domestic NGOs, international operating NGOs, international institutions and national governments (Risse-Kappen 1997) (Risse and Sikkink 1999) (Risse et al. 2001).

One of the most prominent examples of constructivist theory examining the diffusion of international norms is the five-phase 'spiral model' developed by Thomas Risse and Kathryn Sikkink (1999), which tries to capture the specific mechanisms through which international norms can lead to enduring changes in domestic politics. The underlying logic of this model is that transnational advocacy networks put norm violations by the states on the international agenda, they empower and mobilise domestic organisations, and 'they challenge norm-violating governments by creating a transnational structure pressuring such regimes simultaneously from above and from below' (Risse and Sikkink 1999, 5). The model traces what the authors label as the 'socialisation process' of human rights norms, focusing on the causal mechanisms, which they identify as 'phases' that facilitate the internalisation of norms and practices into domestic political arenas. Risse and Sikkink show that this process of norms socialisation is crucial for understanding how the international society transmits norms to its members.

Let us now briefly explore the different phases proposed by the authors. Phase one of the model is the initial state of *repression* perpetrated by the state. At this stage, norm-violating states enact policies of oppression while domestic human rights organisations attempt to document violations and bring them to the attention of the international community. If these domestic advocacy networks succeed in drawing attention to the abuses, there is a transition into the second phase of the spiral model, *denial*. At this phase, once the international community is alerted to the human rights abuses in question, the norm-violating state is placed in the position of having to respond to the accusations of repression. In most instances, this response is to deny the charges levelled against them, often in the form of questioning the legitimacy of human rights norms in general by arguing that state sovereignty should supersede concerns over human rights (Risse and Sikkink 1999, 22–24).

According to the contributors, movement to the third phase – that of *tactical concession* – of the spiral model is based primarily on the strength of the human rights networks and the vulnerability of the state to external pressure. Risse and Sikkink argue that this stage is the most important component in achieving sustainable, long-term human rights improvements. During this stage, governments begin to make concessions and enact policies aimed at ending human rights abuses. Some may even begin to incorporate the language of human rights into domestic political discourse (Risse and Sikkink 1999, 25–28). Completing the third phase successfully, states then move to a fourth, *prescriptive* phase in their internalisation of human rights norms and practices. At this point, norm-violating states are confronted with fully mobilised human rights networks and an increasing level of internalisation of human rights norms, which ultimately force the state to either liberalise their policies permanently or accept some form of substantive constitutional or governmental change (Risse and Sikkink 1999, 29–31). The final phase of the model is *rule-consistent behaviour*. In this last stage, governments institutionalise international human rights norms into actual state practice, thus completing the spiral of policy change proposed by Risse and Sikkink (Risse and Sikkink 1999, 31–33).

While Risse and Sikkink advance their model as a powerful tool to describe the process of how norm-violating states are forced to comply with international standards, their critics argue that the model cannot be generalised to all cases and situations, and is relevant only for smaller and less powerful states (Pace 2001, 9–11). Notwithstanding this criticism, we argue that the spiral model is well suited for assessing the development of women's rights in the two European societies under examination. We argue that the question of societal justice with regards to women's rights is a very specific situation, and employing the model only on two case studies will not run the risk of over-generalisation.

Meanwhile, it has to be emphasised that the protection of women's rights, especially the fight to stop violence against women, constitutes a special case of human rights protection. States that fail to combat violence against women infringe not only on women's rights but also flout the universal human rights to life, freedom, or dignity. In this sense the spiral model that was originally developed for assessing the internalisation of international human rights seems well suited to direct our research. Due to the complexity of the social problem that violence against women presents, as the CEDAW convention also suggests, it is not enough to change public institutions and practices to foster non-discrimination; the private and family spheres also need to be addressed by states via proactive measures. This again would warrant the use of the spiral model for guiding our analysis, as it enables us to address not only the formal governmental levels but also the less formal networks that exist in civil society.

The most important merit of the social constructivist approach is that it demonstrates the very important role of domestic structures in mobilising for and bringing about policy change in the process of transposition of international norms. According to Risse-Kappen (1997), the impact of transnational actors on state policies depends on two factors. First, the impact is contingent upon the domestic structures, i.e. the normative and organisational mechanisms that form the state and structure society, and thus link the two into a polity. Second, the impact of transnational actors on various state practices also depends on the international institutionalisation of a given issue area.

Nevertheless, the spiral model does not shed too much light on what the nature of domestic structures or international norms should look like in order to facilitate rapid adoption of international standards. In a different book, Risse-Kappen offers a more detailed outline of how domestic structures matter when he differentiates three tiers of domestic structure that determine the acceptance of international norms, these being the structure of the political institutions (centralised vs. fragmented), the structure of demand formation in civil society (strong societies vs. fragmented societies), and policy networks (compromise-oriented consensual vs. polarised). Based on these tiers, one can identify six types of domestic structures, each with different implications for the transposal of international norms (Risse-Kappen 1997, 20–25). Thus the differences in the domestic structures – such as having a strong civil society with a compromise-oriented and centralised government – determine the variations in the policy impact of transnational actors.

Yet others argue similarly when they identify several intervening factors, the presence or absence of which determines domestic adjustment due to international pressure (Risse et al. 2001, 1–2). These factors are the following: veto points in the domestic structures, facilitating formal institutions, organisational and policymaking cultures, the differential empowerment of domestic actors, and learning. Although labelled differently, these criteria point in the same direction of the three tiers of domestic structures, calling for a strong civil society, a formal institutional structure, and, most importantly, a consensual policy-making culture that can also include veto-rights for specific actors. In conclusion, one can argue that if the domestic structures are open, i.e. the national government is responsive and civil society is strong, international norms will be adopted more easily. Furthermore, if a society fits all the criteria of a strong civil society, one could argue that there would be no need for international institutional pressure, since this super-society would adjust to the changing international standards on its own.

Going back to the spiral model that we adopted for the purposes of this paper, we argue that the discrepancy between the local implementations of global regulations on violence against women can be explained primarily by the differences between the domestic structures of the states, with international pressure relegated to a secondary role. This is due to the existence of public bodies competent in gender equality matters; these may temper the influence of transnational pressure since the autonomy, degree of specialisation and the function of these bodies determine their transformative potential. As we noted earlier, the relationship between the state and society is critical. The relative strength and autonomy of the state and society from each other, as well as the access civil society has to the political and legal system (and therefore to policy), all determine the character of different policy networks.

Consequently, the existence of relatively strong and mobilised women's movements in society is indispensable for structural changes regarding women's rights in any polity. In cases where the women's movement is weak relative to other groups (e.g. trade unions or religious and professional groups), the adaptation of transnational norms of women's rights is hindered. This is especially true with respect to domestic violence regulation for several reasons. First, the transnational regulations on violence against women bear only normative power in the absence of any sanctions for non-abiding states aside from shaming. Second, in the case of domestic violence, there is no direct infringement of women's rights on behalf of the state; rather, the state acts as a passive arena. Combating domestic violence would require the state to intervene in the private sphere, an action that is contrary to the tendency of liberal states to withdraw from family matters.

At the same time, as we have already shown, the fight against violence against women has been highly institutionalised at the international level since the mid-1990s. The United Nations regulations not only prohibit discrimination against women, but call for states to implement positive measures. Though primarily an economic organ, the European Union has also incorporated the issue of violence against women in its political agenda. However, it should not be forgotten that despite their role in world politics, both the UN and the EU have only normative power in the issue area of women's rights, which might substantially affect their capacity to pressure individual member-states on gender equality issues. This angle casts doubts on the impact international initiatives can have in pushing forward and benchmarking the member states' regulations on domestic violence. What is important to remember is that the adaptational pressure of these international organisations is not sufficient to effect domestic change.

Domestic Violence in the United Kingdom and Hungary

Let us now turn to addressing women's rights and violence against women in our two case studies. Having examined the relevant international norms on domestic violence, we shall now proceed with taking a closer look at the situation in Britain and Hungary. Our analysis is based on a comparative perspective, and we shall concentrate on comparing the role of civil society (women's movements in particular), the character of public bodies, and last but not least, the level of domestic violence against women. The last and concluding part of this paper will present the findings of our comparative analysis.

As mentioned before, the impact of global regulations on domestic structures are transposed by pre-existing practices and institutions. Institutionalised factors, like the legal arena and state/society relations, as well as less institutionalised aspects, like the orientation of the ruling coalition, all influence policy and structural outcomes. Following Caporaso and Jupille's (2001) comparative analysis of the implementation of gender equality policies in France and the United Kingdom, we will assess the developments in domestic violence regulations in Britain and Hungary relative to the role and impact of domestic actors like gender equality agencies and domestic courts as well as women's movements as major mediating factors. At the same time, in tracing the development of domestic policy for the protection of women, we will also attempt to highlight the role of the relevant international documents in this process in order to evaluate what role international pressure has played in directing this policy.

The Role of Civil Society: Women's Movements

In the post-war period, Western European societies experienced massive women's mobilisation. Inspired by the American civil rights movement and the anti-war demonstrations, the women's liberation movement united the issues of women's health and reproductive rights, discrimination in the employment market, etc., under the slogan 'personal is political', which became popular all over the world. Though clearly influenced by American second-wave feminism, women's mobilisation in Britain was originally more related to working class socialism demanding equal pay and equal opportunities in education and work. Nevertheless, with the passage of time, issues like the right to legal and safe abortion, and male violence against women have also become focal points of feminist campaigning in the United Kingdom.

Available research assessing the development and impact of the post-war British women's movement offers an ambiguous and somewhat contradictory picture. In describing the developments of second-wave feminism in Britain in comparison to the second-wave feminism in the United States, some authors (Gelb 1989; Lovenduski and Randall 1993) have highlighted the emergence of small, non-hierarchical organisations failing to engage in nationwide campaigning and reluctant towards cooperation with the state. Gelb and Hart (1999) attribute the gradual institutionalisation and centralisation of women's movements to the recognition that their policy access and influence is restricted due to their informal structure. On the other hand, Nash argues that the adoption of equality legislation in Britain in the mid-1970s marked an opening in the political opportunity structures towards gender equality issues, which could be partly attributed to the country's eligibility requirements to join the EEC, and partly to pressure exerted by women's organisations and trade unions for equal pay during the post-war period (Nash 2002, 317–8). Bretherton and Sperling (1996) also describe a wide network of women's organisations operating at the local community level that are not dependent on the state and actively participate in everyday politics.

However, it should be mentioned that even if the character of women's movement of the 1960s and '70s is disputed, major policy changes were nonetheless introduced during this period (like the legalisation of abortion in 1967, the Equal Pay Act in 1970, and the Sex Discrimination Act in 1975). Whether women's movements of that era might have been decentralised or could have pursued divergent policy objectives is less important for the present paper, as women's mobilisation remained constantly high throughout this period, and the United Kingdom's joining of the EEC merely opened another window of opportunity for women's groups. This historical development has led to the present scenario, in which women's movements' political access and influence in the United Kingdom is relatively high due to strong mobilisation and organisation along different lines of interest.

In Hungary, during the Soviet regime, the imposition of gender equality by authoritarian governments from above resulted in equitable gender regimes resembling those of the Scandinavian countries. Women in communist nations experienced high rates of participation in politics and the labour market, low gender pay gaps, and extensive childcare facilities. However, the public gender equality was only a façade, as the legal and social provisions supporting women's participation in the labour market and political representation did not address domestic inequality in the private sphere (Pascall and Lewis 2004, 375). Authoritarianism did not leave space for any 'genuine' social mobilisation or women's movement.

The post-socialist regime change in Hungary (which, as Chilton argues, was due to the seriously weakened state faced with a highly mobilised opposition society) also brought new impetus to gender equality policy. However, to the disappointment of Western feminists, Hungarian women, unlike other dissident groups, failed to take advantage of the political turmoil. The transition period thus marked the emergence of 'masculinism' (Watson 2000, 369–84) and neo-traditionalist discourse on women in Hungary. In addition to the sharp decline in political and economic participation, this was manifested in the debate on abortion that all newly emerging political parties used as a discursive opportunity to define their own positions (Gal 1994).

We cannot overemphasise the fact that the concept of civil society in Hungary was completely different from its counterpart in liberal democracies. Though it is not the aim of this paper to provide a definition of civil society, it should be stressed that during the Soviet regime in Hungary, society defined itself in opposition to the state (Chilton 1997, 194–5). Therefore, the state-versus-society politics rendered the family as the only anti-political space[1] (Goven 2000) and fostered traditional roles of men and women, counteracting the emancipatory efforts of state feminism. The lack of women's mobilisation and the subsequent emergence of a neo-traditionalist discourse on women in the early 1990s in Hungary can be viewed as a consequence of the previous regime's statist feminism. It is no wonder that the issue of domestic violence was not publicly addressed in Hungarian society: it was regarded as a family matter, and the family sphere was to be protected from any kind of state intervention.

Despite this hostile climate towards any kind of feminist enterprise, the numbers of NGOs dealing with human rights and women's issues increased dramatically after the political transition (Krizsán and Pap 2005, 14). This can only be explained in light of the universal values promoted by the supranational character of international institutions like the UN or the European Union, of which Hungary was eager to become a fully accepted member. This in turn presented an opportunity structure for different movements and NGOs (including women's movements and NGOs) to seek international support to further their interests vis-à-vis their national governments (Pető and Manners 2006).

This was also the case with the establishment of the first Hungarian organisation dealing with violence against women. It was established only in 1994 by several Hungarian women who had participated in an international seminar on 'Violence against

---

1   Anti-politics refers to the disengagement with state-linked political activity in favour of private life and the reconstitution of civil society. It was the practice of acting outside the state. See: Konrád 1984.

Women' at the Women's Commission sessions of the Helsinki Citizens' Assembly, held in Bratislava, Slovakia. The NaNE, i.e. Nők a Nőkért az Erőszak Ellen (Women for Women against Violence) established their office in Budapest with the aim of operating a phone line for women experiencing violence, pressing for the introduction of relevant legislation and providing support services for survivors of violence (Corrin 1999). Other human rights organisations, such as the Women's and Children's Rights Center and the Habeas Corpus Working Group (HCWG), joined NaNE in mounting awareness-raising campaigns about the seriousness of the problem and in compelling the national government to enact legislation that properly addressed the issue of domestic violence. In 2006, the Hungarian state still opposes the work this nationwide NGO performs, and the only support it offers is the occasional donation of shelters for women. Needless to say, the state's stance is a far cry from a national strategy or action plan to combat domestic violence, leaving NaNE (an NGO) to act as the most influential player competent in issues related to violence against women.

The degree of political access and influence on policy exerted by women in the two countries show several differences, which can be attributed to various reasons. In the United Kingdom, women's groups are highly professionalised and mobilised and enjoy a relatively high level of autonomy from the state. This is due to the fact that early on, women's mobilisation was primarily community-based and strongly influenced by the international developments of the time, as our spiral model would predict. The relatively deep historical roots and continuity of women's movement in the United Kingdom also led to British women's groups becoming important domestic actors as well as playing a leading role in new international initiatives.

In comparison, women's mobilisation in Hungary underwent a completely different path of development. It was influenced from the very beginning by international women's movements, where Hungary acted as a norm-taking and not a norm-forming state. Furthermore, the initial positive influence exerted by the first wave of feminism was unable to induce enduring structural changes due to the two World Wars. The post-war socialist state, besides repressing any genuine societal mobilisation, took away all grounds for women's mobilisation by providing access to education, employment, political representation, as well as childcare facilities and legal abortion, rights that women in the Western societies had to fight for. Thus, with the regime change, Hungarian women had to start their mobilisation all over again in a sense. This task was coupled from the beginning with the international institutionalisation of gender equality, as Hungarian women's movements consciously sought influential transnational actors to legitimise their cause.

Public Bodies

In the United Kingdom, the establishment of gender equality machinery dates back to the 1970s. An Equal Opportunity Commission was created in response to the 1975 introduction of the Sex Discrimination Act and the Equal Pay Act. The establishment of the Commission facilitated the UK's entry into the EEC. With time, the position of the Equal Opportunity Commission grew stronger due to both the international and domestic pressure to which the state was exposed. Following the introduction of the Equal Pay Act, several equal pay claims were brought to tribunals, and the European Commission cited the UK for nonconformity with the EC directives (Caporaso and Jupille 2001, 31). In all instances, women's NGOs have played an influential part in both putting violations of the declared norm on the agenda and publicising the issue. This again conforms to the mechanisms of our spiral model that describe the different phases for exerting international pressure on domestic policy-makers. Thus, it can be claimed that the EU's (known at the time as the EEC) pressure facilitated both domestic demands for transforming gender-related policy and the institutionalisation of gender equality machinery in the United Kingdom.

The provisions of the 1995 *Beijing Declaration and Platform for Action*, namely the setting up of national machinery, were endorsed in the Labour Party's platform for the 1997 elections. Whether borne of true commitment or of rhetorical entrapment, the return to power of the Labour Party also marked the establishment of gender equality machinery at the highest political level. The Women's and Equality Unit was established within the UK's Cabinet Office, and the government appointed a Minister for Women as well (Silius 2002, 13). The responsibilities of these entities included the development and promotion of policies on gender-related issues (e.g. employment, health, violence, education, and the environment), co-ordination across the government, and improvement of representation of women at all levels of society.

By the beginning of the 21st century, the gender equality machinery formed in the late 1970s had achieved a rather high degree of institutionalisation (Silius 2002, 12–3). The Equal Opportunities Commission and the women's units enjoy a broad mandate and relative independence from the central government (Caporaso and Jupille 2001, 31), as they are more related to the local government organisations. This is due both to the character of British society, i.e. the mobilisation of women's movements, and the continued flow of international norms for the protection of women, whose demands on the state are ever increasing. Following the recent devolution of power that the United Kingdom experienced, the popularity and linkages with women's organisations of the Commission have only deepened, and women's representation in (local) politics has increased, in accordance with the requirements of Risse's responsive society: strong and formalised, decentralised, and consensual.

As the case of the United Kingdom shows, the institutionalisation of gender equality machinery is high at all levels. Further research could analyse in more detail the effective role and scope of authority the governmental gender machinery has for directing policy on the protection of women. However, the mere fact that the governmental equality machinery co-operates with the Equal Opportunities Commission and the Women's National Commission (an advisory non-governmental public body that acts as the principal medium between NGOs and the government) (Beveridge et al. 2000) as well as the women's units facilitates effective networking between state and non-state actors, enabling them to incorporate their interests regarding gender equality policies in the UK.

In Hungary, the institutionalisation of gender equality is not without antecedents. During the socialist era, Women's Councils were created within the Socialist Party that were immediately dissolved upon the fall of communism. These councils were viewed by many as embodying the normativeness of state feminism, something considered antithetical to the new democratic nature of Hungarian society. However, the second half of the 1990s marked the re-emergence of a national machinery to address women's issues as a requirement of the *1995 Beijing Declaration and Platform for Action*, of which Hungary is a signatory. The Secretariat for Women's Policy was set up within the Ministry of Labour relatively early, in 1995, immediately following the *Beijing Declaration*, in order to precede international pressure.

However, as civil society support for gender issues has been too weak to push from the bottom up to compel the national government to strengthen the agency's position, gender equality policies have been institutionalised only formally. Since its establishment, the Gender Equality Agency has been restructured and integrated into various ministerial departments, gradually losing its resources, its role and scope of authority. From the government office level in 2003, the gender equality machinery was demoted to the level of one small department integrated into the Ministry of Youth, Family and Social Affairs and Equal Opportunities by April 2006. Furthermore, it is less the institutional rank, but the subsuming of gender equality policy into general equal opportunities policy that undermines the legitimacy of a separate gender equality politics in Hungary.

The recent reorganisation of the Gender Equality Agency as well as the reestablishment of the Gender Equality Council (the former inoperative Council for the Representation of Women was dissolved in 2005) during the early autumn of 2006 could serve as a window of opportunity for women's groups to influence policy outcomes. While the initiative demonstrates the government's apparent desire to comply with the international standards, it is the structure of the societal actors that determines the future of the new machinery. To return to our spiral model, it is not enough that Hungarian women's movements can mobilise against and publicise internationally proscribed state action; they must foster rule-consistent behaviour not only on part of the state but also in society as a whole in order to complete the spiral of change.

The lack of political will on the government's part is clearly visible in terms of the minimal support it has given to the gender equality machinery since its inception. To complicate matters, the relevant influential social actors (women's NGOs and human rights NGOs) often harbour conflicting interests. The gender equality policy developments in Hungary show that international pressure was the primary driving force in the government's adoption of legal and institutional changes (which it did in order to comply with the EU *acquis*). Coupled with pressure from the UN vis-à-vis women's rights, the mounting pressure of the EU accession requirements succeeded in bringing Hungary to adopt the *2003 CXXV Act on Equal Treatment and Promotion of Equal Opportunities* as well as the preparation of the relevant policy papers prescribed by EU directives. However, lack of genuine societal support for these initiatives led only to the establishment of a powerless governmental department and the complete devolution of the Gender Equality Agency (the Council for Women's Representation was dissolved, and the Directorate for Gender Equality was headed for extinction). These events clearly fit the logic of the spiral model, namely how Hungary made tactical concessions and adopted prescriptive behaviour to comply with international – primarily EU – norms, which meant the introduction of some policy changes but a lack of any enduring structural change.

The developments in the institutionalisation of gender equality machineries in both countries show that international regulations require similar institutional adaptations, i.e. the institutionalisation of gender equality agencies (a goal of the 1995 Beijing Declaration) so that the compliance with the EU gender equality directives can be achieved. The major difference between the two cases is that while in Britain the legitimacy of the gender equality machinery is less likely to be threatened by the government because it has wide societal support, the institutionalisation of the gender equality machinery in Hungary is merely formal and thus lacks legitimacy on behalf of the state and society alike.

Domestic Violence

Based on our review of the formal settings, we argue that the fight against violence against women started much earlier in Britain than in Hungary. This can be attributed to the differences in political institutions as well as to the disparate ways in which women's movements developed in Western and Eastern Europe. Britain began a nationwide refuge movement as early as 1972 due to the continued pressure of activists to bring the issue on the political agenda. The initial ideas and debates about domestic violence and the creation of refuges for women in the 1970s were profoundly influenced by the slightly earlier developments that had taken place in the United

States (Dobash and Dobash 1992). According to Hester (2005), the development of regulations on domestic violence in Britain owes much to the previous work done in the United States, particularly the work of the Duluth Project in Minnesota. At that time, the UN human rights discourse had not yet been extended to include women's rights and the fight against violence. Therefore, the domestic changes in the UK can be largely attributed to the pressure exerted by civil society. The good practices of the Duluth Program would not have had entered the British context but for the activism of the women's movement in England during the 1970s and 1980s, which Hester considers critical for bringing violence against women onto the policy agenda (Hester 2005, 448). In this sense, the development of British policy on the protection of women conforms to our spiral model, which states that it is the domestic networks that initiate the entire process of policy change. Furthermore, it was the second-wave feminism, of which British (and other Western European) women's activists were a part, that facilitated the institutionalisation of the issue on the international agenda to ultimately be endorsed by powerful transnational actors like the UN.

The developments in the 1990s can thus partly be attributed to earlier domestic changes as well as the possible influence of the United Nations' Decade for Women, followed by the 1993 Vienna Congress, the publication of the DEVAW and the Platform for Action. These events may have served to raise public awareness about gender discrimination and violence against women. Nevertheless, Mullender (1999) attributes the rapid developments in domestic violence regulations that occurred in the 1990s to three violent family crimes that happened within a relatively short period of time. The ensuing policy changes and initiatives to counter domestic violence included the criminalisation of domestic violence (including pro-arrest policies), combined with more holistic community and multi-agency interventions (Mullender 1999, 3–4). The most important of the positive measures introduced included the police-initiated inauguration of an order on domestic violence and police involvement in inter-agency forums, as well as the establishment of designated Domestic Violence Units and other specialist units charged with responding to domestic violence and child sexual abuse.

Even if the major policy changes were introduced due more to domestic pressure than international influence, the governmental changes that have occurred since then show compliance with the international norms that British women's groups may or may have not used to exert pressure on their central government. Since the mid-1990s, changes have been introduced at the governmental level by both inter-ministerial and interdepartmental groups established to consider the policy implications of domestic violence. Within the field of violence against women, the Women's Unit, (renamed 'Women and Equality Unit' in 2001) is responsible for developing and promoting policies on gender-related issues and interdepartmental co-ordination.

In 2001, the government established a Ministerial Working Group to ensure co-or-dinated action to combat domestic violence at the highest level. The group brings together ministers from all major departments, whose mandate is to concentrate on developing integrated policy in the following five key areas: healthcare, accommo-dation for victims, the interface between civil and criminal law jurisdictions, aware-ness-raising and education, and appropriate and consistent response from the police and Crown Prosecution Service (CEDAW 2003, 80 par.365). This activity resembles the centralised concerted effort of different formal bodies in British society to ensure that the state as a whole engages itself in rule-consistent behaviour (our last phase in the spiral model), where the implementation of existing gender policy is not hindered by conflicting sectoral interests.

These undertakings of the government show commitment to combating vio-lence against women, including domestic violence. As the research conducted by Sylvia Walby describing the current situation in the UK and developing a methodol-ogy to estimate the nationwide economic and social costs (Walby 2004) of violence suggests, there is governmental recognition of the major costs that domestic vio-lence incurs for society. The most recent development in the United Kingdom was the 2004 adoption of the comprehensive *Domestic Violence, Crimes and Victims Act*, which entered in force in 2006. In contrast to the previous regulations, the new law places greater emphasis on criminalising domestic violence. It casts the breach of non-molestation orders as a criminal offence, makes common assault an arrestable offence, and extends the law to include same-sex couples as well as non-married and non-cohabiting couples. These features make the act the most comprehensive legislation addressing domestic violence to date.

Though it is too early to assess the impact of the newly introduced regulations, given that they were introduced shortly after the Beijing+5 and Beijing+10 recom-mendations, the British developments could serve as examples of best practice to be adopted by other countries with less comprehensive national regulations to combat domestic violence. The centralisation of a policy issue in this way (as emphasised in the UN recommendations as well as argued by Risse) is necessary to achieve endur-ing structural changes – not only by criminalising the offence but by changing the mentality of society as a whole.

The issue of domestic violence, having been addressed only since the regime change, is a hotly debated topic in Hungary. The old Hungarian proverb 'Money is best when counted, a woman is best when beaten' exposes the deeply rooted na-ture of the problem and speaks volumes about the common popular stance on the issue.

The development of Hungarian regulations on domestic violence as part of gen-der equality politics should be understood in the framework of the ongoing struggle between communist legacies and the newly imposed global and EU demands. As previously noted, it was the normative power of the UN, as well as the eligibility requirements of EU candidacy, that contributed to the institutionalisation of regulations on gender equality (including violence against women) in Hungarian legislation. However, while developments in the gender equality policies in the EU and the western European states have been triggered by the mobilisation of societal actors (namely by the strong influence of second-wave feminism on national and European policy-making), the institutionalisation of gender equality policy in the CEE region embraced a completely different pattern.

Prior to the newly adopted *Amendment to Act XIX of 1998 on criminal proceedings* on domestic violence, legal provisions in Hungary broadly protected human rights, and, though the state adopted the EU *acquis communitaire*, no real changes occurred in legislation on domestic violence until 2006. The issue of domestic violence had previously been addressed in the Penal Code within the wider context of all forms of violence. In actual cases of domestic violence, depending on the circumstances, the statutes on the factors constituting the offence had to be collected from a series of different documents: the Penal Code, the Code of Criminal Offences, and other regulations, such as the Act on the Protection of Children and Family Code (CRR 2000, 66), which posed serious problems for establishing solid cases against perpetrators of violence against women before the court.

Though no significant policy regulations occurred during the late 1990s, this period marked the emergence of publications and research on the issue, all serving the purpose of public awareness raising (the first and second phase of our spiral model). Over the past fifteen years, several studies have been carried out on domestic violence in Hungary, the most important being the works of Krisztina Morvai (1998) and Olga Tóth (1999). Since the end of 2001, the number of research programmes and scientific publications focusing on domestic violence have visibly increased [see for example: Tóth (2003); Tamási (2004)]. The National Criminology Institute has also conducted research – the broadest to date on this subject – analysing criminal statistics between 1997 and 2002. The importance of these publications and research rests in the fact that while gender studies and gender-related research entered academia in the United Kingdom during the 1980s, these Hungarian publications marked the birth of Hungarian gender-related research and initiated the informal inclusion of gender studies into university curricula.

The state's initial neglect of the issue was evident in the Fourth and Fifth Combined CEDAW Report submitted by Hungary in 2000, where domestic violence was treated with a high level of generality (CEDAW 2000). Counter to the official CEDAW report, a shadow NGO Report (2002) was submitted that provided a detailed analysis of the grave situation in Hungary with regard to domestic violence (phase three of our spiral model). As a result, the 2002 Recommendations of the CEDAW (CEDAW 2002, par. 321–322) expressed the Commission's concern about the lack of proper legislation and shelter facilities for female victims of violence, urging Hungary to establish a separate regulation on domestic violence and to organise a zero-tolerance campaign to raise public awareness. Furthermore, the CEDAW recommendations referred to different aspects of domestic violence, calling for a comprehensive and centralised government programme in Hungary as necessary to combat violence against women.

As both the domestic actors and the UN exerted pressure on the Hungarian government (corresponding to the phase one of the spiral model), the drafting of comprehensive legislation on domestic violence became inevitable. However, the government first resisted (phase of denial) the adoption of a separate law on domestic violence, arguing that such a statute would constitute an instance of positive discrimination that the EU would not accept from Hungary (2002, 39). However, the government had to make some concessions (phase four) due to the high mobilisation of societal actors (mass protests, media outcry) after the tragic events[2] that unfolded in September 2002.

The preparation of the new law on domestic violence could have served as an opportunity for open policy-making to include women's NGOs as well as experts in the field. However, during the process, women's organisations could not exert enough influence to prevent the shift from a gendered/feminist policy frame to a gender-neutral one, and thus the debate shifted away from the frame of 'violence against women' towards a 'de-gendered' formulation of violence against the dependent. As Réka Sáfrány (2003) presents in her work, the ongoing parliamentary debates on domestic violence displayed an ideological cleavage between the conservatives and social-liberals, and failed to integrate voices that challenged the status quo of existing gender hierarchies (Sáfrány 2003, 52–8).

At the beginning, both feminist NGOs and related experts were intensely involved in drafting the law. Their involvement led to the definition of the main policy frame, based on the 1997 Austrian model, which prohibits any kind of violence between individuals and mandates immediate police force intervention and eviction of the perpetrator, as well as provides automatic legal aid for the victim (Ébner 2004). The collaboration of the civil society and the government representatives resulted in an initiative submitted by two MPs, on the basis of which two *Parliamentary Resolutions (No. 45/2003 (IV. 16)* and *No.115/2003)* were adopted. These were the first documents

---

2   A fourteen year old girl (S.K.) murdered her foster father, who had been physically and sexually abusing both S.K. and her mother, by shooting him in his sleep. In: Egyetlen lövéssel gyilkolta meg nevelőapját (She Murdered her Foster Father with Only One Shot), in: Magyar Hírlap, 2002.09.05. In addition, a 12 year old boy was strangled to death by his father. Accessed on: 15 March 2006 www.nane.hu/egyesulet/mediafigyelem/tomi.doc

in Hungarian legislative history to elevate the issue of family violence to the level of institutional intervention, and urged the government to introduce effective actions by referring to the international agreements and recommendations that Hungary had already adopted.

After a lengthy legislative process, a decision was reached to *not* sanction acts of family violence in Hungary as a specific crime when Parliament adopted the *Amendment to Act XIX of 1998 on criminal proceedings* on 14 February 2006. According to this amendment, the perpetrator can, in the case of well-founded suspicion of a crime punishable with a prison sentence, be ordered by the judge to stay away from the joint place of residence and the places frequented by the victim for a period of 10–30 days. Restraining orders also prohibit communication by phone or other electronic media, and violation of the rules incurs detention or a fine.

Despite the benefit of the restraining order, i.e. its facilitation of a rapid court procedure, the leading women's NGOs vehemently criticised the amendment and blamed the policy-makers for manipulating constitutional principles (namely property rights and the fundamental right to free movement, which conflict with the basic human right to life and physical integrity) to frame an ineffective statute (2004b). According to the Habeas Corpus Working Group, apart from the law's gender-neutrality in language and interpretation (Krizsán and Pap 2005, 16), the statute is inadequate and even detrimental to the victims, as it does not provide automatic legal assistance for the injured; the perpetrator can be evicted only after a court decision and only for the duration of the legal procedure (2004a). Some other shortcomings were identified in the 6th CEDAW Report, namely that no standard training was provided for any group in charge of enforcing the law, and that the law neither regulated the sort of assistance to be provided for the injured party or perpetrator nor identified the organisations responsible for providing such services (CEDAW 2006, 50).

Notwithstanding this criticism, Hungarian policy to combat domestic violence has undergone important changes since 2002, mainly due to international pressure and concerted women's movement efforts along the lines of what the spiral model of international norm adaptation suggests. Besides the comprehensive law on domestic violence, several other pieces of legislation have been introduced (like the Directive No. 34/2002 of the Ministry of the Interior, Directive No. 13/2003 of the National Police Chief, Act CXXXV of 2005 on the assistance of victims of crime and the alleviation by the state of damage, amendment by Act CXI of 2005 to Act IV of 1978 on the Criminal Code, and Act CXXX of 2005 on the amendment to Act III of 1952 on civil proceedings). Methodology guidelines were also released, training was organised and internal regulations were developed in the police force to ensure effective involvement in combating domestic violence. Some institutional changes have also been introduced: the government launched a pilot *Crisis Centre Service* in 2004 and a National Crisis Management and Information Telephone Service (Országos Kríziskezelő és Információs Telefonszolgálat) in April 2005. It also increased the capacity of shelters and established a secret shelter to host not only victims with children but also lone victims (CEDAW 2006, 35–6).

As our brief review of the development of Hungarian policymaking vis-à-vis domestic violence shows, after the initial reluctance, the Hungarian government was willing to make some concessions and introduce legislative changes due to international pressure and intense public mobilisation. Several major policy and institutional changes have been introduced during a relatively short period of time, the value of which should not be undermined. All of the legal provisions and institutional developments introduced show that measures have been taken to introduce policy and structural changes. However, the final decision *not* to sanction domestic violence as a specific crime leads one to question how far these structural changes really go, and to argue convincingly that present Hungarian legislative changes neither liberalise existing policies nor accept some form of substantive constitutional change. As such, they do not advance beyond the prescriptive phase of our spiral model, and thus pose obstacles to the institutionalisation of international human rights norms into actual state practice.

Conclusion

As our brief review of the development of British and Hungarian policymaking with respect to domestic violence shows, the spiral model of international norm adoption is a powerful explanatory tool. The comparison of our two case studies shows that policy change has been accomplished by similar means, i.e. the interplay of domestic actors and international pressure. Our analysis also indicates that domestic violence regulation in the two nations is headed in the same direction, namely towards centralised and comprehensive regulation, which includes criminalisation of domestic violence as well as the establishment of multi-agency assistance.

As the case of Britain shows, developments in the United States in the 1970s sparked changes in the British regulations on domestic violence. The good practices taken over from America could not have initiated structural changes in the absence of receptive domestic structures, however. The high degree of mobilisation of women's groups during the second-wave feminist movement, as well as the positive inclination of the state towards gender equality, whatever its motivations were, enabled the introduction of substantive changes in policy regulations on domestic violence.

In post-socialist Hungary, where civil society activism in general and domestic violence policy in particular is relatively recent, global social policy and transnational alliances forged at international meetings have enabled local activists to draw on ideas and policy frameworks from outside the nation-state. The newly democratised

Hungarian state acted as a fully norm-taking state, introducing international standards and measures; however, compliance with and internalisation of these regulations was not achieved. As the EU accession negotiations revealed, the stronger the transnational pressure was, the more likely the Hungarian state was to comply. However, in the case of gender equality policy (an issue that holds little importance at the EU level), adaptational pressure was weaker, and adoption of international norms was less efficient due to existing institutional incongruities. Moreover, as the developmental trajectory of domestic violence regulations shows, unless strong societal mobilisation is readily available, policy development is likely to stop before the final phase of the spiral model of transposing international norms.

The international institutionalisation of women's rights brought about by the second-wave feminist movement resulted in the unprecedented growth of international women's NGOs during the UN International Women's Decade (1975–1985). It has influenced public opinion and drawn attention to women's rights violations around the world. Though the impact of the international institutionalisation is less visible on domestic violence legislation in the United Kingdom than in Hungary, the UN policy framework and regulations, especially the CEDAW and DEVAW, have been used by feminists the world over as tools for pressuring their governments to take policy further. This includes pushing for the creation of a more integrated policy linking the various forms of violence against women – domestic violence, rape and trafficking – in a wider framework of gender inequality and human rights violations (Sen et al. 2004).

However, while the application of the spiral model to the case of Hungary is well-grounded and readily available to the researcher, it is less striking in the case of the United Kingdom. This is so because British society ushered in the debate on domestic violence much earlier, at a time when the influence of international actors on domestic developments was still questionable (thus making the application of the spiral model difficult). In contrast, developments in gender equality policy in Hungary's case emerged under relatively powerful pressure from the UN and the EU. In Britain, however, international pressure had not yet gathered steam during the developmental phase of policy-making, and global social policy became important to activists and academics only later as a vehicle for pushing policy even further. Nevertheless, one can still argue that practices rooted in the United States served as an international example, followed, among others, by the British state.

Policy developments in British society can be traced back to second-wave feminism, which was a strong society-based social movement. Its impact can be observed today in the existence of highly professionalised and mobilised women's organisations that enjoy autonomy from the state as well as high level of institutionalisation of gender equality. In fact, Britain is among the leading international actors that facilitated the institutionalisation of the gender issue in the international arena. The policy developments in Hungary can in turn be attributed to various international pressures lacking solid societal support. As the socialist state took away all grounds for women's mobilisation, Hungarian women had to re-learn how to become an influential societal actor. As our study indicates, despite international pressure on governments, women's mobilisation is still relatively weak in Hungary, and, as our spiral model predicts, it will remain so until societal support for gender issues is more prevalent. In order to achieve substantial policy change, Hungarian women have to fight their own battle to secure public support in their push – from the bottom up – for the effective transposition and internalisation of universal norms and values.

References

Beveridge, F., et al. (2000), 'Mainstreaming and the Engendering of Policy-making: A Means to an End?' *Journal of European Public Policy,* 7: 3 (Special Issue), 385–405.

Bretherton, C. & Sperling, L. (1996), 'Women's Network and the European Union: Towards an Inclusive Approach?' *Journal of Common Market Studies,* 34, 487–508.

Caporaso, J. & Jupille, J. (2001), 'The Europeanization of Gender Equality Policy and Domestic Structural Change', in Cowles, M. G., Caporaso, J. & Risse, T. (Eds.) (2001), *Transforming Europe: Europeanization and Domestic Change* (Ithaca and London: Cornell University Press).

Chilton, P. (1997), 'Mechanics of Change: Social Movements, Transnational Coalitions, and the Transformation Processes in Eastern Europe in Eastern Europe', in Risse-Kappen, T. (Ed.) (1997), *Bringing Transnational Relations Back In: Non-State Actors, Domestic Structures and International Institutions* (Cambridge: Cambridge University Press).

Corrin, C. (1999), 'Gender Politics and Women's Political Participation in Hungary', 2006: May 15.

Dobash, E. R. & Dobash, R. R. (1992), *Women, Violence and Social Change* (London: Routledge).

Gal, S. (1994), 'Gender in the Post-Socialist Transition: The Abortion Debate in Hungary', *East European Politics and Societies,* 8: 2, 256–286.

Gelb, J. (1989), *Feminism and Politics: A Comparative Perspective* (Berkeley: University of California Press).

Gelb, J. & Hart, V. (1999), 'Feminist Politics in a Hostile Environment', in Guigni, M., Mcadam, D. & Tilly, C. (Eds.) (1999), *How Social Movements Matter* (Minneapolis: University of Minnesota Press).

Goven, J. (2000), 'New Parliament, Old Discourse? The Parental Leave Debate in Hungary', in Gal, S. & Kligman, G. (Eds.) (2000), *Reproducing Gender: Politics, Publics, and Everyday Life after Socialism* (Princeton, New Jersey: Princeton University Press).

Hester, M. (2005), 'Transnational Influences of Domestic Violence Policy and Action – Exploring Developments in China and England', *Social Policy & Society*, 4: 4, 447–456.

Konrád, Gy. (1984), *Antipolitics* (New York: Harcourt, Brace, Jovanovich Publishers).

Krizsán, A. & Pap, E. (2005), *Equal Opportunities for Women and Men. Monitoring Law and Practice in Hungary* (Budapest, New York: Open Society Institute and Network Women's Program).

Lovenduski, J. & Randall, V. (1993), *Contemporary Feminist Politics* (Oxford: Oxford University Press).

Morvai, K. (1998), *Terror a családban: a feleségbántalmazás és a jog (Terror in the Family. Wife-battering and the Law)* (Budapest: Kossuth Nyomda).

Mullender, A. (1999), *Rethinking Domestic Violence: The Social Work and Probation Response* (London: Routledge).

Nash, K. (2002), 'A Movement Moves ... Is There a Women's Movement in England Today?' *The European Journal of Women's Studies*, 9: 3, 311–328.

Pace, G. R. (2001), 'Human Rights from Paper to Practice: How Far Have We Come?' *Human Rights and Human Welfare*, 1: 1, 9–11.

Pascall, G. & Lewis, J. (2004), 'Emerging Gender Regimes and Policies for Gender Equality in a Wider Europe', *Journal of Social Policy*, 33: 3, 373–394.

Petö, A. & Manners, I. (2006), 'The European Union and Gender Protection', in Lucarelli, S. & Manners, I. (Eds.) (2006), *Values and Principles in European Union Foreign Policy* (London: Routledge).

Risse, T., et al. (2001), 'Europeanization and Domestic Change: Introduction', in Cowles, M. G., Caporaso, J. & Risse, T. (Eds.) (2001), *Transforming Europe: Europeanization and Domestic Change* (Ithaca and London: Cornell University Press).

Risse, T. & Sikkink, K. (1999), 'The Socialisation of International Human Rights Norms into Domestic Practices: Introduction', in Risse, T., Ropp, S. C. & Sikkink, K. (Eds.) (1999), *The Power of Human Rights: International Norms and Domestic Change* (Cambridge: Cambridge University Press).

Risse-Kappen, T. (1997), 'Bringing Transnational Relations Back In: Introduction', in Risse-Kappen, T. (Ed.) (1997), *Bringing Transnational Relations Back In. Non-State Actors, Domestic Structures and International Institutions* (Cambridge: Cambridge University Press).

Sáfrány, R. (2003), *Public and Political Discourse on Domestic Violence in Hungary. The Prospects and Limits of Feminist Strategies* (Budapest: Central European University).

Silius, H. (2002), 'Women's Employment, Equal Opportunities and Women's Studies in Nine European Countries – A Summary', *www.hull.ac.uk/ewsi*.

Tamási, E. (2004), *Bűnös áldozatok* (Budapest: BM Duna Palota Kiadó).

Tóth, O. (1999), *Erőszak a családban* (Budapest: Tárki).

———— (2003), *A családon belüli, partner elleni erőszak* (Budapest: Századvég).

Walby, S. (2004), 'The Cost of Domestic Violence', http://www.womenandequalityunit. gov.uk/research/cost_of_dv_research_summary.pdf.

Watson, P. (2000), 'Politics, Policy and Identity: EU Eastern Enlargement and East-West Differences', *Journal of European Public Policy*, 7: 3 (Special issue), 369–384.

A/RES/48/104. United Nations (1993), 'Declaration on the Elimination of Violence against Women. General Assembly resolution 48/104 of 20 December 1993.' Accessed: 5 December 2005. http://www.unhchr.ch/huridocda/huridoca.nsf/ (Symbol)/A.RES.48.104.En?Opendocument.

A/S-23/10/Rev.1. United Nations (2000), 'Report of the Ad Hoc Committee of the whole of the twenty-third special session of the General Assembly'. Accessed: http://www.un.org/womenwatch/daw/followup/as2310rev1.pdf.

Center for Reproductive Rights. (2000), 'Women of the World: Laws and Policies Affecting Their Reproductive Lives – East Central Europe'. Accessed: 30 May 2006. http://bookstore.reproductiverights.org/womofworlawa3.html.

CEDAW/C/HUN/4-5 (2000), 'Consideration or report submitted by State parties under the article 18 of the Convention on the Elimination of All Forms of Discrimination against Women. Combined fourth and fifth periodic reports of States parties: Hungary'. Accessed: 20 December 2005.

A/57/38. CEDAW (2002), 'Concluding Observations of the Committee on the Elimination of Discrimination against Women: Hungary'. Accessed: 30 March 2006. http://www.acpd.ca/compilation/2006/02-cedaw/2c-2.htm#HUNGARY2002.

CEDAW/C/UK/5 (2003), 'Government of United Kingdom: Fifth Periodic Report of the United Kingdom and Northern Ireland'. Accessed: 10 April 2006. http://daccessdds. un.org/doc/UNDOC/GEN/N03/599/48/PDF/N0359948.pdf?OpenElement.

CEDAW/C/HUN/6 (2006), 'Consideration or report submitted by State parties under the article 18 of the Convention on the Elimination of All Forms of Discrimination against Women. Sixth periodic report of States parties: Hungary'. Accessed: 30 May 2006. http://daccessdds.un.org/doc/UNDOC/GEN/N06/402/22/PDF/ N0640222.pdf?OpenElement.E/CN.6/2005/2.

Commission on the Status of Women (2005), 'Report of the Secretary General on the Review of the implementation of the Beijing Platform for Action and the outcome documents of the special session of the General Assembly entitled "Women 2000: gender equality, development and peace for the twenty-first century"'. Accessed: 10 April 2006. http://daccessdds.un.org/doc/UNDOC/GEN/N04/636/83/PDF/N0463683.pdf?OpenElement.

Habeas Corpus Working Group (2004a), 'Alapvetö észrevételek a távoltartási törvény megcsonkított változatára'. Accessed: March 31 2006. http://www.habeascorpus.hu/jogok/csbe/megcsonkitott.tavoltartas.2004.12.08.h

Ébner, E. (2004), 'Az otthonom az én váram: a bántalmazó családtagot nem lehet kitiltani?' Accessed: 15 May 2006. http://www.mtv.hu/cikk.php?id=1070&offset=0

Women Against Violence Association and Habeas Corpus Working Group (2002), 'Shadow Report on the Realisation of the Convention of the Elimination of All Forms of Discrimination against Women in Hungary'. Accessed: March 15 2006. http://www.wave-network.org/cmsimages/doku/shadowhungary.pdf.

Habeas Corpus Working Group (2004a), 'Alapvetö észrevételek a távoltartási törvény megcsonkított változatára'. Accessed: 31 March 2006. http://www.habeascorpus.hu/jogok/csbe/megcsonkitott.tavoltartas.2004.12.08.htm

Women Against Violence and Habeas Corpus Working Group (2004b), 'Az eröszak nem hajléktalanság. A Nök a Nökért Együtt az Eröszak Ellen (NaNE) Egyesület és a Habeas Corpus Munkacsoport (HCM) álláspontja a kormány családon belüli eröszakkal kapcsolatos, közelmúltban kifejtett tevékenységéröl'. Accessed: 21 March 2006. http://www.habeascorpus.hu/jogok/csbe/az.eroszak.nem.hajlek talansag.htm.

Womankind Worldwide (2004), 'Violence against Women in the UK: CEDAW Thematic Shadow Report 2003'. Accessed: March 12 2006. http://www.womankind.org.uk/upload/CEDAW-report.pdf.omen

Diana Schmidt

Anti-Corruption Advocacy in Contemporary Russia? Local Civil Society Actors between International and Domestic Contexts

Introduction

Over the last decade, anti-corruption initiatives have been booming. Two fundamental phenomena have given additional impetus to a transnational advocacy network (TAN) against corruption since the end of the Cold War: the comparatively high levels of corruption and the emergence of civil society organisations throughout Eastern Europe. Much anti-corruption advocacy is thus focused on this geographic region and characterised by civil society involvement. Of the post-communist states, Russia tends to receive the lion's share of Western aid. Foreign anti-corruption assistance and respective programmes started arriving here in the late 1990s, and President Putin placed the issue high on the agenda upon assuming office in 2000. However, Putin has also established a system of authoritarian governance that negatively affects civil society development in general and the foreign financing of civic advocacy on politically sensitive issues in particular. Moreover, presidential moves against corrupt oligarchs and senior officials appear selective, while endemic corruption remains a pressing problem in all sectors of society. In 2006, a new governmental anti-corruption campaign was launched, comprising international co-operation but also challenging the legitimacy of Russian non-governmental actors and their respective international links.

With respect to theoretical propositions about the transfer of international norms through TAN pressure and international socialisation of a target state, transnational anti-corruption advocacy in contemporary Russia presents a puzzling phenomenon: While conventional TAN models conceptualise target states as responsive, the Russian government is intractable and pro-active at the same time. Its approach certainly does not conform to TAN model forecasts. At the international level, corruption problems in Russia have been the focus of Western donors, observers and media. Nevertheless, pressure from this front has often proven weak or even given rise to counter-productive side-effects on civil society involvement. Russian civil society actors, in turn, are not predominantly oppositional 'norm entrepreneurs', and cannot be said to represent a homogenous category of network actors.[1] But how, precisely, are these civil society actors involved in anti-corruption advocacy on the ground?

---

1   Both practitioners and scholars tend to misleadingly subsume civil society actors as 'NGOs'. Yet in particular in the anti-corruption field it is obvious that local civic initiatives are also led by business and professional associations as well as individual activists, journalists or deputies.

Scholars have essentially conceptualised TANs as a tripartite actor constellation in which domestic groups and international allies put pressure on domestic governments that violate international principles (e.g. Keck and Sikkink, 1998). Ultimately, some presume the successful socialisation of norm-deviant states into norm-compliance through network pressure (e.g. Risse et al., 1999). Based mainly on evidence from human rights and environmental advocacy, these concepts have never been applied to the realm of anti-corruption or to cases where post-Soviet target states are involved. The field of anti-corruption research itself remains ill-theorised and detached from area studies. Importantly, among researchers and policy-makers alike, a preoccupation with outcomes, i.e. success in reducing the level of corruption in a single country, has obstructed the view on inherent socio-political mechanisms of transnational anti-corruption advocacy networking. Given the emphasis placed on the crucial role of civil society as well as the high levels of corruption in the post-Soviet world, one needs to ask what role local civil society actors actually play in these countries.

This chapter thus examines how local civil society actors who are part of TANs and situated within a post-Soviet authoritarian context are involved in the anti-corruption advocacy that is highly relevant to both international and governmental actors. It reintroduces insights gained during a larger research project (cf. Schmidt, 2006a) that brings together – thereby aiming at enhancing both – theoretical work on TANs and empirical evidence on anti-corruption advocacy in Russia.[2] It explores ongoing developments in the anti-corruption sphere at the international level and within the Russian domestic and local contexts. Its main goal is to further our understanding of the *internal workings of TANs* – in addition to, and as a precondition of, their eventual effectiveness (outcomes). It proceeds from the premise that such an understanding could also be enhanced by an analysis of what would conventionally be considered 'unsuccessful' cases. Research should consider the changing agendas and actions of TAN actors by integrating analyses of the advocacy issue at stake as well as the various actors involved. Both issue and actor relations need to be seen within their respective contexts – e.g. international, domestic or local, as illustrated in Table 1. In the case of the anti-corruption TAN, a multitude of actors – situated within different, partly overlapping governance contexts – contribute diverse perspectives

---

2   Empirical findings are based on the analysis of documents and campaign material as well as
     extensive multi-sited field research (2003–2006), including participant observation at international and local events, informal conversations with relevant experts, and about 116 face-
     to-face interviews and background discussions with representatives of international anti-corruption and donor organisations based in Russia and abroad (Berlin, Brussels), as well as with
     representatives of local associations and individuals working on anti-corruption in three Russian cities (Moscow, St. Petersburg, Irkutsk).

on domestic levels of corruption, anti-corruption strategies, and how effective these might be under the given circumstances.

Table 1

	International level	Domestic level	Local civil society
TAN Actors	International organisations and Western donors against corruption	Russian government against corruption	Groups and individuals against corruption
Contexts	Russia as target state on international anti-corruption agenda	Context of Soviet & perestroika legacies, ongoing transformation (authoritarianisation)	Particular regional & local governance context Local anti-corruption efforts
		←——→ ←——→	
		Intersection of international and domestic anti-corruption advocacy	Intersection of domestic, international, local contexts
		←——→	——→

Both TAN studies and the international anti-corruption discourse commonly project Russia as a single unit within the international context. However, as Table 1 demonstrates, it is crucial to differentiate between *domestic* and *local* as distinct operational contexts. Building on case studies of civic anti-corruption advocacy in three cities in different Russian regions (Moscow, St. Petersburg, and Irkutsk), the study behind this chapter adds an intra-national comparative component. This helps determine to what extent local contexts provide different conditions for different forms of corruption, changing principles and practices of civic engagement (and thus different transnational anti-corruption initiatives). The insights generated from these case studies substantiate the argument that transnational advocacy potential also varies *within* the Russian context, depending on the kind and dominance of influences issuing from the international, domestic and local spheres.

Following a brief outline of anti-corruption efforts at the international level, the article describes governmental and non-governmental anti-corruption activities in Russia within this international context, and, against this background, points to some TAN successes and failures involving Russian civil society actors at the local level. The article concludes with a note on the different understandings of both 'civil society' and 'anti-corruption' prevalent across these levels and with a call for a more open-ended, process-oriented analytical perspective on transnational advocacy.

International Anti-Corruption Context

While campaigns against corruption are hardly new, the last decade was the first to witness a turn from understanding corruption as a domestic phenomenon towards regarding it as a 'global problem' requiring counteraction through international campaigns, agreements and regulations. Today, international donors and activists express confidence in the growth of a transnational anti-corruption network, which they predict will become comparable in scope and success to the two principal networks in the issue areas of human rights and the environment. These have exerted significant influence on global and domestic affairs over the past three or four decades.

Evidence on anti-corruption efforts in the international arena suggests that a process parallel to the one deployed in the realm of human rights was indeed set in motion during the 1990s and that the international community has since elaborated common sets of principles against which domestic practices can be measured.[3] A fairly cohesive discourse on corruption as a global threat has since emerged, somewhat similar to the one that endeavoured to frame human rights as a universal good. Within only a few years, international organisations and the 'community of liberal states' were mobilised. Two influential transnationally operating non-governmental organisations, Transparency International (TI) and the International Chamber of Commerce (ICC), have brought about 'a sea change in global attitudes toward corruption' (Galtung 2000, 18; see also Pieth, 1997). TI, in particular, is credited with bringing the issue of anti-corruption onto the international agenda, successfully lobbying for the OECD Anti-Bribery Convention,[4] and fostering the inception of anti-corruption NGOs worldwide. To date, a number of international agreements and codes of good practices have been developed not only by the OECD, the IMF and the World Bank – which have become the 'leading anti-corruption crusaders' (Williams and Theobald, 2000) – but also by the Council of Europe, the EU, the FATF, the UN and others. As the latest example, the UN Convention Against Corruption (UNCAC), which was adopted in December 2003, came into force in December 2005.[5] In addition, *regional* and *sectoral* agreements, networks and action plans are emerging, such as the Inter-American Convention Against Corruption, or, including the post-communist world,

---

3   The Universal Declaration of Human Rights, adopted in 1948, was followed by numerous conventions, specific international monitoring organisations and regional arrangements, the emergence of a huge network of transnationally operating advocacy coalitions and international NGOs, as a result of which a global human rights regime emerged (see Risse et al., 1999: 234).
4   The 'Convention on Combating Bribery of Foreign Public Officials in International Business Transactions' was adopted and opened for signature in November 1997 and entered into force in February 1999 (OECD, DAFFE/IME/BR(97)20).
5   See 'United Nations Convention Against Corruption' at: http://www.unodc.org/unodc/crime_convention_corruption.html [accessed 23/02/2006].

the Group of States against Corruption (GRECO),[6] the Anti-Corruption Network for Transition Economies (ACN),[7] the Extractive Industries Transparency Initiative (EITI)[8] and the UN Global Compact.[9]

With regard to the actor- and issue-related internal workings of the anti-corruption TAN, it is important to mention that many of the international organisations involved are only starting to develop closer co-operation and a more systematic division of labour among themselves. Moreover, advocacy on the issue of anti-corruption frequently overlaps with work on human rights, environmental and, increasingly, anti-terrorism and security issues. This allows the strategic or opportunistic framing of corruption in numerous ways by linking it to different causes, consequences and other phenomena. While such framing is important for keeping the issue on the agenda and widening the scope of action, the linking of corruption to other issues by too many – and, at times, contradictory – causal arrows can be problematic, especially with respect to progress at the local level. Besides the above-mentioned international agreements and instruments at the inter-governmental level, numerous national or multilateral donor organisations provide technical and financial assistance to local civic anti-corruption projects. Over one hundred local NGOs and associations, whose primary mandate is the development and implementation of anti-corruption strategies or campaigning for more transparency, have emerged in countries all over the world.[10] In addition, numerous civil society actors, including

---

6   GRECO, established in 1999 by Resolution (99)5, has been adopted by the following states: Belgium, Bulgaria, Cyprus, Estonia, Finland, France, Germany, Greece, Iceland, Ireland, Lithuania, Luxembourg, Romania, Slovakia, Slovenia, Spain and Sweden; see: http://www.greco.coe.int/ [accessed 11/11/05].

7   ACN, adopted in 1998, involves transformation countries from Eastern Europe / Eurasia: Albania, Armenia, Azerbaijan, Belarus, Bosnia and Herzegovina, Bulgaria, Croatia, Estonia, Former Yugoslav Republic of Macedonia, Montenegro, Georgia, Kazakhstan, Kyrgyz Republic, Latvia, Lithuania, Moldova, Romania, the Russian Federation, Serbia, Slovenia, Tajikistan, Turkmenistan, Uzbekistan and Ukraine, plus collective network members: the EU, CoE, OECD, UN, EBRD, the World Bank, Transparency International and the Open Society Institute (OECD: Anti-Corruption Action Plan for Armenia, Azerbaijan, Georgia, the Russian Federation, Tajikistan and Ukraine, 2003, http://www.oecd.org/dataoecd/60/59/12593443.pdf).

8   Since 2003, about 20 countries have committed themselves to EITI principles, including Azerbaijan, Kyrgyz Republic, Kazakhstan and Mongolia; see: http://www.eitransparency.org/ countryupdates.htm [accessed 11/11/05].

9   The UN Global Compact, operational since 2000, is an international initiative engaging companies and UN agencies, civil society and academia to support universal principles. 'Anti-corruption' was added as the 10th principle in 2004; see: http://www.unglobalcompact.org/ [accessed 11/11/05].

10   Considering only the number of national chapters and chapters in formation working with TI, more than 90 local NGOs are active in 2006 (up from 40 in 1996); see http://www.transparency. org/about_us [accessed 08/05/2006]. In addition, more than 250 local NGOs and associations concerned with national resource revenues are signatories to the 'Publish What You Pay' initiative (excluding TI chapters and transnational organisations; full list at: http://www.publishwhatyoupay.org/english/coalition/members.shtml, accessed 08/05/2006). Moreover, under USAID's anti-corruption programme, numerous anti-corruption coalitions involving civil soci-

NGOs, journalists, business associations and mixed coalitions, are working on single aspects that are somehow related to anti-corruption efforts (e.g. information access, media, rule of law, election observation, environmental protection, human and civil rights, or business ethics), either as their main mandate or as part of a wider work programme. Many of them are well connected internationally, but not necessarily explicitly under the heading of anti-corruption programmes.

Certainly, one can meaningfully speak of a TAN as it is conceptualised in the literature: a network consisting of intergovernmental bodies, foundations, international and domestic NGOs and national governments. These network actors have initiated international agreements that may be considered 'the seeds of an international legal system'[11] in the field of anti-corruption, similar to the early UN proposals for legal and policy reforms in the area of human rights. Indeed, anti-corruption aspects are being incorporated into domestic legislation, and national anti-corruption agencies have been established in many countries, notably throughout Eastern Europe.[12] The anti-corruption TAN even seems to be following an exemplary developmental path, as it has evolved in a highly dynamic way over a short period of time. Still, it has major shortcomings, in particular concerning the nexus between international and domestic initiatives. While human rights TANs are said to have created international tools, agreements and activities that 'make real differences in the daily practices of national politics' (Risse and Ropp 1999, 234), this laudatory assessment does not seem applicable to the anti-corruption sphere. The importance of particular domestic contexts has recently received more attention by some international bodies in this realm. Domestic particularities also form one of the main arguments advanced by Russian state and non-state actors in response to Western efforts of promoting international norms in Russia. But perhaps more importantly, the anti-corruption cause lends itself to the fuelling of mutual recriminations on the basis of value claims and increased competition among states. Governments also instrumentalise the cause to target political opponents, rather than actual corruption problems, in their countries.

Analytically, much research seems pre-occupied with assessing outcomes, even at this early stage of transnational anti-corruption advocacy. This illuminates a major problem in the conceptual foundation of TAN studies as well: their tendency to

---

ety actors have been established in various countries. As a rough comparison, in the field of human rights, Amnesty International has set up 90 country offices since 1961; see http://www.amnesty.org/ [accessed 08/05/2006].

11   Risse and Ropp (1999, 234) on the early UN proposals for legal and policy reforms in the sphere of human rights.

12   Upon adopting the *Acquis Communautaire*, new EU member states and EU candidate countries in Central Eastern Europe (in contrast to old member states) have been obliged to establish anti-corruption agencies and institutions. At the same time, the major international financial institutions have revised their lending policies since 1997 and enacted anti-corruption clauses, which also pertain to their relations with Eastern European recipient countries.

embrace confirmatory research by means of the biased selection of predominantly successful cases in the human rights sphere. The fight against corruption rather resembles other, less successful cases in which the importance of sub-/national contexts seems to have a stronger effect than universal norms. Other recent research on global norms has led to the questioning of the theoretical top-down perspective. For example, Zwingel (2005, 400) concludes from her study on discrimination against women that '[i]nstead of assuming a 'trickle-down' dynamic as a consequence of global agreements [...] the legitimacy and authority of global norms depends on their active interpretation and appropriation within national and local contexts all over the world.' With regard to the promotion of democratisation in Eastern Europe, a group of scholars finds that 'outcomes in postcommunist states, especially Russia, diverge from expectations generated by much of the literature on the power of norms [...] the scope and direction of change within these countries contrasts starkly with the triumphant stories in the international relations literature' (Mendelson, 2002, 242). Substantiating such arguments, this study on transnational anti-corruption advocacy in Russia further demonstrates that our understanding of the *internal* workings of TANs can be enhanced by analysing what researchers have tended to consider as 'unsuccessful' cases – as long as actors, issues and contexts are continuously re-assessed at each level of analysis.

Anti-Corruption Advocacy in Russia – Within the International Context

Efforts to counteract corruption in Russia need to be assessed as processes at the intersection of international and domestic anti-corruption efforts (see Table 1). Governmental initiatives are thus partly in response to increasing international pressure, in keeping with conventional assumptions. Of particular importance here is Russia's precarious rating in the annual cross-national Corruption Perceptions Index (CPI) (and other indices) as well as generally mounting criticism of its increasingly non-democratic course. Russia's ratification of international anti-corruption conventions[13] and anti-fraud customs arrangements between Russia and the EU since 2000, the launching of the Global Compact in Russia in 2001, or its removal from the FATF blacklist of non-co-operative jurisdictions in the fight against money laundering in 2002 certainly have to be seen in this light. However, governmental anti-corruption initiatives are also frequently pro-active presidential measures in the context of power strug-

---

13 Russia ratified the CoE Convention on Laundering, Search, Seizure, and Confiscation of the Proceeds from Crime in 2001, the UN International Convention for the Suppression of the Financing of Terrorism in November 2002, the UN Convention against Transnational Organized Crime in 2004, and the UN Convention Against Corruption and the CoE Criminal Law Convention on Corruption in 2006.

gles and ongoing domestic transformations. Pre-election periods and continued ad-ministrative reforms are of particular relevance here. Measures such as Putin's move against selected oligarchs, revised legislation on party financing, or repeated dismiss-als of senior officials, all allegedly initiated as part of anti-corruption campaigns, fall into this category.

International anti-corruption promotion in Russia has also expanded into local-level initiatives through foreign assistance to civic projects, to particular Russian re-gions, since the late 1990s.[14] TAN research conventionally assumes that international socialisation processes are initiated by domestic NGOs seeking international support. Anti-corruption, in contrast, is a field where a) domestic activities tend to be exter-nally induced, so that non-governmental actors are more responsive than pro-active, and where b) not only NGOs play an active role as local non-state partners. The Rus-sian case illustrates that international anti-corruption promoters are interacting with local NGOs, academic institutions and think tanks, as well as with actors in the busi-ness and media sectors. The role of political parties, although repeatedly mentioned in interviews and conversations with Western diplomats or scholars, is negligible here.[15] Moreover, not all programmes seek to assist civil society actors in pressuring the government. Some, according to multi-stakeholder approaches, place emphasis on developing collaboration with the authorities (at federal, regional, or local levels); others support NGOs in developing anti-corruption programmes at the local level that practically neglect the role of the (federal-level) state. At the same time, local anti-corruption groups are often unaware of the international agreements and inter-governmental activities outlined in the section 'International Anti-Corruption Con-text'.

Throughout the recent years, assessments of anti-corruption efforts in Russia have been mixed to such an extent that many seem contradictory or confusing. Yet closer scrutiny of the chronological course of events and unfolding of relations be-tween various international and domestic actors in this field helps to disentangle the data and provide better insight into the actors' changing expectations and re-sponses. Even the short time span since 2000 is particularly revealing in the Russian

---

14 International efforts to initiate specific, civil society-led anti-corruption initiatives in Russia above all include TI, USAID, the Eurasia and Soros Foundations.

15 As of 2005, legislative changes in the course of Putin's move against the foreign financing of political activities in Russia stipulate that Russian parties are no longer eligible for anti-corrup-tion assistance. More generally, their advocacy potential seems questionable, given the subor-dinate role of the parliament and party system in contemporary Russia and low popular trust in political parties. Although most Russian parties have adopted the fight against corruption as one of their main slogans (CISR, 2004: 5–7; Demidov, 2004: 3), this is of little consequence, or possibly even counter-productive, given that parties also failed to realise anti-corruption agendas during the 1990s (Coulloudon, 2002: 187).

case, since it illustrates that the expectations and approaches of involved actors have taken a number of turns in this period.[16]

The turn of the millennium marked a watershed at the intersection of international and domestic anti-corruption contexts. At the international level, disillusionment started to grow at the sight of slow anti-corruption progress in Eastern Europe. Scepticism has also increased towards civil society involvement in anti-corruption efforts. These concerns are currently even more pronounced in the case of Russia. But it is important to see that they have unfolded at different speeds on various fronts. When Putin assumed the presidency in 2000, hopes among foreign observers grew when he actively pushed the anti-corruption agenda and expressed commitment to civil society development. International indices indeed showed decreasing corruption levels.[17] Yet by 2005, it became obvious that corruption levels were actually on the rise[18] and that the increasingly authoritarian governance under the Putin administration had erected barriers against foreign-funded civic advocacy efforts. Until then, concerns about the low efficiency of anti-corruption efforts, expressed by anti-corruption activists inside the country, had hardly been taken seriously by many international actors. For example, the TI Secretariat in Berlin first expressed alarm at the most recent events, in particular the new NGO legislation,[19] and has subsequently initiated and supported protest activities, whereas TI-Russia had been more critical than the Secretariat from the very beginning of Putin's presidency. Other Russian groups have also presented reform proposals and cited a lack of political will, shifting governmental priorities and frequently revised or postponed reform measures throughout the 2000s. While the Russian government has perceived such voices as increasingly influential, it has not taken their proposals on board constructively. Instead, it chose for a long time to ignore them, and, more recently, has opted to drown them out entirely. In 2006, it launched a new pro-active and multi-faceted anti-corruption campaign that included ratification of international conventions, intensified accusations against notoriously corruption-prone elements of Russian society (e.g. the customs services and an unspecified mass of businessmen and civil servants),

---

16   This article cannot provide more than a brief illustrative summary; for a more detailed discussion on this period, see Schmidt (2006a).

17   See for example the Corruption Perception Indices (CPI) between 2000 and 2003, at TI 'Corruption Measurement', http://www.transparency.org/tools/measurement.

18   See for example the 2005 CPI and the domestic surveys conducted by the Russian think tank INDEM (see 'Diagnostika rossiiskoi korruptsii 2005' at http://www.anti-corr.ru/indem/2005diagnost/2005diag_press.doc, accessed 02/11/2006), both of with have revealed growing corruption in Russia.

19   The new NGO legislation has been part of a broader legal reform package that was approved as 'Federal Law No. 18-FZ of 10 January 2006 on introducing amendments to certain legislative acts of the Russian Federation', which came into effect in April 2006, and will be implemented by means of additional decrees. For a more detailed discussion on the various reactions to the NGO legislation, see Schmidt (2006b).

and corruption probes against senior security, legal and customs officials as well as regional leaders. The administration also deployed more subtle measures, such as radio broadcasts, Internet campaigns and other pro-active extension into the public sphere, most notably through the Duma 'Commission for counteraction against Corruption'. These activities bolster the Russian governmental actors' reputation as co-operative partners in anti-corruption efforts in the eyes of international actors.[20] The developments of the last six years should not only be interpreted as renewed political will (to renew those hopes raised in 2000), but also as an effort to regain control over agenda-setting, data production and information dissemination in this field.

The study of such processes makes it obvious that an analysis of governmental commitments towards the international community and of legislative and institutional anti-corruption reforms alone is insufficient for assessing anti-corruption progress within the country. Initiatives involving civil society actors at the local level require even more rigorous analysis.

Local Anti-Corruption Advocacy – Within Russian Regional and International Contexts

Initiatives against corruption in particular Russian localities need to be understood as processes occurring at the intersection of international, domestic and regional/local anti-corruption contexts (see Table 1). Changes in the international anti-corruption climate, federal-level reforms and changing domestic conditions at large affect the nature of local anti-corruption initiatives. In addition, a number of critical components shape the operational conditions that affect the agendas and behaviour of local anti-corruption activists in a particular city. These include international linkage through the presence of foreign donors, personal connections to local/regional/federal authorities and deputies, the local civil society scene, and prevalent forms of corruption. Overall, the strategies of local activists are forged by their active involvement in local events and indirect involvement in contextual changes. Moreover, anti-corruption at the local level is a highly personalised matter, because chances are higher that action against corruption will be understood as an affront against particular persons, and because collective mobilisation is mostly attributed to the efforts of key individuals. In this light, the study identifies different styles of mobilisation against corruption and modes of international-domestic-local interaction in the three cities. For example, activists in St. Petersburg and Irkutsk are certainly right in their assertion that Moscow-based groups have easier access to funds as well as necessary juridical help (for themselves or when following up on corruption cases) and are gen-

---

20   Author's interviews with EU and UNODC representatives in Brussels, Moscow, and St. Petersburg, 2005/2006.

erally better connected to both international networks and federal governmental circles. Yet within Moscow itself, these advantages may have contributed to the fact that this scene is more clustered internally and that the image of Moscow NGOs is rather questionable in the eyes of the population.[21] In St. Petersburg and Irkutsk, in turn, rather lively civil society scenes have developed since the early 1990s, where (to different degrees) civic rights activists (*pravozashshitniki*), environmental activists, journalists and research groups have played central roles. These activities are partly overlapping, and some of the active organisations reach into anti-corruption without explicitly defining their activities this way and/or without benefiting from anti-corruption-specific grants. While there are no anti-corruption organisations per se in these two cities, a multitude of corruption-related issues is addressed by a variety of organisations, ranging from housing and construction to regional environmental issues, from local SME problems to foreign investment. Importantly, only Moscow hosts specific anti-corruption organisations.

With a view to TAN success, it must be said that federal anti-corruption measures result only rarely from bottom-up pressure. In fact, non-governmental anti-corruption efforts have actually given rise to more backlashes against its initiators than desired reforms. Still, final outcomes may be influenced by local initiatives. The process of amending tax regulations for the business sector is an example where the opinion of local business associations was actively incorporated. Other effects from local initiatives are more long-term and indirect. For example, in the area of access to information, the Moscow-based NGO TI-Russia has been particularly active in promoting a legal reform according to which each federal ministry and governmental executive agency must maintain a website providing certain information on its activities (legal acts, events, statistics and vacancies). Since the legislation was adopted in 2003, the Institute for Information Freedom Development, a small office established in St. Petersburg in 2004, has been furthering this initiative by pushing the relevant agencies to comply with the laws, in some cases launching court cases. Within a short period of time, this effort has achieved considerable success.[22] Indirectly, and in fact unconsciously, this young venture is thus contributing to the continuation and implementation of civic anti-corruption efforts pursued earlier in Moscow. This example shows that advocacy successes do not necessarily result from concerted networking efforts but can also spring from the common concerns of differently situated and uncon-

---

21 As a first cross-regional survey on NGOs and foundations in Russia has shown, Moscow citizens are more critical of civic organisations and donor organisations in Russia. While the reasons for this remain to be studied, the authors of the survey point to the factors of better information and higher educational levels in the capital (Forum Donorov, 2005).

22 By 2004, 53 out of 83 relevant agencies did not yet have their own website. Following a series of letters and correspondences, this number was reduced to 12 in 2005, against which court cases have been initiated (author's interview with the Institute's director, 2005).

nected local activists. However, on the whole civic anti-corruption projects in Russia tend to be less successful. This has not only been due to the increasingly different operational conditions of non-governmental actors in the Russian context but also to tensions at the international-local nexus.

'[T]here are not that many civil society organisations working on corruption. And this is an unfortunate side. Of course you have journalists that provide a lot of useful information.' This statement of a Moscow-based foreign representative only illustrates one side of the coin. Local groups often do not know which international actors are donors and which are not; it is not necessarily obvious.[23] At large, greater exchange of information between international and local non-governmental actors seems necessary to both avoid mutual misperceptions and recognise others' (possible) roles within the network. On both sides, perceptions about each other's *existence* and *changing agendas* have remained considerably vague, if not patently incorrect. Moreover, analysis of international documents and evidence from interviews with international/Western anti-corruption proponents and donor organisations reveals an essential lack of clarification as to who actually represents civil society on the ground and how various non-governmental actors ought to be involved. This has entailed an over-reliance on involving *NGOs* as local partners and has led to a range of questionable projects. For example, only *ex-post facto* were Western-funded resource centres acknowledged as unsuitable strategic entities in Russian cities where local groups tend to both distrust each other and inspire distrust on the part of the population. Furthermore, it was discovered that short-term project results could not be maintained when a new governor had been appointed just after the final report. Where envisioned results could not be attained due to the incompatibility between international/Western and local organisational cultures, new grants consequently tended to be funnelled to other local partners. To compound matters, the issue at stake remains insufficiently debated. Concerns about corruption bring different actors together, but the networking potential has not been fully tapped through interaction, information exchange and debate among anti-corruption advocates. While corruption and anti-corruption are not clearly defined in many assistance programmes, discrepancies between international and local expectations frequently surface only while projects are being conducted. Given the inflexible structures of most grant programmes, it is then often too late to engage in deliberations over locally more appropriate strategies. More constructive relationships between TI-Russia and the TI parent network or USAID as anti-corruption promoters[24] – e.g. in contrast to the USAID-funded anti-cor-

---

23   For example, in several interviews local groups in St. Petersburg listed TI among potential foreign donors for anti-corruption activities, obviously unaware that TI is not a grant-making organisation.
24   TI-Russia has remained in a better position to scrutinise established and largely accepted Western strategies, both within the TI network and vis-à-vis USAID, as long as they have not

ruption projects in Irkutsk – indicate that local expertise is better received when not based on grantee-donor relations.

Several events have thus been ranked differently by anti-corruption proponents on a continuum between 'effective' and 'counterproductive'. The most prominent examples to inspire controversial interpretation (perception and framing) include the increasingly authoritarian governance style in general, the discourse on new terrorist threats, the case against Yukos, and the appointment of regional governors. For example, the authoritarian restructuring of administrative protocol, although criticised by NGOs, is also welcomed by some business actors. The journalistic community has been divided on the issue. The government has used the anti-terrorism agenda to justify some of its unjust manoeuvres against selected opponents as well as against foreign funding of Russian NGOs. On the other hand, the agenda has also raised new hopes among some activists that anti-corruption campaigns might experience a new impetus, since the issue of corruption entered the anti-terrorism discourse when it became clear that bribes made the 2004 Beslan tragedy possible.[25] Furthermore, the Yukos oil company, and along with it Khodorkovsky's foundation *Otkrytaya Rossiya*, are lauded as one of the main Russian donors among journalist and activist communities in Moscow and St. Petersburg. In Irkutsk, however, these entities are perceived less as supportive donors and more as opponents seeking to build pipelines at the cost of local communities and ecosystems – 'buying all the politicians and the media along the route'.[26] The fact that the government has meanwhile put *Otkrytaya Rossiya* out of commission would thus appear to be an instance of clan infighting to some Irkutsk groups while perceived elsewhere as a strike against the beginnings of corporate social responsibility or civil society support from Russian sources. This latter case also points to another relevant dimension of anti-corruption mobilisation: With the exception of the few specialised Moscow-based groups, anti-corruption is 'only' a side-task added to the pre-existing portfolios of various Russian activists and associations engaged in other fields. This kind of piggybacking runs the risk of not only tapping into but also overstraining valuable resources and competencies of local groups. As a consequence, the many possibilities to frame corruption and anti-

---

been involved in the grant programmes of these partners (author's interviews with TI-Russia and TI, 2004–2006).

25 The Beslan tragedy has been linked to the problem of corruption (bribery) by TI-Russia, the TI secretariat in Berlin as well as by President Putin after it became known that the terrorists were able to launch this assault on civilians by paying their way through several security checks with only small bribes. TI-Russia and TI believed that this finally changed the indifferent attitudes of many people in Russia towards corruption (author's interviews with TI, 2004). In Beslan, a southern Russian city, Chechen rebels seized a primary school on 1 September 2004 (traditional school enrolment day) and took more than 1,000 people hostage, including hundreds of pupils and their parents. Three days later, a fire fight between Russian security forces and hostage-takers left over 325 people dead, almost half of them children (e.g. HRW, 2004).

26 Author's interview with environmental activist in Irkutsk, 2005.

corruption may not only create cross-fertilising overlaps, but may also increase the incidence of contradictory interpretations within the network, which may eventually weaken its envisioned effectiveness.

Conclusion

This chapter has summarised some of the findings from a larger study on transnational anti-corruption advocacy in Russia. It started with the question of how local civil society actors in Russia are involved in transnational anti-corruption advocacy. Importantly, different understandings of 'civil society' circulate in the area of anti-corruption advocacy at the international, domestic and local levels. Moreover, a range of civil society actors, from transnational civil society organisations (such as TI) to individual local activists, hold different (and changing) views on what appropriate anti-corruption strategies ought to be. This underlines the importance of considering both actor and issue characteristics within the different contexts contained in transnational efforts. The analysis conducted here also indicates a much wider spectrum of causal and normative conditions of TAN functioning than proposed by existing models, which delimit their focus on ultimately changing the behaviour of norm-deviant states and on NGOs as civil society actors within the domestic context.

Thanks to its transnational network character, the anti-corruption movement may appear unbounded by place in its agendas and actions. However, international, national and local contexts shape actors' perceptions towards both anti-corruption projects and strategic partners – and thus the interpretation of core concepts and expectations – within the movement in various ways. In this respect, this study calls for a more open-minded and unbiased analysis of processes rather than an exclusive focus on outcomes. As in other advocacy realms, researchers working at the blurred boundaries between activism and academia tend to ignore the downsides of anti-corruption efforts. Critics, in contrast, tend to overemphasise the unpleasant consequences of foreign funding and hegemony of Western agendas within transnational networks. Yet the entanglement of international, domestic and local contexts remains insufficiently addressed in the scholarly literature as well as in practitioners' debates on TANs and anti-corruption. In particular, sensitivity to differences between overall governance conditions and reform measures at the national (federal) level and the specific local contexts where civil society actors are situated with their daily activities and routines is crucial. In practice, more deliberation over corruption concerns, local contextual conditions and expectations towards co-operation in this field might lead to more appropriate ways of involving local civil society actors in transnational anti-corruption efforts.

References

CISR 2004. *Anti-corruption field in St. Petersburg: Actors and Activities*, Final report. Prepared within the frame of Think Tank Partnership project 'Mobilising social support to fight corruption in postsocialist countries: cases of Russia and Hungary', St. Petersburg: Centre for Independent Social Research, unpublished document.

Coulloudon, V. 2002. 'Russia's Distorted Anticorruption Campaigns', in S. Kotkin and A. Sajó (eds) *Political Corruption in Transition. A Sceptic's Handbook*, Budapest / New York: CEU Press: 187–206.

Demidov, B. 2004. 'Integrity Assessment', in The Center for Public Integrity (ed) *Global Integrity. An Investigative Report Tracking Corruption, Openness and Accountability in 25 Countries. Russia*: 2–7, http://www.publicintegrity.org/docs/ga/2004Russia.pdf [accessed 10/10/05].

Forum Donorov 2005. *Donorskie i nekommercheskie organizatsii: chto my o nikh znaem. Obzor materialov issledovanii*, Moskva: Forum Donorov.

Galtung, F. 2000. 'A Global Network to Curb Corruption: The Experience of Transparency International', in A. M. Florini (ed) *The Third Force. The Rise of Transnational Civil Society*, Washington, D.C.: Carnegie Endowment for International Peace: 17–47.

HRW 2004. *Joint NGO statement on the Beslan Hostage Tragedy*, http://hrw.org/english/docs/2004/09/08/russia9336_txt.htm [accessed 25/02/2005]

Keck, M. E. and Sikkink, K. 1998. *Activists Beyond Borders. Advocacy Networks in International Politics*, Ithaca / London: Cornell University Press.

Mendelson, S. E. 2002. 'Conclusion: The Power and Limits of Transnational Democracy Networks in Postcommunist Societies', in S. E. Mendelson and J. K. Glenn (eds) *The Power and Limits of NGOs. A Critical Look at Building Democracy in Eastern Europe and Eurasia*, New York Chichester, West Sussex: Columbia University Press: 232–251.

Pieth, M. 1997. 'International Cooperation to Combat Corruption', in K. A. Elliot (ed) *Corruption and the Global Economy*, Washington, DC: Institute for International Economics: 119–131.

Risse, T. and Ropp, S. C. 1999. 'International human rights norms and domestic change: conclusions', in T. Risse, S. C. Ropp and K. Sikkink (eds) *The Power of Human Rights. International Norms and Domestic Change*, Cambridge: Cambridge University Press: 234–278.

Risse, T., et al. (eds) 1999. *The Power of Human Rights. International Norms and Domestic Change*, Cambridge Studies in International Relations, Cambridge: Cambridge University Press.

Schmidt, D. 2006a. *Anti-Corruption Advocacy in Contemporary Russia: Local Civil Society Actors, Transnational Networks and the State*, PhD thesis, Belfast: Queen's University Belfast.

— 2006b. 'Russia's NGO Legislation: New (and Old) Developments', *Russian Analytical Digest* (3): 2–6, http://www.res.ethz.ch/analysis/rad/documents/Russian_Analytical_Digest_3_2006.pdf

Williams, R. and Theobald, R. (eds) 2000. *Corruption in the Developing World*, Vol. 2, The Politics of Corruption, Cheltenham/Northampton: Edward Elgar.

Zwingel, S. 2005. 'From Intergovernmental Negotiations to (Sub)national Change. A Transnational Perspective on the Impact of CEDAW', *International Feminist Journal of Politics* 7(3): 400–424.

*3. Integrating Migrants into Western Societies.
The EU Between Cultural Challenges,
Multiculturalism and New Ideas of Citizenship*

Oksana Morgunova and Dmitry Morgunov

Making Cakes in Scotland. Sweet Memories and Bitter Experiences

Introduction

This chapter represents a case study conducted during the summer months of 2005 in central Scotland and focuses on culturally dependent interpretations of justice and the role of trust in employment relationships. First, the background information, related to the particular host territory, nature of employment, type of companies concerned and the origins and type of migrants will be provided. Second, several conflict situations under investigation will be described and analysed. The findings will be delineated by material from the migrants' web forums.

The Background Information

Region

The area of central Scotland where the company under investigation arranged job contracts for migrants is not densely populated. It experienced the consequences of economic restructuring with the closure of various industrial companies, but at the same time the region fails to supply employees for a variety of existing jobs and businesses. Although since the European enlargement foreign labour accounts for almost three in every 100 jobs in the region, and an influx of approximately 4.000 migrant workers into Tayside has been recorded as of April 2006, the Scottish government agency Communities Scotland reported no impact on employment opportunities for locals.[1] The majority of foreign workers moving into the area has been recruited to fill jobs that the local labour market has failed to supply. The same report states that 15 per cent of companies in Tayside reported signs of increasing tensions as a result of foreign labour.

Tayside, like many other regions in Scotland, is populated mainly by Scots, with only 3% of 'other' ethnicities including a significant share of English and Welsh. The local community has not been subjected to any sizable immigration in the past and appreciates long-term connections to the place via interpersonal relationships established over time. Various studies underline the 'latent racism' in the area with about 10% of the population answering that 'there is nothing bad in hurting somebody

---

1   http://www.communitiesscotland.gov.uk/stellent/groups/public/documents

of a different race.'[2] At this point it is important to highlight that labour migrants in the area are mainly from eastern European countries and are therefore not different racially.

Company

The company concerned, Walker Consultancy,[3] launched an employment program for labour migrants with the focus on the Baltic States. The company is based in the Tayside area, locally owned and permanently employs two people who speak Russian or one of the Baltic languages. The recruitment program was especially successful in Latvia and the company realised, that the majority of prospective clients were Russian speakers. Through the network of the 'Scottish-Russian Forum' voluntary organisation, the agency found a bilingual person to assist with communication. This person became the main informer along with the recruits themselves for this study.

Labour Migrants

The company had more than 100 clients during the researched period. Only three of them spoke Latvian, the others spoke fluent/native Russian and demonstrated varying commands of English. Students constituted a significant share of the recruits and there were a number of married couples. They described themselves as temporary workers and acknowledged their aims firstly as earning extra money and secondly as experiencing life in a foreign country. There were no cases of violent or criminal behaviour recorded by the police involving the researched group of migrants, nor cases resulting in medical conditions for the migrants or a third party. The migrants were allocated to work at a toothpaste factory and frozen food factories. All businesses were located in small settlements.

Mediator

In terms of methodology, this article represents the results of a two-month field study. The mediator provided by the Scottish-Russian Forum conducted participant observations and then discussed the findings with the author and the workers during semi-structured interviews. The study is intentionally reflexive and the personality of the informer-mediator-analyst is therefore of importance. This person (he will be named Misha in this chapter) is a student at one of the Scottish universities. He comes from a Russian-speaking multi-ethnic family, spent his childhood in the Mediterranean and has always studied in an English-language environment. He is bilin-

---

2   For example http://www.cre.gov.uk/downloads/broadening_our_horizons_full_report.pdf
3   All names have been changed for this presentation but the real names of the organisations can be provided on request.

gual but acknowledges difficulties with self-identification in terms of ethnic as well as national belonging. Initially his role was limited to the interpretation of meetings between the workers and the employers, but later he was also called upon to facilitate conflict situations. At this stage his interpretations became more cross-cultural (rather than solely linguistic) in nature. For example, during some of the meetings he had to comment on emotional or rhetorical differences between the sides: What was perceived by the host participants as hostile silence during the conversation was considered normal behaviour in the migrant workers' native culture.

Case No. 1

The first case to be discussed is related to cross-cultural differences in the understanding of work discipline and also provides insights into the varied interpretations of work-related initiative and responsibility.

A group of migrants working in a frozen food factory comprised a couple to be married. Ann and Valdes were students, but Ann's command of English was poor. They worked in different food halls and on one occasion Ann wished to visit her fiancé. She asked for her manager's permission, but for some reason she was not allowed to go to the other production line where he worked. During her break, the young lady went to meet Valdes without asking for anybody's permission. The workers in the various halls wore different protective hats and when entering the other hall she changed her hat. Departing, she ran into another manager who started shouting at her. Instead of asking for forgiveness, Ann burst into laughter and the manager complained. This was her second violation of the rules (she had previously made her work boots shorter) and a disciplinary case was launched.

The Walker company sent Misha to assist with interpreting. Ann gave the following account of the story, stressing the logic of her actions:

- She wanted to see her fiancé to obtain one of the sandwiches he kept in his bag. It was natural to go to him during her break and take one. That was her only purpose.
- She changed her hat because she assumed the hats were needed for health and safety reasons and that every production line had different hats due to safety-related issues.
- She laughed because she barely understood a word of the tirade and found it funny that an adult would lose his temper like that, but she regretted her impulsive reaction.
- Regarding her decision to cut off the upper part of her work boots, she explained that they were too high (she was short of stature) and caused pain, so she decided to improve them.

The manager doubted her version of events and the ensuing dialogue was constructed as a discipline vs. rationality discourse. The manager insisted that Ann had consciously broken the rules several times:

- She violated the rules by opting to leave her station during working hours without asking for permission to do so;
- She did not state the reason for her meeting with her fiancé;
- Her change of hat was seen as part of a pre-meditated plan to remain unnoticed (and therefore a conscious breach of the rules);
- Ann violated health and safety regulations when she made her (personal, but provided by the factory) work boots shorter, a potentially dangerous behaviour (in that a worker made unauthorised modifications to equipment) and a breach of the rules.

Arguing her case, Ann focused on the rationality of her actions. She knew that her actions were harmless. She repeated several times that she was an adult, educated, smart and able to distinguish between potentially harmful and reasonable actions. She did not overtly question the logic of the rules, but expressed doubt about the necessity of some of them and the extent to which they should be followed. For example, in explaining her decision to make alterations to her work boots, she specified that she did not change anything in the lower part of them because she realised that their construction was important for her safety. But the height of the boots was not relevant to the production process in which she was involved: She saved time and effort by making 'improvements' to her footwear without consulting with the manager. She believed it was unfair to take her to task for the breach of discipline: Her behaviour was logical and therefore justified in her eyes.

In analysing this case, one should account for the purely linguistic difficulties in the communication process; however, they do not represent the key issue of the conflict. There is also a cultural component in the confrontation. Lotman (2000, 418) distinguishes between cultures as semiotic systems based on customs and those structured by rules. He notes that within cultures governed by unwritten traditions and customs, any rules and instructions are open for interpretation rather than for automatic implementation or criticism. The arguments on both sides of the conflict situation under investigation were constructed through different Foucauldian discourses: order/discipline vs. rationality. Each concept represented an indisputable system of values for one side and was completely irrelevant for the other: the issues of individual logic were silenced in the managers' position, while the rules did not symbolise authority or guarantee justice in the worker's eyes. It will be argued here that these discourses are culturally specific and locally conditioned.

Although the migrant workers came from Latvia, they represented the Russian-speaking community there. Therefore, their identities can be discussed within the frame of cultural reference imposed by their native language. Historically, the value of individual decisions in the Russian culture has been interpreted ambiguously: Such decisions have been generally criticised when aimed at creating 'extra' profit, but praised when they were related to skills and efficiency. In the identity discourse of the Soviet period, workers were expected to demonstrate an ability to make non-standard decisions by using their 'smekalka' and 'soobrazitel'nost'' (to be witty and smart), both were considered part of the 'tvorcheskiĭ podkhod' (creative approach). Ann's native traditions welcome initiative at the workplace and delegate responsibility for this initiative (including the responsibility for the worker's own safety) to the individual. Ann's decision to fix her footwear would have been considered normal and perhaps even rewarded in her country of origin. Hence she perceived the accusations as unjust and unfair.

The downside of such a 'creative approach' is manifested in its possible violations of technology and alternative approach to discipline. In Ann's case, cultural tradition delegates the right to alter processes and arrangements to the worker and thus downplays the sanctity of the contract per se, allowing some flexibility between the letter and the spirit of legal norms. Ann's arguments demonstrate that she distinguishes between Rules (which she believes are worth complying with) and rules (unnecessary and thus optional), and she makes these distinctions on the basis of her own personal judgements. This stance may be justified under conditions of political and economic instability with a high probability of unpredictable situations (where the established rules are not always efficient and workers' initiative is perceived as justified), but in Scotland it was interpreted as a breach of discipline.

The manager placed the situational locus of control outside of the manager-worker setting in the form of written prescriptions. The idea of justice is represented in his discourse as an immunity of legal norm. The letter and the spirit of the document are inseparable: The manager and worker are not expected to challenge the instructions. An agreement guarantees the personal immunity of both parties with regard to their relationships and safety. According to this perspective, the world is symbolically mapped by rules: Anything which is not defined does not exist.

Without discussing the strengths and weaknesses of both styles of thinking, the case illustrates the significant cultural differences in employment relations which remained latent during the introductory period but created conflict later on because they were not acknowledged or taken into consideration. Here I would like to re-emphasise the absence of physical or phenotypical differences between the migrants and the host population. With less than 3% of an ethnically different population in the area, the local people have not been exposed to the everyday negotiation of cultural differences, although according to the standards of British governance, they are socialised within the norms of sensitivity to ethnic or racial differences. In the absence of visual markers of cultural differences, the cultural differences are not obvious, therefore the migrants from Eastern Europe are not perceived by the hosts as 'strangers,' but as newcomers. Therefore differences in their understanding of discipline and rules are often underestimated.

Here I would like to refer to the aforementioned distinctions between cultures described in Lotman's essay. Lotman also analyses these distinctions within a historic perspective and notes that visual markers, traditionally existing in the form of clothes, job accessories, physical features etc, typically signalled the borderlands between cultures ruled by customs and the ones governed by rules. However, in contemporary society, these markers often disappear, as one of the migrants put it: 'Nothing tells people that I am different – but they do need to be aware of this fact, don't they?'

This observation is supported by material from online communications between migrants from the former USSR. Open access forums are an important part of interpersonal communications between Russian-speaking migrants, and the questions of differences between the migrants and the hosts, as well as migrants of other origins, are subjected to intense discussions in these internet forums. For example, in the Russian-language forum Rupoint, disjunctions in understanding of freedom and rules at the workplace similar to Ann's can be found.[4] In terms of following the rules, the Russian-speaking migrants reflect upon the role of 'avos'' ('Let's hope') in their lives and relationships at the workplace[5]. Migrants reflect on their behavioural differences in business settings and in the decision- making process. They also appreciate the importance of being self-aware of 'being different' in order to communicate effectively.[6]

Case No. 2

The second case consists of numerous observations concerning the workers' trust/ distrust patterns. These observations underscore the importance of independent opinions and non-official sources of information in the lives of the Russian-speaking migrants.

First, one aspect of Misha's role in the communications with migrants will be discussed. During the first company briefing he was introduced to the workers as an interpreter and then translated the directives of the production managers. Misha noticed that the workers initially tended to ignore his presence, but after the end of the official part of the introduction process, they quickly attempted to establish his position within the organisation. When he explained that he was not an employee of the local factory nor a staff member of the HR consultancy which had brought them

---

4   http://www.rupoint.co.uk/showthread.php?t=52560
5   http://www.rupoint.co.uk/showthread.php?t=17317&highlight
6   http://www.rupoint.co.uk/showthread.php?t=25711&highlight

to Scotland, Misha noticed a change in their attitude: The workers seemed a lot more eager to communicate and ask for advice or help. Later, when he came to the premises to collect documents for the Worker Registration Scheme (WRS), the immigrant workers used this chance to ask as many questions related to their life in Scotland as possible. They also called him at home or on his mobile phone. For example, he received calls from the workers asking for directions when they got lost in other cities.

The workers asked his advice when they had conflicts with landlords regarding payment of old electricity bills or savings on heating in private houses. Misha suggested approaching the Walker company directly to discuss these issues, because he believed it would be the most efficient and straightforward way to settle the dispute. But the workers were usually reluctant to do so. The same pattern of behaviour was noted by Ries, who stated that in the Russian-speaking community sharing information about various problems was not necessarily connected to the aspiration to solve an issue quickly and pragmatically. She calls this cultural stance 'litany' and classified it as a rhetorical trope native to Russian culture (Ries 1997).

It is possible to suppose that the workers needed the help of an interpreter or a Russian-speaking local person to clarify various issues due to their inability to speak English. But in practice, such cases were relatively rare. It is feasible that workers were looking for advice from a local person and enjoyed the accessible and free source of information. But there were three other Russian-speaking managers and secretaries in the company and none of them had been asked for advice in the above situations. My argument is that in conflicts or difficult situations, migrants are interested in contacting a source of information which is neutral and independent in their view. As Misha put it in our interview:

> I was not tied by obligations nor controlled by any of the sides. I was less qualified for giving advice about rent or heating, but my potentially unreliable advice was paradoxically more trustworthy for them.

In analysing the migrants' conflict situations, it was necessary to investigate not only the type of agency from which the workers were keen to seek support, but also to identify those institutions the migrants were reluctant to contact in case of difficulties. For instance, there was a case in which a young migrant worker Stas, who, like many of his colleagues, lived in a rough area, was attacked and wounded by his neighbours. After the fight, the young man called the mediator to describe what had happened and asked for advice regarding what he should do. During the conversation it became clear that although this individual had sustained physical injuries, he called Misha before contacting his company, the ambulance or police. It is relevant to note that the interpreter was only briefly acquainted with this person prior to the event, the individual had all the required legal documentation and he was also able to communicate in English. Misha described their conversation: 'When he asked my advice what to do, I suggested seeking medical help. But Stas was reluctant to do it.' Misha also noted that:

- Stas was afraid that the hospital would notify the police. He was convinced that the police were an unreliable and corrupt institution that would have neglected his interests because he was a migrant/stranger.
- He also expressed doubts that his status was actually '…absolutely legal: Because when you are completely white, they will be able to find a black spot.'
- He did not want to cause any trouble for the HR company.

At the same time, he was preoccupied with his future relationship with his flatmates and wanted them to be warned by officials, he was therefore trapped in the vicious circle of his own arguments. Finally, he was forced to change his flat and did so without issuing a formal complaint.

Later in our interview, Misha was asked why he did not report the incident to the company or inform the police. He explained that he appreciated the relationship of mutual trust between him and the workers, and he understood that had he reported the incident, the workers would have considered him an 'informer.' The narratives of contempt for informers as well as the dismissal of complaints of any sort are also widely expressed online,[7] and thus represent a part of a culturally specific understanding of justice: Ideally, a person should deal with difficulties on his or her own without addressing official power structures.

This case illustrates the fact that migrants are not inclined to seek help and advice from official agencies or institutions associated with power, and this position significantly complicates their stay in a new country. Their distrust of official sources of information and power structures is nurtured by the media and social context in their country of origin. Their patterns of behaviour learned at the place of their socialisation do not match the ones of the host country and thus create a potentially dangerous situation for both sides. The migrants need the special services of a cultural and social interpreter, rather than simply translation from one language to another.

This distrust of official structures was also demonstrated by the immigrants with respect to sending off their passports with applications to extend their work permits. The procedure takes about three to four weeks, after which the passport is promised to be returned to the individuals. It was inconvenient to collect the documents at the factory, so Misha had to visit the individuals outside of their working hours in an informal setting. He quickly found that the workers were happy to submit the fee and provide their personal details for the form, but the majority of them declined the request to supply their passports. In this instance, Misha represented the official

---

7   For   example: http://www.russianlondon.ru/forum/showthread.php?t=12088&highlight, http://www.russianlondon.ru/forum/showthread.php?t=12064&highlight,   http://www.russianlondon.ru/forum/showthread.php?t=10661&highlight

side of the situation and they did not ask additional questions, but provided various explanations as to why they could not comply with the rules.

Initially, the migrant workers suggested that they needed their passports for their weekly postal cash transactions. Nevertheless, when this obstacle was removed (the company arranged it so that the local post office would accept photocopies of the passports), the workers were still reluctant to send them off. They provided explanations as to why they should not send away their passports, quoting the opinions of locals. The situation was not remedied even after the head managers of both the HR company and the factory sent out a letter in two languages (Latvian and Russian) specifying the urgency of submitting the passports. Even at this stage, the migrant workers continued to quote the opinions of the local workers who allegedly advised them against dispatching their passports and ignored official information. These arguments suggest, that due to distrust of the officials at any level, the workers resorted to non-official sources of information. Such behaviour would have been natural in their home country. Some of the workers mentioned that they were not convinced of the stability of their jobs and were afraid that they would be powerless without passports in case of a conflict with the employer. To these individuals the passport also held a symbolic meaning, signifying their belonging (see Colic-Peisker and Walker, 2003, Carter, 2004) and their ability to return home. The passport represented a symbolic identity and a security warrant of their independent status in the new country. This case proves that the migrants had predefined stereotypes of power structures as unfair to workers. The British government emerged in this context as an unreliable and vicious power to be regarded with suspicion.

As it was mentioned above the number of non-Russian speakers in the researched group of migrants was small, and therefore it was impossible to draw any conclusions on or comparisons of the patterns of their behaviour. But with regards to the above situation it shall be noted that all three non-Russian (Latvian) speakers got together and searched online for relevant official information to double check the instructions provided by the company. Finally they decided to send their passports to be processed, but posted and insured their postage on their own without participation of the mediator or a company.

Conclusion

The question I would like to discuss now is whether these patterns of trust/distrust are solely culturally or also socially specific. Were the Russian-speaking migrants' patterns of behaviour shaped exclusively by the culture of their native language or were they typical for anyone in unfavourable, unprivileged positions irrespective of cultural dispositions (Bourdieux 1977)?

First, the historic perception of legality in Russian-speaking culture will be noted. In Russian national discourse, justice is perceived as a personal trait rather than an objective social institution: Historically, justice has been associated with truth and honesty as personal qualities, rather than as features of the state. Contemporary socio-linguistic research among native Russian speakers in Russia proves that justice is associated with truth and honesty almost three times more often than with law and legality (Bazovye Tsennosti Rossiyan, 2003, 255). The fact that the same features can be noted in the discourse of Latvian migrants highlights the importance of cultural dispositions, that are inherited through and transmitted by language and habitus (Bourdieu, 1977).

The migrants' attitude to power structures may also have been influenced by the difficulties of the transitional period in post-Soviet societies. Russian identity scholarship suggests that in contemporary Russian-speaking cultures the notions of trust and justice are separate from concepts of legality and power. Research on the 'basic values' of Russian citizens shows that 78.1% of the respondents agreed with the statement 'power is connected to the criminal world' (Bazovye Tsennosti Rossiyan, 2003, 104). The same study demonstrates that the perception of trust was connected to the notion of stability and justice but was surprisingly absent when the respondents were defining the concept of legality. These findings might reflect important characteristics of local conditions and social inequality. The aforementioned study in Russia also demonstrates that 68.1% of those who challenged the idea of justice in contemporary society belong to its most deprived circles in social and financial terms (Bazovye Tsennosti Rossiyan, 2003, 98).

The case studies presented in this article might also be discussed in a wider social and culturally non-specific context. Düvell shows that migrants' discourse on justice has a universal rather than a culturally specific character (Düvell 2005). In the scholar's study on irregular migrants of different origins, he demonstrates that the respondents do not argue their cases in terms of complying with the legal norms of the host countries, but refer to the ideas of humanism and human rights as universal values. Therefore, the interpretations of what is just and fair are reflective of the migrants' unprivileged positions. Similar interpretations of justice are pronounced for various ethnic migrants in the enlarged Europe.[8]

This chapter attempted to prove that migrants' perceptions of justice are culturally defined, locally conditioned, socially influenced and often do not match the ones of their local co-workers. In instances of employment conflicts, the sides tend to relate their experiences in terms of culturally specific interpretations of the universal values of *freedom, truth* and *good.*

---

8   Space does not permit the authors to investigate the conflict between the social role and social status of the migrants in the cases under investigation.

References

Bazovye Tsennosti Rossiyan (2003), Moscow: Dom Intellectual'noĭ Knigi.

Bourdieu, P. (1977) *Outline of a Theory of Practice* (Cambridge University Press)

Carter, J. (2004), Research note: reflections on interviewing across the ethnic divide, *International Journal of Social Research Methodology*, 7:4.

Colic-Peisker, V. and Walker, I. (2003), 'Human capital, acculturation and social identity: Bosnian refugees in Australia', *Journal of Community and Applied Social Psychology*, 3:5.

Düvell, F. (2005) *People should be free to live where they want. How undocumented immigrants justify their behaviour*, paper presented at Irregular Migration – Research, Policy and Practice, COMPAS, Oxford, Annual International Conference, 7–8 July 2005.

Lotman, J. (2000), *Semiosfera: kul'tura i vzryv*. (St. Petersburg: Iskusstvo-SPb).

Ries, N. (1997), *Russian Talk*. (London: Cornell University Press).

David Duncan

Multiculturalism as a Tool for Migrant Integration

Introduction

Within the field of migration research, the past decade has witnessed an increased focus on the attachments that migrants maintain to the people, traditions and the socio-political cultures of their homelands. The consensus maintains that such linkages have become much more intense in recent years, as modern communications technology, proceeding apace with globalisation, has strengthened the networks that connect migrants to other migrants, as well as to their homelands. The result has been the strengthening of transnational communities, which has had effects on concepts of the nation-state, sovereignty, the processes of migrant integration and corollary ethnic relations policies.

This chapter seeks to provide an overview of some of the changes that result from increasing transnationalism and globalisation. While it is often noted that these processes weaken the role and power of national governments, it is important to recognize where governments can continue to exert influence and how they can maximize their influence in regards to the integration of their ethnic communities. While transnational politics are more influential than before, government policy is still the principle deciding force that dictates the function and behaviour of human migration and settlement. Instead of viewing transnational politics as a threat to national politics, it is perhaps more accurate to view the former as being extremely dependent on the latter. For this reason a discussion regarding multiculturalism is timely, for if indeed government policy is an important and effective instrument in managing political migrant transnationalism, then certainly multicultural policy – the umbrella policy used by many Western nations to manage their domestic ethnic relations – is an essential element in influencing the role of transnational politics.

Experiences with multicultural policy have been as mixed as the number of different versions of the policy that exist in practice. The Netherlands has experimented with a number of different approaches that might fall under the umbrella of 'multiculturalism', in that it has long encouraged and supported minority migrant cultural practices within its borders. However, over the course of the past four decades, Dutch policy has evolved to encourage different levels of migrant participation in different aspects of citizenship. As Dutch society becomes increasingly altered by a growing migrant population (nearly half of Amsterdam's population is comprised of foreign-born and their children, for example) (Penninx, 2000a), and as this population finds it much easier to stay connected to the culture of the homeland, it becomes increas-

ingly important to devise ethnic relations policies that stress the successful integration (political, economic, and social) of migrant populations. A multicultural policy
that exists as an approach to integration, and explicitly defines its limits (as opposed
to acting as a set of woolly notions of cultural relativism), may well provide the best
solution for best managing Europe's changing population and avoiding segregation,
while protecting the values from which stem the commitments to tolerance and multiculturalism in the first place.

Growing Transnationalism

Now more than ever individuals can simultaneously think of themselves as members
of two or more societies: efficient and inexpensive transportation allows individuals
to reside in different homes across different national borders, while modern communications technologies allow individuals to remain deeply involved in the political
and cultural happenings of their different homes. As a result, a recent literature has
developed within migration studies, as the influence of transnational ethnic networks
becomes increasingly apparent and pertinent. Alejandro Portes (1997) describes transnational migrant communities as those that comprise

> ...dense networks across political borders created by immigrants in their quest for eco-
> nomic advancement and social recognition. Through these networks, an increasing
> number of people are able to live dual lives. Participants are often bilingual, move easily
> between different cultures, frequently maintain homes in two countries and pursue eco-
> nomic, political and cultural interests that require their presence in both.

Consequently, much evidence does exist (and continues to be collected) that demonstrates that the impact of transnational communities on both the sending and
receiving countries is undoubtedly extensive, affecting the political, economic and
social processes of the countries involved. On the political front, understandings of
national citizenship are changing, which affects further our understanding of the
processes that govern our political communities. Traditionally, political theories have
worked within the paradigm of a container-model of the nation-state, that is to say, a
bounded demo which assumes the exclusive loyalty of its citizens towards their single state. Transnational migrant networks challenge both of these presuppositions,
as they create overlapping memberships between territorially separated and independent polities.

   The increasing economic influence of transnational communities has been noted
by a number of sources, as remittance payments currently exceed US$60 billion each
year and a number of developing migrant-sending countries are becoming increasingly reliant upon them (Vertovec, 2001). The transfer of remittance funds is largely
facilitated by strong transnational networks, which allow for the success of migrant-

operated systems of trust-based financial networks.[1] The economic influence of transnational migrant communities is often readily transferable into political influence, as diaspora communities with significant financial means are able to influence political outcomes in the countries in which they no longer reside. For example, Croatian emigrants contributed nearly 80% of the funds donated to political parties during the 1990 election campaign (Vertovec, 2001).

The political influence that migrants exert in receiving countries has grown in recent years as well, as immigrants acquire citizenship that allows them to participate in new political arenas. The United States, Australia and much of Western Europe host large populations of dual-nationals, estimated to be in the millions of people. This number has increased greatly since 1997, when the Council of Europe abolished its 1963 convention that placed restrictions on multiple nationalities (European Convention on Nationality 1997). The issue of dual citizenship and multiple nationalities has generated heated debate in numerous countries, as questions regarding the loyalties and political allegiances of transnational migrants are deliberated (often through a haze of polemic), leading to different approaches taken by different Western countries.[2]

However, from these debates can be rescued legitimate concerns regarding the changing nature of citizenship, and the effects on societal well-being that might result from increasingly common and strong transnational communities. The Parekh Report (2000), otherwise known as The Future of Multi-ethnic Britain, provides a comprehensive overview of race relations in Britain. Summarising one migrant's impressions of community belonging, the individual is quoted: '[i]t is not unusual, particularly in the modern world, for some of my loyalties to be transnational – I have feelings of kinship and shared interests with people in at least two different countries.' While the report does not go on to probe the implications of this statement for multiculturalism or our model of the nation-state, the statement may be seen as presenting challenges to both.

While in past decades one's citizenship would entail full participation in the community, Rainer Bauböck (2002) suggests that for migrants, one's second citizenship

---

1   The flow of money from migrants to their homelands often relies upon the 'hawala' network of informal banking transactions, which by operating often virtually on trust alone, allows for the covert movement of incredible sums of money around the world.

2   A small number of European nations, Austria for example, insist that nationality is a singular entity, and attempt to enforce this commitment with respect to their naturalised immigrants. Another group of countries, the United States in particular, does not officially condone dual nationality, but does not demand evidence to prove that immigrants have renounced previous citizenships, thus generally ignoring the issue altogether, while hoping that new immigrants will have a primary loyalty to their new country of residence. A third perspective acknowledges and promotes the rights of its dual nationals to partake in processes (such as voting) of the second country of citizenship.

'carries the essential benefit of free movement between two societies to which they are linked by residential and family ties. Yet even this formal overlap does not generally imply a full and simultaneous participation in the legal order and political life of two states'. The possibility of such an ambivalent state of citizenship for dual nationals has been alluded to by Adrian Favell (1998), who describes such a position as one that can provide transnational migrants with a distinct advantage:

> ... immigrants, classically between two (or more) cultures ... are good indicators of the power to be found by playing on the line between belonging and non-belonging. To be able to refuse norms, or choose when and where they might be useful to follow, is a rare power, and a somewhat problematic concept for the theory of socialization that must be at the heart of any sociological theory. To discover a new form of anomie as a source of social action and capital, might indeed be the most interesting and paradoxical discovery to be made from charting the contemporary politics of belonging...

These examples make pressing the importance played by integration policies. As the ties that connect migrants to their homelands (particularly political culture) grow stronger, the failure of migrant communities to successfully integrate can lead to consequences of transnationalism that benefit very few, while harming very many. Many regions of Europe have seen the increased ghettoisation of migrant communities, while North America – its own immigration flows increasing – is attempting to avoid such results. If transnationalism is making it easier for migrants to stay connected to their previous cultures, then transnationalism risks increasing the barriers to migrant integration within host cultures.[3] Needed, then, is an ethnic relations policy that places integration at the core of its mandate.

Multiculturalism

The term 'multicultural' can be both descriptive and normative. At a basic level, most Western countries can be considered to be multicultural as their inhabitants comprise a multitude of different ethnicities cohabitating in one state. However, when discussing 'multicultural policy' with reference to migrant populations (as this chapter does), the term signifies a certain approach to ethnic relations. Concepts of multicultural policy differ widely, but at a fundamental level the multicultural model is founded upon a commitment to the tolerance of different cultures and the official recognition in national institutions of these cultures.

Multiculturalism as an official government policy began in Canada, where it was introduced by Pierre Trudeau in 1971. Not a set of codified rules and principles to which policy-makers strictly adhere, it is more useful to regard multiculturalism in Canada as a constantly evolving approach to migrant integration. As has been the case in

---

3   Steven Vertovec writes that 'transnational connections enable migrants as never before to maintain collective identities and practices ... [which also] has a significant bearing on the culture and identity of the second generation' (Vertovec, 2001).

other countries that followed Canada's lead, multiculturalism has undergone an often ad-hoc evolution as it attempts to adapt to new challenges. First and foremost, Canadian multicultural policy seeks to modify the terms of integration: by treating all cultures and their people as legitimate, multiculturalism works to better accommodate and encourage ethnic diversity. As a result, integration is now considered a two-way process (Kymlicka, 1998, 46). While immigrant groups are expected to adapt to their host country's laws, the host population is also expected to cooperate in the accommodation of different cultural practices in order to ensure that the rules and functioning of common institutions do not unduly disadvantage immigrant groups. The goal is to encourage immigrant groups to share in the country's common institutions: by accommodating different cultural practices within these institutions, Canada hopes to encourage immigrant participation and integration within them.

While encouraging the diversity of cultural practices, Canadian multicultural policy does not permit practices that violate Canadian law. Canada's Multiculturalism Act is subordinate to the Charter of Rights and Freedoms, the Human Rights Act, and the Criminal Code. While multicultural policy is intended to facilitate negotiation regarding the terms of integration, it is not intended to renegotiate fundamental values or law. Thus, in the case of Canadian multicultural policy, the goal has been to integrate migrants into Canadian institutions while allowing them to retain and celebrate their own cultural heritages. This differentiates it in practice from the concept of multiculturalism as a tool to promote egalitarianism, relativism, or other woolly liberal ideas. Instead, Canada's approach has been much more pragmatic: not solely based on grand philosophical notions of cultural equality, Canadian multiculturalism is instead indicative simply of an approach to migrant integration based on the idea that migrants whose cultures are treated as legitimate will better integrate into Canadian society. Based on the assumption that most immigrants to Canada are there to stay, the multicultural project has been one of giving them the best opportunity to acquire citizenship and participate within Canadian society.[4]

The Case of the Netherlands

This sets Canada apart from many of its Western colleagues, as many European nations, for example, have struggled with questions regarding the extent to which migrants should integrate within particular institutions of their adoptive countries. Prior to 1974, immigration was for the most part welcomed throughout Western Europe, the result of a need for immigrant labour. However, following changes to the European economic structure, this demand was significantly reduced, which ushered

---

4   Canada is unique among most Western nations in that over 80% of its immigrants become Canadian citizens.

in the era of unsolicited migration to the continent. As immigration continues and immigrant populations increase with high birth-rates, European countries continue to wrestle with different policies aimed at managing their evolving national ethnic make-up.

In order to facilitate an examination of the different approaches used by different countries to reconcile democratic values with the inclusion of cultural diversity, Rinus Penninx (2000a) distinguishes three different aspects of citizenship. First is the political dimension, which refers to whether or not immigrants are regarded as full members of the political community. Second is the socio-economic dimension of citizenship, which refers to the social and economic rights of immigrants and is contingent on their access to the same institutions and facilities (e.g. social housing and welfare benefits) that can be accessed by natives. Third are the rights to cultural and religious expression that can be enjoyed by migrant groups.

Looking specifically at the Netherlands, Han Entzinger (1999) determines four different phases apparent in the approach to integration during the country's post-war years: avoidance, ambivalence, ethnic minority and integration. 'Avoidance' describes the era from 1950 to 1961, as the expanded labour market encouraged immigration (mostly from Indonesia) that was at best reluctantly tolerated by the receiving population. The policy during this period was one of assimilation: while immigrants were offered some of the trappings of the burgeoning welfare state, by way of dispersed housing and strong government pressure from social workers, Indonesians were strongly pressured into joining an unchanging model of Dutch society (Vermeulen and Penninx 2000). While Penninx's second category is partly met during this era, his first and third aspects of citizenship are absent, as there was little push to involve immigrants in the political sphere of the country, while assimilationist policies did not encourage distinct cultural expression.

Entzinger describes the period of 1961 to 1980 as one of ambivalence towards migrants. Immigration rates were increasingly rapidly (1961 marked the first year of an immigration surplus) with many more Surinamese, Moroccans and Moluccans arriving (Vermeulen, 1997). In contrast to their treatment of the Indonesian migrants, Dutch authorities resisted strong assimilationist policies towards these new groups, as it was presumed that the greater cultural difference between these groups (as opposed to the Indonesians) and the Dutch would prevent successful assimilation (Entzinger 1999). The manifestation of Penninx's third category of rights to cultural distinctiveness became very apparent during this period, as policies were introduced to help preserve migrant cultures, through language programmes and other forms of cultural support. While these immigrants were granted full access to the provisions of the welfare state, it was still assumed (by both Dutch officials and many immigrants themselves) that they would return to their native countries. As a result, policies were created to help smooth their transition once they were to return home (Lucassen and Penninx 1997). The primary upshot of this period of 'ambivalence' was the seg-regation – both culturally and economically (job market performance of immigrants was especially poor) – of migrants, as many did not speak the language of their new country, nor had much involvement in, or knowledge of, their receiving culture.

By the mid-1970s the divisive effects of transnationalism could already be seen in the Netherlands. As the Moroccan population of the country increased, community organisations – mostly religious[5] – began to flourish. Beginning in 1973, the Moroc-can government, in an attempt to exert influence over its emigrants, set up organisa-tions known as 'Amicales' throughout the Netherlands, Belgium and France (Heel-sum, 2002). While these organisations were purported to help Moroccans in Europe establish cultural and social activities, it became clear that they were simply a control apparatus designed to quell left-wing opposition to the Moroccan government that had been gaining support in Moroccan communities throughout Western Europe. While retarding the participation of Moroccan immigrants in Dutch community af-fairs, these Amicales also exacerbated divides within the Moroccan immigrant com-munity, pitting those who supported the Moroccan government against those who wanted nothing to do with the authorities of the country which they had left.

After recognizing in 1979 that most migrants who had arrived in the Netherlands over the previous few decades were there to stay, the government became one of the first in Europe to form a long-term ethnic relations policy. This came in the form of a report entitled 'Etnische Minderheden' (Ethnic Minorities), that acknowledged that immigrants were settlers and not temporary visitors and as such required a pol-icy to facilitate their permanent incorporation into Dutch society (Vermeulen and Pennix 2000). The report focused on migrant groups – particularly those who were of low economic standing. The term 'ethnic minority' then came to mean an ethnic group with low socio-economic status over a period of a number of generations (Ver-meulen, 1997). The policy was aimed at Surinamese, Moluccans, Antilleans, refugees and Romany, and its goal was to prevent these groups from becoming problems for Dutch society. As ethnic groups who were not economically disadvantaged were not affected by this policy, it is clear that the aim of the policy was not the cultural integration of minority ethnic groups, but rather the mitigation of the risks posed to greater Dutch society by poor ethnic-minority groups.

Indeed, during that time the Dutch government continued its extended support of minority cultural practices that encouraged the type of de facto segregation of Entzinger's previous period of 'ambivalence'. During the late 70s and early 80s, the

---

5   The largest category of Moroccan organizations in the Netherlands is religious, see: Heelsum, Anja van: Explaining trends, developments and activities of Moroccan organisations in the Neth-erlands. Paper for the Sociaal Wetenschappelijke Studiedagen, Amsterdam, May 30–31, 2002.

Dutch government considered religious facilities to be essential to the functioning of minority communities (Vermeulen, 1997) and from 1976 to 1983 it played a large role in the construction of mosques and Hindu temples throughout the country. While the federal government put an end to its involvement in such projects in 1983, local governments continue to promote and fund the establishment of these places of worship, and today the Netherlands is home to almost four hundred mosques (Vermeulen, 1997). Similar is the state of religious schooling in the country, for as privately run schools are entitled to the same funding received by state-run schools, the Dutch government fully funds over thirty Islamic schools (Vermeulen, 1997). This period of 'ethnic minorities' (1979 to 1994, according to Entzinger's classification) might be considered to satisfy all three of Penninx's categories, for migrants were on the receiving end of the social welfare privileges of the country, were supported in the preservation of the culture and customs and were now considered to be permanent residents and encouraged to participate in the political processes of their new country.

During this time cultural diversity was often discussed as though it were an end in itself, or had some sort of intrinsic value. The term 'multiculturalism' was often used to describe the collection of Dutch policies during the 1980s, which had promoted the maintenance of immigrant cultures not to encourage the return of immigrants to their home countries, but to build and strengthen a Dutch multicultural society. The barriers to political membership within this society became astonishingly low, for even voting rights were extended in 1985 to anyone who had resided in the Netherlands for three years, regardless of citizenship (Rex, 1991). While political integration had increased among migrants, their cultural integration into Dutch society was not following suit. As the Dutch welfare state moved close to crisis during the early 1990s, a dialogue was initiated regarding the duties of individuals versus the role of government. An upshot of this dialogue was a discussion regarding the responsibility of migrants to better integrate within the Dutch society that had been providing them with full social welfare support.

In 1994 the report 'Contourennota integratiebeleid etnische minderheden' (Framework memorandum: integration policy ethnic minorities) appeared, which defined integration as 'a process leading to the full and equal participation of individuals and groups in society, for which mutual respect for identity is seen as a necessary condition' (Entzinger, 1999, 24). This report ushered in Entzinger's fourth phase of Dutch migrant policy, which he has described as 'integration'. This present phase resembles more Canada's policy of multiculturalism, which stresses integration within a bilingual (English and French) framework. While provisions to eliminate disadvantages faced by migrants in all fields of public policy were continued, as were programmes aimed at low socio-economic migrant groups, the government has begun placing a greater onus on migrants to make an effort to participate in Dutch society.

Currently it is mandated (by the threat of fines) that all permanent migrants (except those from EU and EES countries, Switzerland and the US) must take 600 hours of language and special orientation classes, while the Dutch government has reduced funding for sending-country language training (Penninx, 2000b). The premise holds that migrants with Dutch language training and education have higher rates of naturalisation – a move by Dutch officials to encourage greater integration (both symbolic and practical) within Dutch society (Bevelander and Veenman, 2006).

Reconciling Integration, Multiculturalism, and the Concerns of Host Populations

If multiculturalism is to serve as a policy to successfully manage domestic ethnic relations, it must concern itself not only with the needs of migrant groups, but also with the needs of the host population. Multicultural policy that lacks public support will face serious challenges if the public harbours resentment against the ethnic minorities of the country. Multicultural policy that provides only for the preservation of minority cultural practices does little to improve the economic status of minority groups and risks the balkanisation of various ethnic communities. Instead, multicultural policy ought to be viewed as a tool for *integration*: promoting diversity as a useful goal, not necessarily an end in itself, but because it provides the foundations for productive relationships between ethnic communities and government. As a result, such promotion of diversity should occur only in areas where increased integration is a foreseeable and likely result. In short, the idea of successful multiculturalism is to encourage migrant participation in common institutions by reducing any cultural barriers to their participation, so long as any resulting changes to these institutions do not violate established law or contradict the established values of the host country. Thus the parameters, or limits, to multiculturalism must be made explicit; not only will this encourage a specific type of desired integration, but will also assuage the host population that their fundamental laws and values are not suffering a process of renegotiation.

In this respect Australia has been successful in ways that most other 'multicultural' countries have not, as they have emphasised the limits to Australian multiculturalism as follows:

- multicultural policies require all Australians to accept the basic structures and principles of Australian society – the Constitution and the rule of law, tolerance and equality, Parliamentary democracy, freedom of speech and religion, English as the national language, and equality of the sexes;

- multicultural policies impose obligations as well as conferring rights; the right to express one's own culture and beliefs involves a reciprocal responsibility to accept the right of others to express their views and values;
- multicultural policies are based upon the premise that all Australians should have an overriding and unifying commitment to Australia, to its interests and future first and foremost (Office of Multicultural Affairs 1995).

Multicultural theorist Will Kymlicka (1998, 67) states that 'this is the type of explicit statement that we need in Canada [and elsewhere]', even though he does find the third limit somewhat troublesome.[6] This type of policy stipulates a two-way process of integration: host countries will adapt to accommodate diverse cultural practices within an explicit framework, while migrants – encouraged to participate within public institutions – will also be encouraged to maintain the cultural practices of their homeland, provided they do not contravene established law.

In an age of strong identity politics, a commitment to individual rights in a multicultural environment is necessary to maintaining a cohesive force and avoiding a fractured society. In today's climate of increasing transnationalism, the pieces of a fractured society would not be limited to internal groups and interests, but would invite a stronger and more influential transnational political dimension. Governments still have the power and ability to control migrant political transnationalism by encouraging integration, and multiculturalism has an important role to play in securing its country's ethnic relations and protecting its values and laws. Successful multiculturalism must be considered as a tool and an approach to migrant integration and is to be maintained with a strong commitment to the values to which it owes its very success and existence.

References

Bauböck, R. (2002), 'Political community beyond the sovereign state: Supranational federalism and transnational minorities', in Vertovec (ed.) (2002), *Conceiving Cosmopolitanism: Theory, Context and Practice* (Oxford: Oxford University Press).

Bevelander, P. and Veenman, J. (2006), 'Naturalisation and Socioeconomic Integration: The Case of the Netherlands', in *Working Paper Series: Research on Immigration and Integration in the Metropolis* (Vancouver: Metropolis).

Entzinger, H. (1999), 'Towards a model of incorporation: the case of the Netherlands' Forthcoming.

European Convention on Nationality, Strasbourg, 1997.

---

6   Kymlicka states that the third limit, in its present form, 'overstates the sort of allegiance that states can rightfully demand from their citizens.'

Favell, A. (1998), 'To belong or not to belong: the postnational question', in Favell and Geddes (eds) (1998), *The Politics of Belonging: Migrants and Minorities in Contemporary Europe* (Aldershot: Ashgate).

Heelsum, A. (2002), 'Explaining trends, developments and activities of Moroccan organisations in the Netherlands', paper presented to the Sociaal Wetenschappelijke Studiedagen, Amsterdam, May 30–31.

Kymlicka, W. (1998), *Finding Our Way* (Oxford: Oxford University Press).

Lucassen, J. and Penninx, R. (1997), *Newcomers: Immigrants and their descendents in the Netherlands, 1550 – 1995* (Amsterdam: Het Spinhuis).

Parekh, B. (2000), *The Future of a Multi-Ethnic Britain* (London: Profile Books).

Penninx, R. (2000a), ‚Integration of Immigrants in Europe', paper presented at the Working Together for the Future: Partnerships in Immigration Research and Policy Conference, Toronto, Ontario, Canada, March 22–25.

—— (2000b), ‚Integration of Immigrants in Europe: policies of diversity and diversity of policies', paper presented to the conference Herausforderung Integration: Migrationspolitik für schweizerische und europäische Städte, Bern, Switzerland, April 13 and 14.

Portes, A. (1997), 'Immigration theory for a new century: Some problems and opportunities', *International Migration Review* 31, 799 – 825.

Rex, J. (1991) ‚The political sociology of a multi-cultural society', *European Journal of Intercultural Studies* 2:1, 7–19.

Vermeulen, H. and Penninx, R. (2000), *Immigrant Integration: the Dutch case* (Amsterdam: Het Spinhuis).

Vermeulen, H. (1997), *Immigration policy for a multicultural society* (Brussels: Migration Policy Group).

Vertovec, S. (2001), 'Transnational Challenges to the "New" Multiculturalism', paper presented to the ASA Conference, Sussex, March 21 – 24.

'What is Multiculturalism?' Canberra: Department of the Prime Minister, Office of Multicultural Affairs, April 1995.

Aleksandra Wyrozumska

Enhancing Inclusion in the European Union. The Model of a European Stakeholder Citizenship

Introduction

In the last decades of the 20th century, some traditional notions of state sovereignty have become challenged by economic globalisation, growing concern with human rights and European integration. The comparative research on citizenship policies in the EU member states has established that the residence requirements for naturalisation are becoming shorter, states are showing increasing tolerance for dual citizenship and the *ius sanguinis* modes of citizenship acquisition are being gradually replaced by the *ius soli* rules (Howard, 2005; Vink, 2005; Aleinikoff and Klusmeyer, 2000). Drawing on these empirical findings, it has been noted that the national citizenship policies of European states reveal a steady tendency towards becoming more inclusive (Bauböck, Ersbøll, Groenendijk and Waldrauch, 2006). Not all of the states, however, confirm the *democratic convergence hypothesis,* and some have even made their regulations stricter than before. With the sole exception of refugee regulations, the EU has no formal policy competence in nationality law. The role of the European Union is limited to exercising soft pressure which however ought not to be entirely disregarded – particularly concerning the issues of long term migrants' integration and statelessness.

What is particularly interesting about the socio-political changes is the fact, that immigration and the EU integration have neither evoked a cosmopolitan citizenship, nor have they preserved traditional citizenship formations (Joppke/Morawska, 2003). As a consequence, the terms of inclusion, so central to the normative theory of citizenship, have to be redefined as well. Against that background, an attempt to establish *a priori* criteria for inclusion is not feasible in the context of the EU. First of all, given the scope and pace of socio-political changes in the last two decades, these criteria would very soon be challenged. Secondly, an *a priori* definition would be insensitive to the socio-cultural context which interprets normative principles. Terms of inclusion are set on the basis of normative criteria, which are constantly redefined by individuals whose demands and preferences change according to the social, political and economic constraints or possibilities that they encounter. However, while a universal definition of inclusion cannot be developed, different modes of exclusion can nonetheless be identified and limited. The prospective model of national citizenship should be capable of living up to these requirements.

The traditional models of national citizenship either rely on the fixed terms of inclusion and exclusion, often difficult to defend from a moral perspective, or prematurely disregard the sovereign powers of the state actors. The chapter shall therefore critically evaluate particularistic ethnic and republican models of citizenship, as well as cosmopolitan and liberal conceptions (Bader, 2005a+b; Soysal, 1994). Having mapped different modes of exclusion in the EU, it will be argued that traditional models of citizenship are not capable of limiting all the patterns of exclusion identified in the EU member states. Finally, a model of stakeholder citizenship is put forth, being the most promising prospective model of national citizenship limiting exclusion yet responding to social demands (Liebert, 2004; Bauböck, 2005b). The major assumptions of the model are the following: firstly, acknowledgement of multiple and cross-cutting national or other identities, secondly, enhancing participation of stakeholders, and thirdly, focus on limiting *both* internal and external exclusion of stakeholders.

The Problem of Just Inclusion

In general terms, citizenship accounts for a formal relationship between an individual and a state and is usually associated with specific rights and duties. Yet the very term implies different meanings, depending on the type of polity and the scope of duties and rights associated with the membership status (Marshal, 1949/1965). Citizenship, according to David Lister, is a 'Janus-faced' phenomenon evoking both inclusionary and exclusionary practices. It sets down the terms of membership within a particular society and henceforth serves as a historical justification and a locus of legitimacy. As a consequence, those patterns of exclusion which have become deeply embedded in a historical context are usually difficult to eradicate when social reality changes.

Moreover, citizenship not only grants individuals different rights but constrains people's powers in two different ways (Perczyński and Vink, 2002). Firstly, at the individual level, citizenship imposes duties and obligations towards the state and the community. Secondly, at the societal level, citizenship reveals an inclusionary and an exclusionary nature. These two mechanisms have become a source of a major tension between contemporary understandings of democracy and citizenship. For instance, ancient Greek or Roman democracies were highly exclusivist in their denial of migrants', women's and slaves' right to citizenship. On the other hand, respect for liberal values implies that not only the type of governance but also the terms of membership in a polity should be based on consensus, and contemporary democracies differ from their predecessors by respecting the individual's right to redefine his or her membership status.

The goal of this section is to present and evaluate traditional models of citizenship. Before doing that, the term 'model' needs to be clarified. Models, as presented in this chapter, are analytical tools helpful in mediating between empirics and normative theories. Referring to Sartori's 'ladder of generalisability', one could say that models are located below such general, normative concepts as 'citizenship', 'ethnicity' or 'republicanism' (Sartori, 1984) but certainly 'above' indicators. Models of citizenship remain ideal-type constructs which cannot be simply attributed to a particular state's citizenship law. For instance, a model of an 'ethnic citizenship' consists of all the attributes characterising this particular model and no attributes belonging to a different one. The observable citizenship regimes have developed into rather eclectic entities, where, for example, ethnic principles mix with liberal ones. Therefore, when analyzing contemporary citizenship regulations it is possible to establish that a particular principle, say ethnicity, informs one form of citizenship acquisition applicable to specific category of people. However, another type of citizenship acquisition applicable to another category of people may be based on an entirely different principle. The role of the models is therefore to structure and organize our observations but also to assess each model's normative justifications for defining inclusion in a state.

What makes the traditional models vulnerable to criticism is the fact that they rely on the fixed terms of inclusion and exclusion. Citizenship models reflecting particularistic assumptions, namely ethnic and republican models, are united by the principle of priority for compatriots. In the ethnic model, the tie between compatriots is established on the basis of the *ius sanguinis* principle, while in the republican model relies on the *ius soli* tenet. In the ethnic model, the population entitled to set the terms of inclusion and exclusion is a culturally defined 'imagined' community of common ancestry. In the republican model, the criteria of membership are twofold. Firstly, only the inhabitants of a state can be its full-fledged members. Secondly, only those migrants who can contribute to the 'common good' of a state can take up residence in the state and aspire for full membership status. While in the ethnic model, citizenship is granted unconditionally to fellow co-ethnics, in the republican model, it is withheld once an individual leaves the state. Looking at the opposite side of the spectrum, the cosmopolitan model disapproves of all the preferential criteria and calls for citizenship based upon universal normative standards and freedom from state-imposed limitations. In this liberal model, which adheres to the *ius domicile* principle, individuals residing in a particular polity are automatically entitled to full membership status – regardless of their ethnicity.

Ethnic, republican and liberal models are well illustrated by Michael Walzer's membership metaphor (Walzer, 1983). According to Walzer, citizenship can resemble a membership in a family, club or a neighbourhood. If a state grants citizenship automatically on the *ius sanguinis* basis to all nationals or gives preference to co-ethnic immigrants, then a state acts like a family. The 'exclusive' club membership corresponds with the republican model's giving preference to those individuals who can contribute to the common good or well-being of the community. Finally, states act like neighbourhoods if they are open to including as full and equal members all non-nationals either born or residing in a territory of that state. The cosmopolitan model, though not envisaged by Walzer, advocates a 'portable' membership status, associated not so much with belonging to a particular community but rather with a bundle of universal rights that are attached to it.

Particularism unites quite diverse approaches under the principle of *'priority for compatriots,'* (Bader, 2005a) ranging from liberal democratic or moderate patriotism in political philosophy (Nathanson, Fletcher), liberal nationalism in political philosophy (Miller, Kymlicka, Tamir) or in social sciences (Joppke), defenders of social-democratic welfare states (Walzer, Offe), and finally extreme nationalism. The extreme ethnic stance subscribes to the principle described by Geller: 'Ethnic boundaries should not cut across political ones.' (Gellner, 1993). Nationalists call for a particular political order in which ideational ethnic boundaries overlap with the territorial frontiers of a state. Ethnic homogeneity is conceived as a necessary condition to achieve unity and integration in a state. The advocates of an ethnic nation-state argue that membership status in a political community should be inherited. As a consequence, only a titular ethnic group is authorised to set the terms of inclusion and exclusion in a state.

The principle of congruence of ethnic and territorial boundaries is entirely exhausted today and was never a feasible option even in the past (Bauböck, 1994). Nationalists' idea of a homogenous collectivity 'owning' the state and setting the terms of inclusion itself is in conflict with the modern vision of a democratic state in which an ethnic or a national majority has to respect at least the basic universal standards and constitutional rights of minorities. The ethnic model, especially in its extreme form, finds no justification for its disregard of non-nationals' rights to participate in the process of defining inclusion. The shifting of borders coupled with large-scale migration has eventually made it impossible to think of Europe as a continent of homogenous nation-states. Furthermore, constrained as they are by the contemporary standards of human rights and non-discrimination, states cannot impose strong cultural assimilation programmes on the non-nationals who already reside within their borders (Joppke, 2006). States also cannot entirely close their borders and simply prevent all non-nationals from entering. For that reason, even in a mild form, the ethnic model is highly contested given its reluctance to grant membership status to long-term residents.

In the republican model, priority to compatriots guarantees sustainability of social and welfare arrangements, which the metaphor 'club membership' illustrates perfectly. For republicans, membership in a political community is a value in itself and hence imposes duties on its members. The titular population does not close the borders of its state to non-nationals, however, it keeps them open only for those individuals who can contribute to the common good of the state. In practical terms, a titular population admits only those individuals whose skills are in demand. Republican particularists acknowledge that the nation-state is a myth, however, they argue that a redistribution of welfare presumes a certain level of trust and solidarity within a community. As Offe puts it, there is always a trade-off between inclusiveness and solidarity (Bader, 2005b). In his view, the high diversity among states, regions or continents makes it more difficult to attain a 'common denominator' for solidarity on the global or continental than on the national level. Therefore, according to Offe, redistribution is most effectively conducted within states.

Republican exclusivism is highly contested in the EU context. First of all, restricted access – or selective admission policy – to the markets of some western European states is not justifiable vis-à-vis citizens of the other member states. Such limitations undermine the egalitarian status of EU citizenship, which in principle should not distinguish between the rights of the old and the new member states' national citizens. Secondly, the opinion that a welfare state requires 'closure' in order to be sustainable has been contested from the point of view of both normative political thought and economics. Thirdly, although nation-states remain prior arenas for redistribution, this fact does not prevent the establishment of a number of unitary welfare standards at the EU level. Common, though relatively low, welfare standards should be accessible for the poorest member states but at the same time equally binding for all (Schmitter, 2000).

A serious shortcoming of ethnic and republican particularism is its disregard for transnational and global moral obligations (Bader, 2005b). The new socio-political reality imposes on states special obligations that reach beyond their own citizens or even residents (Bauböck, 1994). These obligations concern relations with specific populations that may have resulted from active involvement in the affairs of another country, from geopolitical proximity or from historic ties. Transnational obligations concern such phenomena as reparative duties (compensation for historical injustices such as slavery, colonialism and imperialism), refugee protection and family reunification. Global moral obligations are derived from universal solidarity with other peoples or countries. They oblige states to fight poverty, discrimination and grand injustice (Bader, 2005b). Although global moral obligations are still vaguely defined, they do entail an imperative for the better-off states to compensate the worst-off. The argument for unlimited inclusion or entirely open borders has been often brought up in this debate. The proponents for open borders would argue that given the deep economic discrepancies between the states, entirely open borders and hence unlimited inclusion is a basic device to fight poverty in the world. The opponents of unlimited inclusion maintain that opening borders is not an effective means to fight poverty because it is not the worst-off who emigrate. As a result, unlimited inclusion is still a contested principle, leaving space for arguments in favour of maintaining some exclusionary practices. In sum, with the exception of the arguments for maintaining limited border control, particularism is a deeply contested approach.

The cosmopolitan model of citizenship derives standards for inclusion from universal moral duties and prudential obligations (Soysal, 1994). It supports unrestricted freedom of movement and international redistribution. For cosmopolitans, the egalitarian principle of equal liberties precludes all ascriptive privileges. In other words, the *ius soli* or *ius sanguinis* criteria for citizenship acquisition are morally no more defensible than social class or gender. Free mobility is recognized as an important principle in itself and a necessary condition to pursue other basic rights. In the cosmopolitan model, the decision to emigrate and take up residence in another state is entirely dependent on the individual's free will. Therefore, states' limitations on immigration are generally precluded as violating this basic right.

With respect to national citizenship, cosmopolitans argue that it has been gradually becoming obsolete. In their view, citizens' rights are now guaranteed by universal human rights, which are not derived from states' exclusive competences. Cosmopolitans therefore expect a general convergence towards liberal and inclusive citizenship, eventually leading to an overlap between national and EU citizenship. And yet, although national citizenship regulations have indeed come to reflect universal human rights, it is still state actors who decide on the extent to which these universal norms are to be implemented (Joppke, 2002, 339–366). The EU has also very limited means at its disposal to prevent a regression into more exclusionary practices.

The liberal, *ius domicile* model of citizenship resembles a neighbourhood type of membership. The principle underlying this model is that all individuals subject to the governance of a given state should be able to aspire to full-fledged citizenship (Dahl, 1989). In this respect, the model attempts to reconcile democracy's inherent exclusivism and tendency towards closure with liberal voluntarism. It can certainly be considered an asset of the model that it enhances inclusion within the borders of a state by fostering the naturalisation of long-term migrants. In the early nineties, the liberal model was still regarded as sufficient to enhance inclusion in the European Union (Hammar, 1990). However, drawing predominantly on liberal individualism and negative freedoms, the model is neutral with respect to fostering equality between individuals who are in possession of formal citizenship status but nonetheless do not have equal access to some of the provisions that citizenship status guarantees. The liberal model has therefore not been sufficiently inclusive either with regards to exclusion of individuals with former citizenship status or the cases of exclusion which the *ius domicile* or neighbourhood model does not consider.

In sum, particularism and universalism correspond poorly with the complex so-cio-political reality of the European Union. Firstly, both can be challenged by the transnational and global moral obligations that states respect nowadays (Bauböck, 1994). Secondly, while particularism rejects going beyond a nation-state, cosmopolitanism dismisses it prematurely (Soysal, 1994). The liberal model of national citizenship ultimately does respond to most patterns of internal exclusion (that is within the borders of a state), however, it fails to promote equality of individuals with formal citizenship status (for instance, by being gender-sensitive) or respond to external (outside the state borders) cases of exclusion.

The next section first identifies and discusses different internal and external patterns of exclusion in the EU. The model of stakeholder citizenship is then presented as a potential device limiting exclusion in the EU in a more successful manner than the traditional citizenship models.

Internal and External Modes of Exclusion in EU Member States

Why is inclusion so difficult to attain? Firstly, because the political map rarely represents perfectly stable borders. Secondly, international migration during the post-war period has posed a challenge to European democracies. The first problem manifests itself in 'priority for compatriots' and cross-border extensions of national citizenship. The latter is illustrated by the problem of denizens[1] exclusion from political rights. As Joseph Carens notes, 'citizenship in the modern world is like feudal status in the medieval world. It is assigned at birth, for the most part it is not subject to change by the individual's will and efforts, and it has a major impact upon that person's life chances.' Although free movement of people and the right to readmission have in principle become hallmarks of modern citizenship practice, national citizenship still serves as a control device that either forbids the entry to a state or limits states' obligations towards resident non-nationals – even in EU member states (Bauböck, 2005a).

The liberal model of Tomas Hammar aims at identifying internal modes of exclusion which conflicted with liberal-democratic standards of inclusion. According to this model, the exclusionary nature of citizenship is manifested by the three gates of entry that non-citizens need to pass upon entering a host state (Hammar, 1990). The first gate of entry concerns immigration regulations, which define who is eligible and upon what conditions to enter a host state legally. The second gate of entry applies to immigrants who have entered a state legally and have therefore become subject to the regulations defining permanent residency status. The third gate concerns the naturalisation procedure, namely requirements a resident needs to fulfil in order to

---

1   A *denizen* is an old British term to describe 'an alien to whom the sovereign has by letters of patent under the prerogative granted the status of a British subject but who has not been allowed to hold public office or obtain a grant of land from the Crown' (Hammar, 1990).

become a full-fledged citizen of a host state. Drawing on the liberal-democratic definition of inclusion, Hammar's model overlooks the fourth obstacle, consisting of the
internal inequalities between citizens included in our model. A necessary condition
for achieving inclusion 'from within' concerns the empowerment of those groups
that do not enjoy equal access to certain provisions that citizenship guarantees despite possession of full citizenship rights.

Modes of exclusion

(A) Internal exclusion (inside a state's borders).	(B) External exclusion (outside a state's borders).
Alienation, full exclusion of migrants: no entry or exclusion of illegal migrants.	*Denial I*, full exclusion concerning non-nationals.
Denizenship, residence status in a host state or partial citizenship status.	*Denial II*, full exclusion concerning former nationals residing outside the states borders.
Naturalisation, ius soli basis.	*Fuzzy citizenship*, partial citizenship status granted to external nationals, concerning socio-economic but no political rights
Socio-economic exclusion of persons with full citizenship status, i.e. unequal position of naturalised persons or women in a segmented market.	*Naturalisation, ius sanguinis* basis.

Each of the four modes of internal exclusion poses different normative or empirical
challenges and hence requires specific policy arrangements. While the first mode
of internal exclusion (alienation) is considered to be a hard case from the normative
and political perspective, the second, third and fourth modes constitute easy cases
(Bader, 2005b). The first gate of entry is a hard case because the arguments for maintaining border control are legitimate even for democratic states. Other entry gates
constitute soft cases, given the fact that in principle, most democratic states grant
all individuals subject to their governance citizen status (Dahl, 1989). For that reason,
they are less restrictive than the first entry gate.

Denizenship, as a socio-political phenomenon, has had a significant impact on
West European democracies. A large group of denizens, composed mostly of former
guest-workers and their children, decided to establish themselves in the host states
instead of returning to their countries of origin. As a consequence, they have kept
the status of legal residents but have not been granted citizenship in the host state.
The advocates of denizens' inclusion point to the fact that a long period of residence

should be sufficient for acquiring citizenship of that state. Although some restrictions may be justifiable with respect to the first generation, exclusion of the second or third generation already born on the territory of a host state is difficult to justify.

The third mode of exclusion concerns naturalisation practices. It usually takes its most severe form when membership in a polity is ethnically defined. Under such conditions, dominance of the *ius sanguinis* rule makes naturalisation on the *ius soli* basis very difficult or even unattainable. It is important to note that in the EU states, we can observe a gradual relaxation of *ius soli* naturalisation practices. Finally, the fourth mode of exclusion, 'from within,' results from internal socio-economic inequalities within states. Some social or ethnic groups may not enjoy equal access to the rights or public goods guaranteed by citizenship, despite possessing formal citizenship status. Therefore, combating exclusion from within entails empowerment of the underprivileged groups, in which EU institutions have been actively assisting the member states.

External modes of exclusion are initiated outside the states' borders. The first and a rather straightforward mode of exclusion, Denial I, concerns external non-nationals. Denial II applies to external co-ethnics who have lost their citizenship either as the result of shifting borders or emigration. If a state's predominant acquisition principle is *ius soli* or *ius domicile*, external populations of co-nationals do not enjoy preferential treatment unless they decide to take up residence in their state of origin. However, if the acquisition rule is dominated by the *ius sanguinis* principle, external nationals can expect preferential treatment during the naturalisation procedure. Fuzzy citizenship, constituting a third mode of exclusion, consists of incomplete citizenship status granted on the *ius sanguinis* basis to former nationals and their offspring without the requirement of taking up residence in the state of origin (Fowler, 2004). Fuzzy citizenship is similar to denizenship in that neither extends political rights. However, as long as denizenship status is ascribed on the *ius soli* basis, fuzzy citizenship can be acquired exclusively on the *ius sanguinis* principle. The external naturalisation procedure, constituting the last mode of exclusion, differs from internal naturalisation by virtue of the fact that it is granted solely on *ius sanguinis*. The internal and external naturalisation procedures therefore enhance different modes of membership in a political community (blood-based or residential) and address different populations (ethnic and non-ethnic).

A Model of Stakeholder Citizenship

As long as the demands for deeper internal inclusion are compatible with the liberal, *ius domicile* model, the demands for external inclusion are generally believed to be made solely in the name of particularistic motivations. Put differently, demands for internal inclusion are thought to facilitate democracy while demands for external exclusion foster ethnic nationalism.

However, these first observations should not lead to the premature conclusion that particularistic motives are first of all devoid of legitimacy and secondly undemocratic. Quite to the contrary, these arguments are based on valid normative grounds. Citizenship accounts for a formal relation between a citizen and a state, therefore – by definition – there is some element of 'closure' involved. Secondly, citizenship is a locus of states' legitimacy which implies that state actors are still entitled to initiate some exclusionary practices – though limited by transnational obligations and universal standards. It is also wrong to assume that all aspects of inclusion can be determined in reference to democratic principles: Not only are these principles being increasingly contested, but their interpretation also changes with time. For instance, Greek democracy was highly exclusive by denying citizenship rights to women or slaves. Nowadays a state depriving over fifty per cent of its population of citizenship would not even be classified as democratic. Moreover, contemporary interpretations of the major democratic principles differ across academic and national traditions. The definition of inclusion will therefore continue to be highly dependent on cultural context. From that perspective, it is premature to argue that demands for internal inclusion necessarily facilitate democracy while demands for external exclusion promote ethnic nationalism. Particular demands for inclusion should not be permanently associated with a given model of citizenship, as for instance the external inclusion of compatriots within an ethnic model. Individuals may have various, not only particularistic, motivations for demanding external inclusion.

External inclusion can be equally well demanded as a transnational compensatory practice. Citizenship is defined by two components: territoriality and membership. Shifts of borders affect territorial dimensions but not ideational membership status. For these reasons, external nationals who were left outside the frontiers of their state in the course of political border shifts have strong grounds to maintain or reclaim their citizenship status. Citizenship has a strong bearing on the identity of each individual person, and its deprivation constitutes a form of identity violation. Thus, reacquisition of citizenship by former nationals or their offspring can be a transnational compensatory practice.

A model of citizenship living up to these expectations would need to separate individuals' motives for demanding wider inclusion from the models of citizenship which traditionally presume specific motivations. In other words, such a model would need to be open for contestation of the democratic principles and the terms of inclusion and exclusion.

A practical proposal accommodating diverse interests and cross-cutting normative approaches is stakeholder citizenship (Bauböck/Ersbøll/Groenendijk and

Waldrauch, 2006). The model of stakeholder citizenship links national and transnational ties in order to reconfigure individuals' membership bonds. The development of transnational activism, a result of intensive migration in Europe and the development of citizens' rights in the EU, requires new forms of participation challenging the conventional models of citizenship. It rests on the assumption that given the high mobility of individuals in such complex and overlapping polities as those in the EU, individuals may have their 'stakes' in different states. A stakeholder is therefore a person who has an interest in a given state's policies and who is affected by the decisions taken by the government of that state. As a consequence, a stakeholder need not be a citizen of a given state but just a resident. The model of stakeholder citizenship is concerned with enhancing participation and rights of all stakeholders in public decision-making. As some authors have noted, the most proper framework to achieve that goal is not representation but deliberation, because it allows for an open-ended process of redefining the democratic principles informing the patterns of inclusion and exclusion (Dryzek, 1990). The deliberative framework would permit easy discussion and changing of the rules defining the membership in a polity. What is important, those who do not constitute its fully-fledged citizens, but who are affected by the policies, would be also entitled to participate in the process of defining formal membership.

Concerning its applicability, stakeholder citizenship has two dimensions. The first is individual and the second is territorial. Stakeholder citizenship is individually differentiated when people have stakes in more than one polity, usually when one polity is a country of origin (birth) and the other a country of residence. When a states' law tolerates multiple loyalties, individually differentiated stakeholdership manifests itself through dual citizenship. Although multiple loyalties or cross-country identities seem to be recognized in an individual dimension (i.e. how people perceive themselves as members of political communities), there is still a considerable resistance to legal change, which is acceptance of dual citizenship. The arguments in favour of individually differentiated stakeholdership are as follows (Aleinikoff and Klusmeyer, 2002). Firstly, recognition of multiple loyalties reflects deeply felt affiliations, connections and loyalties. In a highly mobile, transnational society people develop multiple and cross-country links which are important components of their identities. Maintaining these ties is often affected by the possibility to acquire or maintain citizenship of the state where one has stakes, especially regarding political rights (voting) and property rights. Secondly, stakeholdership promotes naturalization and integration of residents. Often people are not willing to apply for citizenship of their country of residence if in consequence they loose the citizenship of their country of origin. As a result, long term residents, very often well-integrated, cannot exercise political rights in their country of residence for they do not possess citizenship of that state.

Thirdly, stakeholdership facilitates free movement between states because it allows to acquire full rights in the countries were people come to have their stakes located. Finally, this particular model of citizenship promotes inclusiveness based on both *ius soli* and *ius sanguinis* criteria which is applicable within and outside the borders of a state.

The arguments against stakeholdership in an individual dimension concern most often the following issues: voting in two countries, military service and conflicts of laws regarding such issues as for instance taxation. Critics have argued that voting in two states creates some sort of instability and political flux. Furthermore, they have pointed to the fact that individuals who have never participated in the political life of a given state but are granted with political rights- can be prone to manipulation or populism (Kis, 2004). The first argument is not valid because vote-casts from two different states are not aggregated. The second argument brings in reasonable concerns. However, it should not be forgotten that acquisition of stakeholder citizenship applies only to those co-ethnics who *still* take interest – or still have 'stakes' – in their states of origin and whose well-being depends on maintaining these ties. In so doing, stakeholdership rejects ethnic priority for compatriots and recognizes the ideational aspect of a formal membership. In order to avoid the danger of manipulation, the criteria for third generation naturalisation should be automatically granted on the *ius soli* basis. Externally, naturalisation of former nationals' offspring should be automatic only as long as the persons concerned decide to take up residence in the country of their grandparents' origin. Resolving conscription with dual loyalties was still a problem in the 19th century, however, nowadays many countries have either abolished conscription or require a civil service as its substitute. Moreover, in the times of peace and political stability, military conflict between the European states is basically impossible. Thirdly, the conflict of laws is also less and less possible in an economically and politically integrated Europe.

The territorial dimension of stakeholdership promotes functionally overlapping jurisdictions. The idea has been functionally and normatively justified (Frey/Eichenberger, 2000, 1323–1334). The functional proposal has been developed by Frey and Eichenberger under the name Functional, Overlapping, Competing Jurisdictions (FOCJs), which are established in borderland territories, creating semi-autonomous jurisdictions which would also have a right to taxation. FOCJs take over only some functions of national citizenships of the two (or more) states involved. In return, they minimize the costs of human and capital flows. In practice one person could be a citizen of state 'A' with respect to functions 'X' and 'Z' but, together with someone from a state 'B', a citizen of FOCJs with respect to function 'Y'. Normatively, from the perspective of ethnocultural justice, nation-state tends to be inherently unjust because state-building aims to achieve a highly centralized and standardized political entity

(Kis, 2001). Ethnocultural justice requires that the cultures of minorities are also recognized in the process. For that reason, in case of heterogeneous territories an exclusive jurisdictions should give way to overlapping jurisdictions if the criteria for ethnocultural justice are to be fulfilled. Admittedly, territorial dimension of stakeholdership is more difficult to be achieved than individual. Although in principle democratic states possess all capacities to do so, they usually lack the external, overarching frame. This is not the case in the European Union, which facilitates decentralization and empowerment of regions.

In the individual and the territorial dimension, stakeholder citizenship reaches beyond the boundaries of nation-states by entitling all concerned stakeholders to full-fledged participation. Given internal exclusionary practices, stakeholdership not only fosters denizens' inclusion but also empowers underprivileged social or gender groups who possess formal citizenship status but do not have equal access to all the provisions it offers. By acknowledging multiple and cross-cutting national identities, stakeholdership allows individuals to keep or aspire for dual citizenship.

Conclusions

It has been acknowledged that some of the traditional notions of state sovereignty have become deeply eroded over the last two decades. EU member states have therefore been faced with the necessity to redefine not only the formal relationship between an individual and a state but also the terms of inclusion and exclusion. While a universal definition of inclusion is not attainable in a polity as complex and rapidly evolving as the EU, existing patterns of internal and external exclusion have been identified in the EU and confronted with the traditional models of citizenship: ethnic, republican, cosmopolitan, and liberal. It turns out that the traditional models are not successful devices in terms of limiting exclusionary practices in EU member states.

The major shortcomings of the respective citizenship models can be highlighted in comparison to the external and internal modes of exclusion. In this chapter, the ethnic model has been disregarded for preserving strong internal exclusionary practices, affecting the denizen population most severely. The republican model has also been contested for fostering a selective admission policy vis-à-vis citizens of the other member states. The cosmopolitan model, on the other hand, has been rejected for its premature disregard of the prerogative of legitimate state actors not only to participate in the process of setting the terms of inclusion and exclusion but to also maintain some limited exclusionary practices concerning the first gate of entry. Finally, it has been established that the liberal model does not successfully limit external exclusionary practices.

The article argued for stakeholder citizenship as the most promising prospective model of national citizenship in terms of limiting exclusion in the EU and responding to the complexity of social demands. In comparison to the traditional models, stakeholdership not only successfully enhances internal and external inclusion but also fosters stakeholders' participation. By recognising multiple and cross-cutting identities, stakeholdership also allows for an open-ended process of redefining the patterns of inclusion and exclusion.

References

Aleinikoff, A. and Klusmeyer, D. (2002), *Citizenship Policies for an Age of Migration.* (Washington: Carnegie Endowment for International Peace).

Aleinikoff, A. and Klusmeyer, D. (2000) *From Migrants to Citizens* (Washington: Carnegie Endowment for International Peace).

Bader, V. (2005a) 'Reasonable impartiality and priority for compatriots. A criticism of liberal nationalism's main flaws', *Ethical Theory and Moral Practice*, 1–21.

Bader, V. (2005b), 'The Ethics of Immigration', *Constellations* Volume 12, no 3.

Bauböck, R. (1994), *Transnational Citizenship* (Aldershot, Edward Elgar).

Bauböck, R. (2005a), 'Citizenship policies: international, state, migrant and democratic perspectives', *Global Migration Perspectives*, no 19, Jan.

Bauböck, R. (2005b), 'Expanisve Citizenship-Voting beyond Territory and Membership' in *PS-Online*, Oct. 2005.

Bauböck, R; Ersbøll, E; Groenendijk, K. and Waldrauch, K. (2006), *Acquisition and Loss of Nationality. Policies and Trends in 15 European States* (Amsterdam: IMISCOE research, Amsterdam University Press).

Dahl, R. (1989), *Democracy and its Critics* (New Haven: Yale University Press).

Dryzek, J. (1990), *Discursive Democracy: Politics, Policy and Political Science* (Cambridge: Cambridge University Press).

Fowler, B. (2004) 'Fuzzying Citizenship, Nationalizing Political Space: A Framework for Interpreting the Hungarian 'Status Law' as a New Form of Kin-State Policy in Central and Eastern Europe' in Jeda, O; Kántor, Z; Majtenyi, B; Halász, I. *The Hungarian Status Law: Nation Building and/or Minority Protection*, (Budapest and Sapporo: Slavic Research Centre)

Frey, B. and Eichenberger, R. (2000), 'A Proposal for a Flexible Europe', *The World Economy*, Oct. 2000, pp. 1323–1334.

Gellner, E. (1993), *Nations and Nationalism* (New York: Ithaca, Cornell Uni Press).

Hammar, T. (1990), *Democracy and the Nation State* (UK: Aldershot Gower Publishers).

Howard, M.M, (2005), Variation in Dual Citizenship Policies in the Countries of the EU, *International Migration Review*, forthcoming.

Joppke, C. (2006), 'State neutrality and anti-veiling laws in France and Germany', forthcoming.

Joppke, C. and Morawska, E. (2003), *Towards Assimilation and Citizenship: Immigrants in Liberal Nation-States*, (UK: Palgrave).

Joppke, C.. (2002), 'The Legal-Domestic Sources of Immigrant Rights: The United States, Germany, and the European Union' , *Comparative Political Studies*, 34(4) 339–366.

Kis, J. (2001), 'Nation-Building and Beyond', in: Kymlicka, W. and Opalski, M. (2001), *Can Liberal Pluralism be Exported? Western Political Theory and Ethnic Relations in Eastern Europe*. (Oxford: University Press).

Kis, J. (2004) 'Miért megyek el szarazni' (Why am I taking part in the voting), *Népszabadság*, Nov 20.

Liebert, U (2004): 'European Social Citizenship. Preconditions for Promoting Inclusion', in: Magnusson, L. & Strath, B. *A European Social Citizenship? Preconditions for Future Policies from Historical Perspective* (P.I.E Peter Lang: Bruxelles, Bern, Berlin).

Marshal, T.H. (1949/1965), 'Citizenship and Social Class', *Class, Citizenship and Social Development. Essays by T.H. Marshall* (Anchor Books: New York).

Perczyński, P. and Vink, M. (2002), 'Citizenship and Democracy: A Journey to Europe's Past', *Citizenship Studies*, vol. 6, No. 2.

Sartori, G. (1984), *Social Science Concepts. A Systematic Analysis* (Beverly Hills: Sage).

Schmitter, P. (2000), *How to Democratize the European Union... And Why Bother?* (NY: Rowman and Littlefield Publishers).

Soysal, J. (1994), *The Limits of Citizenship*. (Chicago: Uni Press).

Vink, Maarten, (2005), Patterns of Citizenship Liberal Trends, Convergence and the Politics of Nationhood <http://www.personeel.unimaas.nl/m.vink/patterns_of_citizenship.html> (updated 15.08.2006).

Walzer, M. (1983), *Spheres of Justice: A Defence of Pluralism and Equality* (New York: Basic Books).

4. Restituting Expropriated Property in Post-Socialist Countries. The Limits of Legal Justice

Csongor Kuti

Justice and Reparation

Introduction

This chapter explores the justice of post-communist reparation schemes, focusing on the three Baltic States, Poland, Germany, the former Czechoslovakia, Hungary and Romania. It deals with two fundamental justice problems that transitional property reparation schemes have to address: why property injustices have to be mitigated, and why former property owners enjoy a privileged status in comparison with other victims of past injustices? Answering the first question, the analysis concludes that neither international law, nor general principles of justice, nor even domestic constitutions recognise a general right to restitution. Therefore, while answering the second question, the inquiry identifies the possible arguments that may justify property restitution.

However, the three possible answers, recognition and protection of rights, past harm, and political persecution do not adequately explain why former property owners are favoured over other victims. In these conditions, the chapter concludes that property restitution schemes do not have an exclusively reparative nature, moreover, restitution was deliberately linked with structural reform, and due to this duality, the scheme features a mixed distributive-reparative character. This, however, represents a real problem for the rule of law, taking into consideration the fact that material justice is the arch enemy of formal rationality, constitutes a serious threat to the rule of law.

Transitional Rule of Law

Writing on the Central and East European transition to democracy, Preuss notes that 'the principle of the rule of law [...] was even declared the principal guide of all the political actions of the revolutionaries.' In this context, Preuss wonders what the true meaning of the 'rule of law' could be: protection of legal rights? Prohibition of legal retroactivity, immunising rights acquired in the past from takings? Or simply the requirement that changes be carried out legally? (Preuss 1993)

One radical answer is given by Elster, who notes that 'transitional justice is often characterised by stark departures from the rule of law. The desire for thoroughness trumps the desire for justice.' (Elster 1998) Teitel takes a different approach, arguing that for natural lawyers, the predecessor regime's immorality determines the necessity for a 'fresh start.' (Teitel 2000, 11–27) Prior arbitrariness that often resulted in unequal lawmaking and unjust outcomes must be overturned: Rule of law regimes cannot be founded on immoral grounds. Posner and Vermeule argue that transitions should respect liberal norms, 'at least to the extent necessary for and consistent with, the consolidation of liberal democratic institutions.' (Posner and Vermeule 2004)

The constitutional courts of the transition countries faced the challenge of reconciling demands for justice and demands for legality. The Hungarian Constitutional Court (HCC) constructed the concept of 'the rule of law revolution,' which led to the conclusion that legal certainty is more important than necessarily partial and subjective justice. (AB 11/1992) Consequently, the Court could deny former owners' rights to claim the return of their properties taken during the previous regime(s).

The Czech Constitutional Court (CCC) argued that precisely the notion of a state ruled by law warrants retroactive justice. (Proháczka 2002, 118–119) The CCC refused to regard the communist regime as a 'Rechtsstaat,' and maintained that preventing retroactive punishment (this reasoning applies mutatis mutandis to property restitution as well) would mean to prefer the legal certainty of perpetrators to the legal certainty of citizens (victims). (Proháczka 2002, 145–147)

The Slovakian (SCC), and to a considerable degree, the Romanian Constitutional Court (RCC), represent a third – preservationist and deferential – approach to transition. The SCC fashioned an attitude labelled as 'silly' by scholars, as it talked about the legislators' competence to decide when, and in which form, bills relating to restitution would be adopted. (Proháczka 2002, 174) Concerning the RCC, the initial deferential attitude has started to gradually shift in the past years. Recently, in a 2005 decision, the Court endorsed a view maintaining that legalisation of a historical injustice cannot be accepted in the name of legal stability. (Decision no. 375/2005)

Teitel holds that even if certain measures 'threaten the conventional rule of law, what supports their use [...] is that they are justified [...] by the future aim of constructing a more liberal state.' (Teitel 2000, 187–188) More than fifteen years after the fall of communism in Central and Eastern Europe, the suspicion arises that the 'illiberal' measures did not necessarily result in a 'more liberal' outcome.

Property (Re)Distribution

Two broad and distinct goals were entwined by most of the property redistribution schemes: to compensate individuals for property losses and to resettle property relationships so as to achieve certainty in possessions (a precondition for the creation of an efficient market economy). Such is the case in Hungary, where, as already mentioned above, property compensation had a declared social goal. Or, in Poland, the Constitutional Tribunal (PCT) identified 'a beneficial social aspect' of the compensation scheme dealing with the properties left beyond the Bug River. (Judgement of 15 December, 2004) A similar conclusion was reached by the Estonian Supreme

Court (ESC), arguing that '[o]wnership reform is a specific task of the state in building up a rule of law state and a market economy.' (Decision of 22 December, 2000) The Lithuanian Constitutional Court (LiCC) has argued that '[t]he restoration of the rights to land was the basic means for implementing of land reform.' (Judgement of April 20, 1999)

Contrary views have been voiced, for example, by the CCC (Judgement of 24 March, 2004) and the Latvian (LaCC, Judgement of April 20, 1999) courts, which both held that the goal of restitution laws is (reparative) justice, i.e. the rectification of past wrongs. Although commentators identified, at least at the moment of its adoption, additional purposes in the Czechoslovakian scheme – speeding up privatisation and developing a market economy (Cepl 1991) – it seems that in 2004 the CCC managed to discover a narrower ratio legis for restitution.

By adding additional aims to property reparations, a strong distributive is created. Kutz notes that because on one hand communist takings of property generally maintained a semblance of legitimacy[1], post-communist reparations are being pushed towards a more distributive approach. (Kutz 2004, 298) The UN Human Rights Committee (UNHRC) held, in Somers v. Hungary, that objective criteria of compensation have to be applied equally and without discrimination. (Decision of 29 July 1996) Macklem considers this language as urging governments to pay close attention to the demands of distributive justice. (Macklem 2005) A couple of years earlier, the HCC had already argued that the constitutionality of the compensation law has to be assessed on the basis of distributive justice, taking into consideration not merely the interests of the victims, but also the concurrent constitutional tasks. (AB 15/1993)

Forms of Reparation

There are three major forms which the actual reparations could take: in kind restitution, monetary equivalent, and vouchers. It could hardly be argued that there were 'pure' systems, in the sense of embracing solely one of the options enumerated above. Regularly, one of these prevailed, but out of objective necessity, the other forms of compensation occurred too, at least in the form of exceptions.

The Baltic States: Military Occupation

From August 1940, Estonia, Latvia and Lithuania were incorporated into the Soviet Union. Briefly interrupted during WWII, Soviet rule resumed after the war and gained stability with the 1949 collectivisation and mass deportations. (Mertelsmann 2003, 11–14) The Latvian legislature, in a 1996 declaration, stressed that 'the USSR [...] il-

---

1 The HCC's rulings, declaring the nationalisation decrees unconstitutional, played a significant role in paving the way for the compensation legislation.

legally and without compensation expropriated property.' ('Declaration on Occupation of Latvia', the Saeima, 22 August, 1996)

The Estonian compensation scheme envisaged the return or compensation for unlawfully expropriated property. Concerning land, it was envisaged to be returned, as a rule, according to its former boundaries. In cases of property in the form of shares, certificates etc., or of property that was destroyed, compensation was to be paid. This compensation took the form of vouchers which could be used in the privatisation process. (Principles of Ownership Reform Act, 1991)

Latvia enacted a scheme which provided for the renewal of property rights. (Law 'On the Land Reform in the Republic of Latvia Rural Regions,' 1990) When such renewal was not possible, compensation vouchers (certificates) similar to those in Estonia were issued. These could have been either converted to cash or used in the privatisation process. (Land Reform Act, 1997)

Lithuania contemplated restoration of rights to properties nationalised or 'otherwise unlawfully made public.' (Law On the Procedure and Conditions of the Restoration of the Rights of Ownership to the Existing Real Property, 1991) Restoration, as in the previous two cases, took two forms: in kind or compensatory (in case of land, either by other plots or financially).

Poland: the Struggle for Restitution

Poland has not yet enacted a comprehensive norm for the regulation of nationalised properties, (Dembour and Krzyzannowska-Mierzwska 2004) although quite a number of bills have been taken into consideration by the Parliament. According to commentators, the Polish situation is the result of a combination of factors, including an extraordinarily fragmented legislature with conflicting agendas, limited financial capacity and various private interests. (Youngblood 1995)

There is one special act for the compensation of the properties left beyond the Bug River due to the exchange of population between Poland and the former Soviet republics, which was already mentioned above. (Offsetting the Value of Property Abandoned Beyond the Present Borders of the Polish State Against the Price of State Property or the Fee for the Right of Perpetual Usufruct Act, 2003) The compensation formula essentially consists of the right to offset (credit) the value of the abandoned properties against either the price of state property or the fee for perpetual use of such property. (Broniowski v. Poland, European Court of Human Rights (ECHR), Judgement of 22 June, 2004) Further, there is also legislation providing for the restitution of religious properties. (Jaskaunas 2003)

Germany: Fairness, Justice and the Social State

The Federal Constitutional Court (FCC) has stated that compensation is based on principles of fairness, justice and the social state. The main principle of compensation was declared to be equal treatment, but the financial situation of the state and other obligations arising from reunification were to be taken into consideration too. (European Commission for Democracy Through Law, Opinion no. 277/2004) The Joint Statement of the two German states regarding the resolving of property issues spoke about the necessity of 'a socially acceptable balance (sozial verträglicher Ausgleich) between the competing interests, while taking into account the need for legal certainty and clarity and to protect the right of property.' (Wittek v. Germany, ECHR, Judgement of 12 December, 2002) Germany also opted for in kind reparations. By way of exception, property that could not be returned was compensated. (Kutz 2004)

Former Czechoslovakia, Hungary and Romania

The Czech and Slovak reparation laws were guided by the principle of restituting the original property to the entitled persons.[2] Financial compensation was to be granted in cases where restoration of property was not possible.[3]

The Hungarian compensation law (Law no. XXV of 1991) envisaged a different scheme, opting for compensation as a rule and restitution as an exception (only church properties were returned). Compensation embraced the form of vouchers which could be used in the privatisation process. As in Germany, equal treatment was made a basic principle of compensation. (Democracy Through Law, Opinion no. 277/2004)

In Romania (Law no. 18/1991), restitution was combined with original distribution of property (in the case of land). Compensation was the rule in the case of properties which could not be restituted. This could take the form of similar plots, stock company shares, privatisation vouchers or money; even combinations of these were possible. (Law no. 18/1991, art. 1)

---

2   Law on extrajudicial rehabilitation, 21 February 1991, no. 87/1991 Coll. of Laws art 3, and Law on modifying ownership relationships with respect to land and another agricultural properties, 21 May 1991, no. 229/1991 Coll. of Laws. (See also CCC, I. US 754/01 Decision of 23 November 2003, available on the World Wide Web at URL: http://test.concourt.cz/angl_verze/doc/1-754-01.htm.)

3   Law on extrajudicial rehabilitation, 21 February 1991, no. 87/1991 Coll. of Laws, section 13; See also Kopecký v. Slovakia, ECHR Judgement of 28 September 2004, Application no. 44912/98, para. 23; Law on modifying ownership relationships with respect to land and another agricultural properties, 21 May 1991, no. 229/1991 Coll. of Laws, art. 8.

Fundamental Questions

Reparations or Not?

The first question that needs an answer is whether communist takings of property demand reparations or not. Undoubtedly, Article 8 of the Universal Declaration of Human Rights creates a right to effective remedy for acts violating fundamental rights guaranteed by constitution or by law. A similar provision is reiterated by the International Covenant on Civil and Political Rights. Commentators note, however, that it does not necessarily create an obligation to compensate every type of violation. (Orentlicher 1994) In addition, none of the major international documents recognizes a right to restitution.

In Somers v. Hungary, the UNHRC held that 'there is no right, as such, to have (expropriated or nationalised) property restituted.' (Decision of 29 July 1996) A similar conclusion was reached by the ECHR in the case of Jasiūnienė v. Lithuania, where the Court stated that the Convention does not guarantee the right to restitution.

Nonetheless, the obligation of successor regimes to repair the wrong done by their predecessors is unequivocally formulated. (Meron 1991, 171) Moreover, it may also be invoked that general principles of international law also assert the requirement of prompt, adequate and effective compensation for the expropriation of property. But in James and others, the ECHR pointed out that the principles in question apply exclusively to non-nationals; thus, they do not govern the treatment accorded by the states to their own citizens. (James and Others v. United Kingdom, Judgement of 22 January, 1986)

Interestingly, the HCC, in an early decision, declared unconstitutional a number of nationalisation laws and decrees. The Court held that the norms in question were targeting the property of certain social groups, and thereinafter aimed at the eradication of private property, with both goals being in conflict with the requirement of public utility. (AB 27/19) The Czechoslovakian legislature declared null and void all judgements, convictions and confiscation ex tunc (from the day of their pronouncement); thus, the original owners' rights were considered as surviving without interruption. (Glos 2000)

Although, to make things more complicated, two different groups of communist-era property deprivations have to be distinguished. On one hand we have takings resulting exclusively from the actions of the domestic governments, such as 'common' nationalisation of property, as part of various – land and economical – reforms; confiscation, as a penal sanction (usually accompanying convictions for 'political crimes'), as a consequence of absence (taking of vacant property) or of deprivations of citizenship (a measure illegal by itself). On the other hand are losses of property endured as a consequence of international agreements regarding population exchanges along the redrafted boarders of post-war Central and Eastern Europe.

Property Lost as a Consequence of Population Exchange

In these cases, bilateral treaties attempted to resolve the fate of property left behind by those who had moved across the border. Such treaties were sometimes characterised by a certain haste, which resulted in leaving the most important questions – namely those related to the payment of compensations – unresolved. (Broniowski v. Poland, ECHR, Judgement of 22 June, 2004) This was the case of the Czechoslovakian-Hungarian agreement of 1946 (HCC, AB 45/2003), or the Republican Agreements, concluded by the Polish Committee of National Liberation in 1944 with the neighbouring Soviet Socialist Republics of Ukraine, Belarus and Lithuania. (Broniowski v. Poland, ECHR, Judgement of 22 June, 2004)

Both the HCC (AB 45/2003) and the PCT (Judgement of 15 December, 2004) recognized the government's obligation to adequately compensate the repatriated citizens. However, the HCC stressed that the state had wide discretion to decide how it intended to fulfil its obligation. The PCT arrived at a similar conclusion, when it stated that 'the [...] particular institutional solution [...] remains within the legislative autonomy.' (Judgement of 19 December, 2002) The HCC also stressed that the possibility of compensation could be contemplated only in those cases in which the state gave up its right to vindicate Hungarian citizens' property left abroad through international agreements. The argument explained that the Hungarian State had no obligations stemming from the damages caused to its citizens' property by other states, especially in that the assets located abroad are not part of the Hungarian state's patrimony. (1043/B/1992)

In Estonia, the law on ownership reform provided that restitution or compensation of property belonging to persons who left Estonia on the basis of agreements entered into with Germany had to be resolved through an international agreement. (Law on the Fundamentals of Ownership Reform, June 1991) The ESC found unconstitutional (violation of the principle of legal clarity) the legislature's omission to comprehensibly establish the rights of resettled persons and of the users of the properties which belonged to them. (Decision of 28 October, 2002)

Property Losses as a Consequence of Various Domestic Takings

This group can be broken down into two subcategories: formally legal-, (land reform or criminal confiscation) and illegal takings. Kutz argues that 'expropriation on its own is not a categorical wrong [...]; it does not by its very nature vault to the head of the line for repair.' (Kutz 2004)

The HCC declared some of the nationalisation decrees as unconstitutional, exactly because their goal could not be defended on the basis of social need, while their finality was the liquidation of an entire property class. (AB 27/1991) The HCC's arguments back Sadurski's critique (Sadurski 2003) of Posner and Vermeule: Communist takings were not advancing a pressing social goal, but did significantly undermine the market (basically terminating it); thus, they differ fundamentally from 'normal' takings.

But the HCC decision is not the sole example of unconstitutional takings. Failure to comply with obligations assumed through international conventions is also illustrative in this sense. Another good example is a Romanian decree which led to the nationalisation of a large number of houses and apartments. (Brumarescu v. Romania, ECHR, Judgement of 28 October, 1999) The act disregarded existing constitutional guarantees (Constitution of Romania, 1948, art. 10), providing for expropriation without any compensation. The LiCC (Ruling of 27 May 1994) has found that the 'nationalisation and other unlawful socialisation of property' was started by the occupation government (i.e. Soviet Union). Therefore, steps had to be taken towards the restoration of people's rights.

In light of the arguments exposed above, as a rule, there is no compelling obligation for successor regimes to mitigate the property losses caused by previous governments. Neither international law nor general principles of law create such an obligation. Thus, if no unequivocal right to reparations and no corresponding obligation to provide relief exist, it remains to be seen: Which principles justify a property reparation scheme?

However, it must be added with equal emphasis that under those circumstances in which illegality/unconstitutionality can be demonstrated, there are strong reasons to recognize the 'survival' of former property rights, even if the state withholds the discretion to decide upon the concrete form of the compensation which may be granted in these cases. In these situations, the right to compensation should be recognized as flowing from the state's lack of compliance, rather than made a function of an ex gratia allotment.

The major problem with ex gratia restitution is that governmental benevolence does not equate with justice. This constitutes one of the main controversies of the Hungarian compensation law (Law no. XXV of 1991): The preamble speaks about the principles of the rule of law and the society's sense of justice, but at the end of the day, the entire scheme is made a function of the state's generosity. The HCC has had a major role in turning justice into grace. This can be traced back to a vision entailing that the sealing of the past as well as the new redistribution have to be done in conformity with the Constitution, from the point of view of past, current and future owners. (HCC, AB 28/1991) Given this attitude, it was not possible to speak about the former owners' rights. To explain this peculiar solution, the Court made use of the civil law institution of novation. This – as the Court explained it – meant that old obligations were renewed, upon a new legal basis, to a new extent and in new terms. According to the Court's rationale, the application of this method is permissible because – as already mentioned – the takings had an unusual character, as they were targeting the systematic eradication of private property. (HCC, AB 28/1991) A markedly different point of view has been voiced by the RCC, which stated that 'it is inconceivable to apply private law norms in a domain belonging without any doubts in its entirety to the domain of public law.' Therefore, 'the state does no wise appear as a simple debtor of obligations,' nor do 'the former owners or their heirs have the status of creditors.' (Decision nr. 73 of 19 July, 1995)

Why Do Only Certain Losses Deserve Compensation?

The second fundamental question is why only certain losses deserve compensation. There are three possible justifications to discuss: the recognition and protection of rights, the idea of past harm and the principle of political persecution. (Teitel 2000, 132–134)

In a post-communist context, it is rather difficult to ground property restitution on the idea of rights. The takings were effected upon seemingly legal grounds, save for the exceptions discussed above. Furthermore, the right to property is neither the sole nor the paramount fundamental right recognized by post-communist constitutions. Thus, the fundamental question still remains unanswered: why losses of property are regularly compensated, while, for instance, former restrictions on the freedom of speech or conscience are not. One argument in favour of property restitution could be that the objects of property rights physically exist (existed); thus, they can be returned or compensated, while speech has only a potential existence. In other words: Restrictions upon speech burdened or prohibited the exercise of this freedom, but the disappearance of the authoritarian regime automatically resulted in the disappearance of the restrictions. At the same time, however, the political change did not automatically entail repossession of taken property. Another way out of this dilemma is offered by the previously mentioned HCC decision, which declared a number of nationalisation decrees unconstitutional. (AB 27/1991) But note that the HCC is pointing towards a formal deficiency (lack of compensation), and absent such a feature, the scheme could hardly be justified on a rights-based approach.

The principle of past harm as a normative value does not offer enough guidance in justifying property reparations, at least in the post-communist context. That is because it is simply too sweeping. As Elster remarked, 'essentially everybody suffered under communism.' (Elster 1992) István Pogány noted that 'the economic consequences of expelling Jews from certain sectors of employment [...] was at least as severe, for the individuals concerned and for their families, as the confiscation of property proved for others.' (Pogány 1997, 171) The obvious result, to which the principle of past harm has to therefore lead, is universal and equivalent reparations.[4]

Hence, the third justification, namely political persecution (discrimination) needs to be addressed. The above-mentioned HCC decision maintained that the notion of public utility does not extend to takings that stigmatise or discriminate against individuals or groups. (AB 27/1991) Discriminative taking, as a ground for restitution, appears perhaps most obvious in the case of Holocaust restitution. In Hungary, after the fall of the right-wing regime, between 1945 and 1947, a number of acts provided for the return of immovable and movable goods and regulating the fate of heirless properties. (Prime Minister's Orders no. 7590/1945, 3630/1945, 10.480/1945, 300/1946, 12.530/1946, 6400/1947, 5280/1947, and Governmental Decree no. 13.160/1947.) In post-war Czechoslovakia, all transactions that occurred on the basis of racial or political persecution under the German Reich were annulled. (Macklem 2005) Of course, Holocaust reparations take place in an entirely different context: The confiscation of Jewish assets was part of a genocidal program, which makes these claims more compelling. (Kutz 2004)

A paradoxical counter-example is represented by the CCC's decision on the 'Beneš decrees.' The act in question identified as enemies of the nation persons of German and Hungarian ethnicity, with the aim of subjecting them to property confiscation. The presumption of enmity was refutable if these persons could demonstrate their loyalty to the Czechoslovak Republic. However, the Court found the presumption of responsibility a 'just sanction,' a 'proportionate response' to Nazi aggression, and not a nationalistic form of revenge. (Judgement of 8 March, 1995)

In any case, the criterion of persecution does not give an explanation that satisfactorily justifies property reparations. It helps in drafting the pool of beneficiaries to distinguish those persecuted – the confiscation of dissident's assets is the paradigm – from all the others who may also have suffered some property losses. Still, not only property owners were persecuted under communist regimes, and from a moral perspective, other forms of persecution cannot be considered to be less worthy of compensation than expropriation. (Offe and Bönker 1993)

In this context, it is worth noting, for example, that the Hungarian legislature did design a scheme for the (monetary) compensation of those who were illegally deprived of their lives or liberty on political grounds. (Law no. XXXII of 1992) This approach, however, merely widens the class of the privileged, and therefore cannot avoid the kind of criticism which is phrased by Elster: 'as it would be absurd to indemnify everyone, it follows that one should not compensate anyone.' (Elster 1992)

---

4   As former Czech president Václav Havel asked: '[i]f everyone suffered, why should only some be redressed?" (Wilson 1992)

In conclusion, it can be stated that the reasons underlying post-communist property compensation schemes do not satisfactorily justify the distinguished treatment enjoyed by former property owners. Offe and Bönker note in this respect that '[t]he concentration on property losses primarily reflects the strategic importance attached to property reform and the greater political leverage of former property owners compared with other victims of the communist regime.' (Offe and Bönker 1992)

The Ferryman's Puzzle

According to the classical puzzle, a ferryman has to safely cross a wolf, a goat and a cabbage to the other side of the river, his problem being that only two of the three fit in his boat in the same time, and he is the only one who can row. The dilemma is how to pair up the passengers in a way that prevents them from harming each other. Post communist societies of Central and Eastern Europe faced a similar, although more complicated puzzle: They had, in a relatively short period, to deal with past injustices, to secure the preconditions of a market economy and to create and entrench a new elite.

To their misfortune, in the majority of the cases, the worst solution was chosen, namely to take on all the passengers in the same time, with the obvious risk of having the ferry sunk by the overload. Perhaps the river looked temptingly narrow; perhaps it was too enticing to talk about market economy in terms of justice. The mixture of reparative and distributive justice that resulted from this was not the consequence of some grand theory of property or justice. Rather, what currently is called 'transitional justice' is explicable by external political values stemming from the political exigencies of the time. (Teitel 2000, 147)

It was wrong to link questions of reparation with questions of redistribution, because they simply cannot justify each other. It is theoretically untenable for property restitution or compensation to target an even distribution because this would better facilitate the emergence of a market economy. It is equally untenable to compensate property-related injustices of the previous regime because a market economy is contingent upon privately owned property.

When reparative concerns are linked with structural reform, the whole scheme – including reparations – can only be upheld on grounds of distributive justice. The conclusion to which the HCC has arrived, namely that the concept underlying a partial compensation is of distributive character, because the compensation scheme pursues property reform goals, is inevitable. (AB 15/1993)As a consequence of such an approach, the majority of Central and East European restitution programs present problematic features, which call into question the justice of restitution.

First, there is no compelling judicial argument for the mitigation of past expropriations at large. It is indeed up to the government whether it wishes to link redistribution of property to pre-existing holdings. Nevertheless, in a number of significant, albeit less numerous exceptions, it is possible to point to an actual past injustice or failure of the government to fulfil its promises towards the claimants. In these cases, it is wrong to derive the right to claim and the corresponding obligation to compensate from governmental gratitude.

Second, the distinction made between former property owners and the rest of the society can be defended only by reference to the social dimension of the property reforms. The analysed normative values (past harm, breach of fundamental rights and political persecution) used to define the circle of beneficiaries do not adequately explain why other victims are excluded from the scheme.

The principle of past harm is too sweeping, because virtually everyone experienced some kind of loss under the authoritarian regimes. The principles of violation of fundamental rights, or of political discrimination, work in case of Holocaust restitution (discriminative takings as part of the genocidal project) but are difficult to sustain in a post-communist context. While politically motivated takings may be a legitimate ground to claim reparations, they do not essentially distinguish themselves from other forms of political persecutions, unless the market economy reasons are brought into play.

In this context, the Hayekian statement, according to which 'any policy aiming directly at a substantive ideal of distributive justice must lead to the destruction of the Rule of Law' (Hayek 1991, 59) constitutes a very serious objection that post-communist restitution programs must face.

References

CCC I. US 38/02, judgement of 24 March 2004, <http://test.concourt.cz/angl_verze/doc/1-38-02.html>

CCC Pl. US 14/94, judgement of 8 March 1995, <http://test.concourt.cz/angl_verze/doc/p-14-94.html>

CCC, I. US 754/01 Decision of 23 November 2003 <http://test.concourt.cz/angl_verze/doc/1-754-01.htm>

Cepl, V. (1991), 'A note on the restitution of property in post-communist Czechoslovakia', Journal of Communist Studies 367

Constitution of Romania, 1948, <http://www.constitutia.ro/const1948.htm>

Declaration on Occupation of Latvia, adopted by the Saeima, on August 22, 1996

Dembour, M-B., Krzyzannowska-Mierzwska, M (2004), 'Ten Years On: The Voluminous and Interesting Polish Case Law', E.H.R.L.R., 5, 517–543

Democracy Through Law, Opinion no. 277/2004, CDL-AD (2004) 009, comments by rapporteur László Sólyom, <http://www.venice.coe.int/docs/2004/CDL(2004)012-e.asp.>

ECHR, Broniowski v. Poland, Application no. 31443/96, Judgement of 22 June 2004

ECHR, Brumarescu v. Romania, ECHR, Application no. 28342/95, Judgement of 28 October 1999

ECHR, James and Others v. United Kingdom, Application no. 3/1984/75/119, Judgement of 22 January 1986

ECHR, Wittek v. Germany, Application no.: 37290/97, Judgement of 12 December 2002

Elster, J. (1992): 'On Doing What One Can: An Argument Against Post-Communist Restitution and Retribution,' *East European Constitutional Review*, Vol. I, no. 2

Elster, J. (1998) 'A framework for the study of transitional justice', *European Journal of Sociology*, 39 (1):7–48

ESC Case no. 3-4—5-02, Decision of 28 October, 2002, <http://www.nc.ee/english>

ESC Decision 3-4-1-10-2000, of 22 December, 2000, <http://www.nc.ee/english>

Glos, G.E. (2000), 'Restitution of Confiscated Property in the Czech Republic', *Czechoslovak Society of Arts and Sciences* <http://www.svu2000.org/issues/glos.htm>

Hayek, F. (1991), *The Road to Serfdom* (Chicago: University of Chicago Press)

HCC 1043/B/1992

HCC AB 11/1992

HCC AB 15/1993, 1543/B/1991

HCC AB 27/1991, 91/E/1990.

HCC AB 28/1991, 1160/A/1991

HCC AB 45/2003, 960/B/1995

International Covenant on Civil and Political Rights, General Assembly. resolution 2200A (XXI), 21 U.N. GAOR Supp. (No. 16) at 52, U.N. Doc. A/6316 (1966), 999 U.N.T.S. 171, <http://www1.umn.edu/humanrts/instree/b3ccpr.htm>

Jaskaunas, P. (2003), 'Vilnius Lost', *Legal Affairs* 63

Joint communication of the Hungarian Ministry of Foreign Affairs and the Ministry of Finances no. 8004/1991

Kutz, C. (2004), 'Justice in Reparations: The Cost of Memory and the Value of Talk.' *Philosophy & Public Affairs* 32, no. 3

LaCC, Case No. 04/01(99), Decision of 20 April, 1999, <http://www.satv.tiesa.gov.lv/Eng/Spriedumi/04-01(99).htm>

LaCC, Case No. 2002 -17 – 0103, Decision of 10 January 2003, <http://www.satv.tiesa.gov.lv/Eng/spriedumi/17-0103(02).htm.>

Land Reform Act, 1997, subject of several amendments, consolidated text published in the State Gazette RT I 2001, 52, 304

Law 'On the Land Reform in the Republic of Latvia Rural Regions,' 1990

Law 'On Land Privatisation in Rural Regions,' 1992

Law no. 18/1991, consolidated text republished in the Official Gazette no. 1 of 5 January 1998

Law No. I-1454 On the Procedure and Conditions of the Restoration of the Rights of Ownership to the Existing Real Property, 1991, <www.litlex.lt/Litlex/Eng/Frames/Laws/Documents/78.HTM>

Law no. XXV of 1991

Law no. XXXII of 1992

Law on extrajudicial rehabilitation, 21 February 1991, no. 87/1991 Coll. of Laws

Law on Judicial Rehabilitation, 23 April 1990, no. 119/1990 Coll. of Laws

Law on modifying ownership relationships with respect to land and another agricultural properties, 21 May 1991, no. 229/1991 Coll. of Laws

Law on the Fundamentals of Ownership Reform, June 1991

LiCC, Ruling of 8 March 1995, <http://www.lrkt.lt/doc_links/main.htm>

LiCC, Ruling of 20 June 1995, <http://www.lrkt.lt/doc_links/main.htm>

LiCC, Ruling of 27 May 1994, <http://www.lrkt.lt/doc_links/main.htm>

Macklem, P. (2005), '1 Rybná 9 Praha 1: Restitution and Memory in International Human Rights.' 16 European Journal of International Law 1.

Meron, T. (1991), Human Rights and Humanitarian Norms as Customary Law (Oxford: Clarendon Press)

Mertelsmann, O. (ed.) (2003), The Sovietization of the Baltic States, 1940–1956 (Kleio: Tartu University Press)

Offe and Bönker (1993), in 'A Forum on Restitution: Essays on the Efficiency and Justice of Returning Property to Its Former Owners', East European Constitutional Review, 2

Offsetting the Value of Property Abandoned Beyond the Present Borders of the Polish State Against the Price of State Property or the Fee for the Right of Perpetual Usufruct Act, 2003

Orentlicher, D. F. (1994), 'Addressing Gross Human Rights Abuses: Punishment and Victim Compensation.' in: Henkin and Hargrove (eds.) (1994), Human Rights: An agenda for the next century (American Society of International Law)

PCT K2/04, Judgement of 15th December 2004, <http://www.trybunal.gov.pl/eng/summaries/documents/K_2_04_GB.pdf>

PCT K33/02, Judgement of 19th December 2002, <http://www.trybunal.gov.pl/eng/summaries/K_33_02_GB.pdf>

Pogány, I. (1997), *Righting Wrongs in Eastern Europe*, (Manchester: Manchester University Press)

Posner, E. A., Vermeule, A. (2004), 'Transitional Justice as Ordinary Justice', *Harvard Law Review*, January 2004

Preuss, U. K. (1993), in 'A Forum on Restitution: Essays on the Efficiency and Justice of Returning Property to Its Former Owners', *East European Constitutional Review*, 2

Prime Minister's Orders no. 7590/1945, 3630/1945, 10.480/1945, 300/1946, 12.530/1946, 6400/1947, 5280/1947, and Governmental Decree no. 13.160/1947

Principles of Ownership Reform Act, 1991, subject of considerable amendments, consolidated text published in State Gazette RT I 1997, 27, 391

Procházka, R. (2002), Mission Accomplished. On Founding Constitutional Adjudication in Central Europe, (Budapest: Central European University Press)

RCC Decision nr. 73 of 19 July 1995, published in the Official Gazette no 177 of 8 August 1995.

RCC Decision nr. 375 of 6 July 2005

Sadurski, W (2003),'"Decommunisation", "Lustration", and Constitutional Continuity: Dilemmas of Transitional Justice in Central Europe'. European University Institute, Florence, Working Paper Law No. 2003/15, <http://cadmus.iue.it/dspace/retrieve/1758/law03-15.pdf>

Teitel, R. G. (2000), *Transitional Justice* (New York: Oxford University. Press)

UN Human Rights Committee, Somers v. Hungary, CCPR/C/57D/566/1993, Decision of 29 July 1996

Universal Declaration of Human Rights, General Assembly resolution 217 A (III) of 10 December 1948, <http://www.un.org/Overview/rights.html.>

Wilson, P. (ed.) (1992), *Open Letters: Selected Writings, 1965–1990* (Alfred A. Knopf)

Youngblood, W. R. (1995), 'Poland's Struggle for a Restitution Policy in the 1990s', *Emory International Law Review* 645

Katerina Koleva

Restitution of Expropriated Property in Eastern Europe. The Restrictive Approach and Available Remedies with a Special Emphasis on the Case Law of the European Court of Human Rights Related to Restitution[1]

Introduction

This chapter exhibits the approach adopted by former communist countries to address restitution issues. This approach has necessarily been a restrictive one. While all of the states endeavoured to strike a balance between the interests of the former owners against those of the state and society as a whole, they could and did not always succeed in restoring justice. Many former owners and their heirs tried to fill this lacuna in seeking reparation for past injustices beyond the boundaries of their own countries.

For reasons of space, comparative law aspects will be presented in the form of a summary of the key problematic issues of property transformation.

Restitution in Eastern Europe and its Limitations

The fall of the Berlin wall marked the beginning of a difficult period of transition for the former communist countries towards democracy and a market economy. Both of these objectives required a profound transformation of property. The former communist countries faced the phenomena of privatisation and restitution of property, which turned out to be the greatest challenge of their transitional period (Barkan, 2000). Restitution is deemed not only to contribute to the development of a market economy, but also has a deeper social and moral impact and is generally considered a step towards addressing and repairing past injustices (Barkan, 2000).

Restitution is a highly controversial and complex issue. The remedying of expropriations, most of which occurred several decades ago, had to strike a 'fair' balance between different historical, political, economical, moral and diplomatic factors. The victims' wish to have the expropriated property returned in due time or receive an equivalent compensation on the one hand and the need to establish a new moral national identity and reconcile society on the other were at odds. Issues such as the general unwillingness to open still sensitive issues about responsibility for World War

---

1 The views expressed in this chapter are solely those of the author and do not in any way represent those of the Court.

II, the dearth of financial resources, misgivings about the adverse effects of restitution on new owners who had acquired expropriated property in good faith, anticipated difficulties related to the lack of updated ownership registers, and new political strategies on development and progress (such as investment and market economy rather than reopening the issue of historical injustices) had to be taken into account.

In addition, the fragile balance between competing interests had to be achieved in an atmosphere of pressure from the outside: international organizations (such as the EU and NATO, see Karadjova, 2004, 334), NGOs (Eizenstat, 1998) and even individual states tried to influence the process.

In these circumstances, restitution was bound to be limited to certain expropriations, certain property and certain beneficiaries. This reality was sometimes stated explicitly in the laws providing for restitution (for example, the preamble of Act No. 87/1991 on Extra-Judicial Rehabilitations of the Czech Republic and Slovakia stated that it was adopted with the aim of mitigating the consequences of certain infringements of property rights) or elaborated in the case law of the supreme and constitutional courts (for example, the judgment of 22 November 2000 of the German Federal Constitutional Court stated that the legislature was not obliged to have regard to the real value of the property; it had to situate the indemnifications in the context of other measures associated with German reunification). Those Eastern European countries which opted for restitution at all (all former communist countries with the exception of Russia, Ukraine, Belarus, Poland and Serbia) had to address two key matters: scope and form.

The Scope of Restitution

The scope of restitution concerns the temporal limits of restitution, the property to be restituted and its beneficiaries.

The Temporal Limits

Unlawful expropriations were carried out before the communist regimes came to power as well – during World War II, for example. Not every country was willing to turn the clock that far back, especially since restitution was – at least initially – perceived as a means of restoring the situation that had existed immediately before communism.

After its unification, Germany decided not to restitute in kind any property that had been expropriated in the Soviet Occupied Zone between 1945 and 1949. The governments of the Soviet Union, the German Democratic Republic and the Federal Republic of Germany agreed that these expropriations could not be revoked or revised (Joint Declaration of the FRG and the GDR on the Resolution of Outstanding

Property Issues of 15 June 1990, a constituent part of the Unification Treaty of 31 August 1990). However, former owners (natural persons) were entitled to partial compensation under the Act Governing State Compensation for Expropriations Carried Out on the Basis of the Laws or Other Powers of the Occupying Force of 27 September 1994. No restitution or compensation was provided for expropriations carried out before 1945. A number of other countries opted for a similar solution. Bulgaria, Romania, Croatia and Albania limited restitution to expropriations committed during the communist period.

By contrast, Law XXV of 1991 and XXIV of 1992 in Hungary provided for compensation back to 1 May 1939, thus covering the period during World War II. The Czech Republic opened up the possibility of restoring possessions expropriated between 1938 and 1945 and after 1948, but chose not to remedy expropriations carried out immediately after the war (Cepl, V.).

The choice was, as a whole, dependent on how sensitive the respective country was to expropriations carried out before the advent of communism.

The Property to be Restituted

Restitution and compensation concerned, in general, both moveable and real property. Normally, restitution is provided for when former owners have not been compensated for the expropriation. Certain countries allowed the return of the property, even if the former owner had been compensated (see, for example, Law on Restitution of Property Nationalised under the Territorial and Urban Planning Act, Bulgaria).

Property that had in the meantime been acquired by third parties is to be restituted if the acquisition was unlawful, by means of an unlawful advantage or abuse of power (see for Bulgaria Section 7 of the Law on Restitution of Ownership of Nationalised Real Property of 1992, for the Czech Republic Section 4(2) of the Extrajudicial Rehabilitation Act of 1991 and for Estonia Section 12(3) (3) of the Principles of the Property Reform Act of 1991). These provisions were apparently inspired by the belief that during the communist period, the privileged of the day had unlawfully taken advantage of their position.

The Beneficiaries

This question concerns the eligibility of foreigners and legal persons to benefit from restitution. A number of countries preferred to bar foreign citizens from making claims – in the Czech Republic, Croatia, Lithuania, Romania, and Slovakia, only their own citizens could claim restitution.

In Bulgaria, this issue is dependent on the type of property – in principle, foreigners are eligible for the restitution of farm and forestland; however, they must sell the property within three years (Sections 3 and 8 of the Forests Restitution Act and section 3 of the Agricultural Lands Act).

In Germany, legal entities are excluded from restitution and compensation with respect to property expropriated during 1945–49. In Slovakia, legal entities are not eligible for the restitution of land. Under section 4 of Act No. 229/91 on Adjustment of Ownership Rights to Land and Other Agricultural Property only real property originally owned by individuals could be restored.

The Form of Restitution

The majority of the countries at issue opted for restitution in kind and, where not possible, for compensation (the Czech Republic, Bulgaria, Romania, the Former Republic of Macedonia, Lithuania, Latvia, Germany, Lithuania, Estonia, Slovakia and Albania). Hungary alone decided not to restitute in kind, but to compensate.

In any event, former owners tended to receive compensations which usually did not correspond to the current value of the property – either the compensation was originally conceived as partial (Hungary and Germany) or provided in the form of bonds or vouchers (Hungary, Germany, Bulgaria, Lithuania, the Former Republic of Macedonia, Latvia, and Slovenia) and not in cash. Albania limited restitution and compensation in kind to 10,000 square metres (Section 4(1) of the Restitution and Compensation of Property Act no. 7698 of 15 April 1993, as amended by Law no. 8084/1996). The maximum amount of compensation for expropriated property in Croatia is limited to 3,700,000 Croatian kunas (Section 58 of the Act on Compensation for and Restitution of Assets Taken under the Yugoslav Communist Regime).

Conclusion

The above examples show that the Eastern European countries have applied a more or less restrictive approach in remedying the injustice of past expropriations. Certain groups of former owners and expropriations carried out during particular periods were excluded from restitution; others received partial compensation which did not correspond to the market value of the property at the relevant time, and even those persons whose property had been returned did not always receive the full value, given the condition of the property. In addition, time limits for claiming restitution or compensation ensured that the process would not last indefinitely, serve as a restriction of restitution as well.

Non-National Instruments of Redress with Respect to Expropriations and Their Limits

Victims of expropriations who were not remedied by the adopted national restitution measures searched for other options for obtaining redress. In practice, they could complain to the UN Human Rights Committee and to the European Court of Human Rights. Another avenue explored by the descendants of Jews who settled in the United States and tried to file restitution claims before the US courts (for example, *Garb v. Poland*, the latest judgment of 3 March 2006 of the US Court of Appeals, Second Circuit) will not be discussed here. Such claims are bound to be unsuccessful given that states enjoy immunity before each other's courts.

The International Covenant on Civil and Political Rights

The UN International Covenant on Civil and Political Rights does not guarantee the right to property or restitution. Nevertheless, its Article 26, which prohibits discrimination, has had certain relevance with respect to property rights. Pursuant to the First Optional Protocol to the Covenant, the Human Rights Committee (the body established to monitor compliance with the Covenant) is competent to examine individual applications.

In a series of cases concerning restriction on restitution based on citizenship, the Human Rights Committee concluded that the requirements of residence and nationality for persons lodging restitution claims were unreasonable and that the denial of restitution or compensation to the claimants constituted a violation of Article 26. The Commission considered that because the State party was itself responsible for the departure of the author in seeking refuge in another country, it would be incompatible with the Covenant to require the author to satisfy the condition of citizenship (see, for example, *Marik v. Czech Republic*, Views adopted on 26 July 2005). Examination of such complaints was possible because, unlike Article 14 of the European Convention on Human Rights, Article 26 has an autonomous existence and does not depend on the application of other rights guaranteed by the Covenant.

The Human Rights Committee prepares 'views' which it forwards to the member state concerned as well as the claimant and includes the annual report on its activity submitted to the UN General Assembly. Accordingly, as is evident by their very appellation, the views do not have a legally binding character and are generally unable to provide individual remedies to violations. They are considered an instrument of political pressure and are used by individuals in the hope of receiving a more positive response to their grievances (Karadjova, 357).

The European Convention on Human Rights ('the ECHR')

Some former owners who were unsuccessful in obtaining restitution at the national level sought protection under Article 1 of Protocol No. 1 to the European Convention on Human Rights (the Convention). Article 1 of Protocol No. 1 reads as follows:

'Every natural or legal person is entitled to the peaceful enjoyment of his possessions. No one shall be deprived of his possessions except in the public interest and subject to the conditions provided for by law and by the general principles of international law. The preceding provisions shall not, however, in any way impair the right of a State to enforce such laws as it deems necessary to control the use of property in accordance with the general interest or to secure the payment of taxes or other contributions or penalties.'

Most applications have, however, been unsuccessful due mainly to the following reasons: 1) the fact that the Convention does not guarantee the right to restitution (incompatibility *ratione materiae*); 2) the fact that the expropriations occurred before the Eastern European countries ratified the Convention (incompatibility *ratione temporis*); 3) the reservations made by certain countries (Estonia and Latvia) in respect of their property reform when ratifying the Convention. They have been found to satisfy the requirements of Article 57 of the Convention (see *Kozlova and Smirnova v. Latvia* and *Shestojorkin v. Estonia*). In addition, the Court accords a wide margin of appreciation to the member states in terms of implementing social and economic policies, which necessarily narrows its scrutiny to the particular facts (Mahoney, 1998, 4).

General Principles

Applicability Ratione Temporis *or Limitation of the Court's Temporal Jurisdiction*

According to the well-established case law of the ECHR, the provisions of the Convention do not bind a Contracting Party in relation to any act or event which took place or any situation which ceased to exist before the date of the entry into force of the Convention with respect to that Party (*Malhous v. the Czech Republic; Broniowski v. Poland*, § 123 and *Von Maltzan and Others v. Germany*, § 82). This conclusion is in compliance with the general principles of international law and, in particular, with Article 28 of the Vienna Convention of 1969 on the Law of Treaties, which provides for the non-retroactivity of treaties ('Unless a different intention appears from the treaty or is otherwise established, its provisions do not bind a party in relation to any act or fact which took place or any situation which ceased to exist before the date of the entry into force of the treaty with respect to that party.'). The purpose of this limitation is to preclude complaints about events dating from a period when the respondent State was not in a position to foresee the international responsibility or legal proceedings to which these events might give rise (*Blečić v. Croatia*, § 68).

The Doctrine of 'the Margin of Appreciation'

The Convention's doctrine of the margin of appreciation is considered an interpretation tool necessary for drawing the line between what is properly a matter for each community to decide at the local level and what is so fundamental that it entails the same requirement for all countries (Mahoney, 1998, 1). Under Article 1 of Protocol No. 1, this concept comes into play in relation to the aim pursued by an interference with the right to property, as well as in the context of the proportionality test (Winisdoerffer, 1998, 18). With respect to restitution, the margin of appreciation additionally underlines the Court's conclusions that the Convention does not provide for the right to restitution and does not apply retroactively.

As it was summarised in the case of *Von Maltzan and Others v. Germany* (§ 74):

> Article 1 of Protocol No. 1 cannot be interpreted as imposing any general obligation on the Contracting States to return property which was transferred to them before they ratified the Convention. Nor does Article 1 of Protocol No. 1 impose any restrictions on the Contracting States' freedom to determine the scope of property restitution and to choose the conditions under which they agree to restore property rights of former owners [...]. In particular, the Contracting States enjoy a wide margin of appreciation with regard to the exclusion of certain categories of former owners from such entitlement [...]. On the other hand, once a Contracting State, having ratified the Convention including Protocol No. 1, enacts legislation providing for the full or partial restoration of property confiscated under a previous regime, such legislation may be regarded as generating a new property right protected by Article 1 of Protocol No. 1 for persons satisfying the requirements for entitlement.

Accordingly, issues related to the form of restitution (see, for example, *Szechenyi v. Hungary* and *Jasiūnienė v. Lithuania*, § 40–41), the amount of compensation (see, for example, *Von Maltzan and others v. Germany*, § 91 and 105), citizenship and residence requirements (*Gratzinger and Gratzingerova v. the Czech Republic*, § 48) or other conditions for obtaining restitution (for example that only natural persons are entitled to seek restitution, see *Valová and Slezák v. Slovakia*) fall within the large margin of appreciation of the state and thus outside the scope of Article 1 of Protocol No. 1.

The wide margin of appreciation is also of importance when the Court examines a complaint on its merits and makes an assessment as to whether a 'legitimate aim in the public interest' (see *Pincová and Pinc v. the Czech Republic*, § 48) exists.

Applicability Ratione Materiae

The applicability *ratione materiae* shows that Article 1 of Protocol No. 1 applies only when the interferences at issue concern the applicant's 'possessions.' It is closely related to the state's margin of appreciation as it is the state which sets the conditions for restitution, and thus the actual meaning of a possession. The relevant principles with respect to 'possessions' have been summarised in the case of *Kopecky v. Slovakia* (§ 35):

> 'Possessions' can be either 'existing possessions' or assets, including claims, in respect of which the applicant can argue that he or she has at least a 'legitimate expectation' of obtaining effective enjoyment of a property right. By way of contrast, the hope of recognition of a property right which it has been impossible to exercise effectively cannot be considered a 'possession' within the meaning of Article 1 of Protocol No. 1, nor can a conditional claim which lapses as a result of the non-fulfilment of the condition [...].

Accordingly, applicants who did not meet the conditions for restitution set by their national laws did not have an existing possession or claim which was 'sufficiently established to be enforceable' (*Gratzinger and Gratzingerova v. the Czech Republic,* § 74) and their complaint was considered incompatible *ratione materiae* with the Convention.

It follows that based on the provisions of the Convention and its established case law, the Court considered that it lacked competence to contend with most limitations relating to the scope and form of restitution. However, certain issues concerning restitution were found to fall within the scope of Article 1 of Protocol No. 1 and have been examined by the ECHR. Some of these cases are presented briefly below.

Restitution Cases Falling Within the Scope of Article 1 of Protocol No. 1

Failure of the State to Provide Compensation or to Restitute Property Once Compensation/Restitution has been Awarded

The case of *Broniowski v. Poland* concerned the failure of the state to provide compensation to a large number of persons who had been 'repatriated' from the so-called 'territories beyond the Bug River' (which became part of Belarus, Ukraine and Lithuania after World War II). In 1944 Poland signed agreements with the above states and undertook the obligation to compensate the repatriated persons. Ever since, Polish law has continuously upheld their entitlement to compensation under a certain scheme. However, this legislative scheme did not work well in practice, and thousands of people, although entitled to compensation, did not receive any. The Court determined that it had temporal jurisdiction to examine the complaint because it concerned entitlement to compensation vested in the applicant named above under Polish law at the time of the ratification of the Convention. It later found that the applicant had possessions according to the definition in Article 1 of Protocol No. 1, as domestic legislation had continuously provided for his compensation, and that its lack as well as the state of uncertainty in which the applicant found himself for many years placed a disproportionate and excessive burden on him.

As required by Article 46 of the Convention final judgments of the Court are binding on the respective Contracting State and are transmitted to the Committee of Ministers of the Council of Europe, which supervises their execution.

In general the enforcement measures include (1) payment of the monetary compensation which the applicant may have been awarded; (2) other individual measures where a mere monetary award cannot achieve full redress (for example, reopening of criminal proceedings) and (3) general measures, aiming at preventing new violations of the same kind (Sundberg, 567).

Taking into account that the violation in the above case concerned a situation which affected about 80,000 other persons, the court ruled for the first time in the operative provisions of a judgment on the general measures that the Respondent State should take to remedy a systematic defect at the origin of the violation found (see Cases Pending for Supervision of Execution, 5 July 2006, p. 114–115). It was obliged through appropriate legal measures and administrative practices to secure the property rights of the Bug River claimants or provide them with equivalent redress in lieu (§ 194 of the judgment on the merits).

On 6 September 2005 the applicant and the Polish Government reached a friendly settlement about the individual and general measures to be taken by the State. The applicant received payment of about 60,000 Euros. A number of legal provisions were changed and new adopted in order to facilitate the redress of the Bug River claimants (for example, provisions for State tortuous liability for omissions to enact legislation, legislation providing for the creation of a special compensation fund, several provision of a law, restricting the rights of partially compensated claimants were declared unconstitutional, a new draft law on the compensation of the Bug River claimants was submitted in the Polish Parliament etc.). However, as of 5 July 2006, pending the entry into force of the new law, the implementation of the Bug River claimant's rights is to a large extent suspended (see Cases Pending for Supervision of Execution, 114). The consideration of the case will be resumed by the Committee of Ministers at their meeting in October 2006.

Similarly to *Broniowski*, in the case of *Kirilova and Others v. Bulgaria* the applicants were entitled to receive particular flats offered in compensation for the expropriation of their properties. The flats were never constructed due to the municipality's financial difficulties, and the applicants did not obtain another form of reparation. Accordingly, the continuing failure to provide them with the compensation awarded was found to be in breach of Article 1 of Protocol No. 1.

The Court decided that the question about the pecuniary and non-pecuniary damage to be awarded to the applicants was not ready for decision, and with regard to the possibility that an agreement between the parties be reached, reserved it (§ 142 of the judgment on the merits). On 12 December 2005 the Secretariat of the

Department for the Execution of Judgments of the European Court of Human Rights requested from the Bulgarian Government information as regards the evaluation of the situation at national level concerning persons who are in similar situation to that of the applicants in the present case (see Cases Pending for Supervision of Execution, 25). This information is awaited and the consideration of the case will resume at the meeting of the Committee of Ministers in October 2006.

In the case of *Jasiuniene v. Lithuania* the Court found a violation of Article 1 of Protocol No. 1 on the ground that the domestic authorities had failed to provide compensation in land or money to which the applicant was entitled pursuant to a final judgement of the domestic courts. The applicant was awarded a compensation for pecuniary and non-pecuniary damage amounting to 9,000 Euros (§ 52 of the judgment).

Revision of a Final Judgement Awarding Restitution/Compensation

In the case of *Brumarescu v. Romania* the applicant was able to recover the possession of a house expropriated in 1950 and thereafter sold by the state to other persons. On complaint of the new owners, the procurator general of Romania intervened and reopened the restitution proceedings. The applicant's restitution claim was dismissed in the fresh proceedings. The Court found that the initial recognition of the applicant's title to the property represented a 'possession' and that the applicant was subsequently deprived of it without compensation and in breach of the principle of legal certainty, which placed a disproportionate and excessive burden on him.

In a judgment of 23 January 2001 the Court determined the measures to be taken by the State to redress the above violation. The Romanian State was to return the property at issue to the applicant or to pay him its current value and to provide him with a compensation of 15,000 US-Dollars for non-pecuniary damage. It seems that this judgment has not yet been enforced and its consideration will resume at the Committee of Ministers' meeting in October 2006.

Effects of Restitution on Third Parties

The restitution of expropriated property often affected the third parties who had acquired it in the meantime. It is the Court's view (*Pincová and Pinc v. the Czech Republic*, § 58) that:

> [T]he attenuation of old injuries [should not] create disproportionate new wrongs. To that end, the legislation should make it possible to take into account the particular circumstances of each case, so that persons who acquired their possessions in good faith are not made to bear the burden of responsibility which is rightfully that of the State which once confiscated those possessions.

In the case of *Pincova and Pinc v. the Czech Republic* the original owner of the property obtained restitution and the applicants, who had meanwhile bought the property from the state, were ordered to vacate it and were reimbursed the purchase price. The ground for allowing restitution was that the applicants had acquired the property at a price lower than its actual value at the relevant time. The Court found that although the deprivation was lawful and pursued a legitimate aim (to provide redress for expropriations that had occurred during the communist regime), it did not strike a fair balance: The compensation in the amount of the purchase price paid in 1967 did not take into account the applicants' personal and social situation (as it was apparently no longer related to the value of the property) or the fact that the property constituted the applicants' only housing, in which they had lived for forty-two years. The applicants were awarded 35,000 Euros as compensation for the pecuniary and non-pecuniary damage sustained (§ 68 of the judgment).

Final Remarks: Restitution and Justice

It is more than understandable that the former owners of expropriated property who were unable to obtain restitution perceived the whole process as unfair. However, views in support of complete restitution based solely on issues of morality and justice are one-sided and do not take account of the complexity of the problem necessitating a compromise. And compromises normally mean sacrifice.

The question arises whether any justice at all could be achieved through a large-scale compromise; similarly, which is the appropriate forum to evaluate the individual approach of each state with respect to restitution?

As a whole, the former communist countries were to a very large extent willing to provide remedy for past injustices. When assessing their approach and its restrictions, one must not lose sight of the fact that restitution developed in a particular context – that of transition to a democratic society and a market economy. The purpose of this transition was not only to face the injustices of the distant past and to give legitimacy to the present, but to facilitate societal progress as well. It is very tempting to believe that the latter would benefit all members of society.

References

Publications

Karadjova, M. (2004), 'Property Restitution in Eastern Europe: Domestic and International Human Rights Law Responses', *Review of Central and East European Law*, No. 3.

Mahoney, P. (1998), 'Marvellous Richness of Diversity or Invidious Cultural Relativism?', *Human Rights Law Journal*, Vol. 19 (1998), No. 1.

Sundberg, G.E. (2001), 'Control of Execution of Decisions under the ECHR – Some Remarks on the Committee of Ministers´ Control of the Proper Implementation of Decisions Finding Violations of the Convention', in: Alfredsson, G. et al. (eds.) (2001), *International Human Rights Monitoring Mechanisms*, (The Hague: Kluwer Law International).

Winisdoerffer, Y. (1998), 'Margin of Appreciation and Article 1 of Protocol No. 1', *Human Rights Law Journal*, Vol. 19 (1998), No. 1.

Internet-Based References

Barkan, E. 'Restitution and Amending Historical Injustices in International Morality, European Union Centre of California', Working Paper 11/2000, <http://www.eu center.scrippscol.edu/publications>.

Cepl, V. 'Restitution of Property in Post-Communist Czechoslovakia', Working paper No. 3 General Series, Centre for Central and Eastern European Studies, University of Liverpool, <http://www.liv.ac.uk/history/research/ceg_pdfs/Book3.pdf>.

Eizenstat, S. 'Testimony before the US House International Relations Committee of 6 August 1998 on Property Restitution in Central, East Europe', <http://www.resti tution.org/us/eizenstat.898.html>.

Garb v. Poland, judgment of 3 March 2006 of the US Court of Appeals, Second Circuit, <http://caselaw.lp.findlaw.com/data2/circs/2nd/027844p.pdf>.

Judgment of 22 November 2000 of the German Federal Constitutional Court, <http:// www.bundesverfassungsgericht.de/entscheidungen/rs20001122_1bvr230794. html>.

Cases Pending for Supervision of Execution as of 5 July 2006, Council of Europe's Home page dedicated to the execution of Judgments of the European Court of Human Rights <http://www.coe.int/T/E/Human_Rights/execution/>.

Case-Law of the European Court of Human Rights and the European Commission of Human Rights

Blečić v. Croatia [GC], no. 59532/00, ECHR 2006-...

Broniowski v. Poland [GC], no. 31443/96, ECHR 2004-V.

Broniowski v. Poland [GC], no. 31443/96 (friendly settlement), 28 September 2005.

Brumărescu v. Romania [GC], no. 28342/95, ECHR 1999-VII.

Brumărescu v. Romania [GC] (Article 41), no. 28342/95, ECHR-I.

Gratzinger and Gratzingerova v. the Czech Republic [GC] (dec.), no. 39794/98, ECHR 2002-VII.

Jasiūnienė v. Lithuania, no. 41510/98, 6 March 2003.

Kirilova and Others v. Bulgaria, nos. 42908/98, 44038/98, 44816/98 and 7319/02, 9 June 2005.

Kopecký v. Slovakia [GC], no. 44912/98, § 35, ECHR 2004-....

Kozlova and Smirnova v. Latvia (dec.), no. 57381/00, ECHR 2001-XI.

Malhous v. the Czech Republic (dec.), no. 33071/96, ECHR 2000-XII.

Pincová and Pinc v. the Czech Republic, no. 36548/97, ECHR 2002-VIII.

Shestojorkin v. Estonia (dec.), no. 49450/99, unreported.

Szechenyi v. Hungary, no. 21344/93, Commission decision of 30 June 1993.

Valová and Slezák v. Slovakia, no. 44925/98, 1 June 2004.

Von Maltzan and Others v. Germany (dec.) [GC], nos. 71916/01, 71917/01 and 10260/02, ECHR 2005-...

Damiana Gabriela Otoiu

Restitution Policies and National Identity in (Post)Communist Romania. The Case of the Jewish Community

'Transforming Socialist Property'[1]

Viewed as a central dimension of the economic, political and social process which affected post-socialist countries, the restoration of the private property was considered the fundament of a new system in which the market economy replaced the planned one and where the individuals played the former role of the State (CeFRes, 1997, 5).

Nevertheless, starting from the mid-nineties, this thesis of a radical gap between the socialist and the post-socialist use of property was progressively dismantled. First, its contenders started by explaining the limits of a 'transitology' literature[2], which presupposed a predicted and predictable evolution, a gradual and compulsory succession of developmental phases (e.g. Kornai 1990). The principle of a linear evolution, imposed by the 'transitology' paradigm, was deconstructed and replaced, starting from the question whether this paradigm constitutes a valid conceptual framework, which may be properly applied in relation to the multiple post-communist spaces.

Secondly, the proponents of the revision of the 'transitology' thesis continued with the remark that the post-socialist regime of property had not been established only upon the reconstruction of the presocialist property (from between the two world wars), but also in relation to principles, legal terms and political practices inherited from communism. This is, in fact, anthropologist Katherine Verdery's most important thesis:

> I suggest that, contrary to those who see de-collectivization as a process of *(re)creating private* property, it is better understood as a process of *transforming socialist* property. Socialism was not a property void; it had its own structure of property rights, a structure that had a long afterlife in the course of dismantling socialism [...] Old power structures renew themselves in radically changed circumstances (Verdery, 2003, xiv).

Starting from the concepts formulated by the post-socialist studies and especially from the necessity of taking into account the recent past as a general framework for analyzing the (re)construction of private property in the countries of Central and Eastern Europe, this chapter builds on two complementary approaches.

On one hand, I am discussing the legislation area, as the means whereby (to use Claus Offe's terms, Offe, 1997, 85) 'the dilemmas of justice in post-communist transitions' were resolved in Romania. Borneman, a law anthropologist who argues that

---

1   Title borrowed from Verdery, K. (2003, xiv).
2   For a critical presentation of the transitology approaches, see Dobry, Michel (2000, 585–614)

the pursuit of retributive justice is a crucial element of the postcommunist (German) *Rechtsstaat*, assumes that 'when socialist states dissolved, socialist normative system went with them' (Borneman, 1997, 16). My study tries to question this statement, presuming the existence of continuity between the socialist and post-socialist regime of property.

On the other hand, my reflections concern the possibility/ impossibility of an 'ethnic reading' of the restitution legislation. My hypothesis is that 'the nation' is reflected in the legal structure, especially in the case of the property regime (this is also the central assumption of Alexander Karn's study on the restitution policies developed in the former Czechoslovakia and in the Czech successor states: Karn, 2000). Hence, I presume that the legislative redefinition of the private property and the public debates around the restitution laws could tell us something about how the legislators have constructed an 'other' through the restitution policies. Moreover, I presume that the definition of the 'citizen' and of the 'nation' by means of the restitution policies is still 'coherent' with the recent past, that these 'Romanian people', whose civil rights, including the right to property, are re-defined, and whose heritage of the former Party State[3] is restored, represent (during post-socialism, exactly like during socialism) 'an organic nation, by the ethnic understanding of citizenship' (Barbu, 2001, 23; the author makes this remark while discussing the understanding of citizenship as it emerges from the Romanian Constitution of 1991).

I have chosen to examine in greater detail the case of the Jewish community in Romania because it seems particularly relevant for two reasons. Firstly, the Jewish communities in Eastern Europe were 'victims' of a double spoliation – by the Nazis and their Aryanization policies and by the communists, following nationalization. A second reason why I have chosen this case study regards the double quality of the members of the Jewish Community: they are both, part of an ethnic and of a religious minority. Therefore, I deem this to be an illustrative, while by no means a typical, case, which may underpin a wider reflection on the status of the 'foreigner-outsider' and of the 'minorities' in particular, as reflected in the post-socialist property regime.

I will mainly analyse the case of the Jewish communal property (which means the works, the artefacts and especially the buildings belonging to the Jewish communities and organizations). I have restricted my study to the communal and organizational Jewish assets principally firstly because I consider that an 'ethnic reading' of the reprivatization is not (necessarily) supported by the level of individual property[4],

---

3   Decree no. 30/ 18 January 1990, M.O., No. 12/19 January 1990 (Art. 1 : 'All the patrimony of the former Romanian Communist Party will pass to the State, and will be considered goods belonging to the entire people').

4   The legislation of restitution for individual properties doesn't exclude the members of different ethnic or religious communities, but imposes citizenship and residency requirements for regaining assets (or even for owning land and real estates).

but could be valid on the level of communitarian assets (assets that belong to the different ethnic or religious communities).

Secondly, the restitution of the property expropriated from the Jewish communities has both, a highly symbolic and a considerable material dimension. The transfer of ownership of the places of worship, cemeteries, former schools, etc, often coincides with a moment of revival of the Jewish Communities in Central and Eastern Europe, as remarked by Horel (Horel, 2002): the reopening of history research institutes, mostly forbidden during communism, the (re)foundation of Jewish schools and museums, etc.

A third reason for focusing our research on this specific type of property is our interest for the study of actors involved in the elaboration of restitution policies. While the members of the Jewish communities generally try to recover their properties through individual claims, several organizations give expression to the claims regarding the communal properties: local communities, regional and international associations, like the World Jewish Restitution Organization (see Eizenstat, 2004).

However, I must also mention the fact that, despite the obvious distinction between communal and individual property, the confusion between these two types of property/ laws is very recurrent in the public discourse or the daily discourse of my informants. For instance, after the elaboration of the Law no. 501/2002 pertaining to the restitution on religious properties, one of my interviewees bitterly noticed: 'They [the Jews] always had a privileged status. Maybe should I convert to their religion, in order to get my family's house back'.

In the first part of this article, I will briefly trace the 'history' of property expropriation that affected the Jewish Community surrounding World War II (the 'aryanization') and after the instauration and the consolidation of the communist regime (the 'nationalization'). Subsequently, I focus on politics elaborated in Romania for providing compensation or restitution to the Jewish Community for these expropriations. After this review of the historical background and of the post-communist restitution policies, I will explore the 'ethnos'-based (Priban, 2004) rhetoric of restitution.

'Damn them, they'll cry, but finally they'll shut up...'[5] –
'Romanianization' and Nationalization of the Jewish Assets

Several waves of expropriation affected both the Jewish community and individuals.

The first laws for the 'Romanianization' of Jewish property were voted in July – August 1940, during the royal dictatorship of Charles the 2nd. The national legionary state continued the 'Aryanization' of the Jewish property between September 1940 and January 1941, in 1941 a National Commission for Romanianization was established within the Ministry for National Economy to manage 'Aryanized' property. The available figures allow one to understand the width of this phenomenon, both at the level of individuals and at the level of the community: until 1943, 75 385 persons[6] were banished from their apartments; between July 1942 and August 1944, based on the Decree-Law no. 499 /1942, 1 042 buildings belonging to the Jewish communities (temples, synagogues, prayer houses, hospitals, schools, cemeteries, etc.) were confiscated (The Federation of Romanian Jewish Communities. The Centre for the History of Romanian Jews 1993, 344).

After the instauration of the communist regime, like in the case of Czechoslovakia or other countries of Central and Eastern Europe, several normative acts were adopted, which invalidated the process of Aryanization and proclaimed the restitution of 'Romanianized' properties (for instance the Law for the abrogation of anti-Jewish legislative measures, adopted in Romania in December 1944). In fact most of these assets were not effectively restituted. One should mention, however, that a law on heirless and unclaimed Jewish property was passed in 1948[7]. This law allowed the local communities to retrieve all the movable and immovable assets belonging to the deported Jews, in order to be used for helping the poor. But the main beneficiaries of this law were the Federation of Jewish Communities (based in Bucharest) and the Jewish Democratic Committee (an organization founded in 1945 by the communists in an effort to exercise a better control over the Jewish community). The main task of this so-called 'Democratic Committee' was the 'political enlightment and mobilization [...] of the Mozaic clergy and Mozaic faithful', which means (according to Bercu Feldman, the Committee's Secretary) 'to increase the Jewish working people's love and attachment for the USSR, to mobilize Jewish working people more actively in the

---

5   Says 'comrade' Iosif Chisinievski (a Jew himself) during 'The meeting of the Political Bureau of the C.C. – RWP' (Central Committee of the Romanian Working Party) from January 14, 1953 (while the political bureau was discussing the possible abolition of the Jewish committees and organizations). See Rotman (1996, 241).
6   After WWII, some 350 000 Jews still lived in Romania (Rotman 2004, 31; Wasserstein 2000, 6).
7   Decree no. 113/ June 30, 1948 (Decretul no. 113 cu privire la bunurile rămase de pe urma evreilor, victime ale unor măsuri de persecutie, decedati fără mostenitori, in *Colectiune de legi, decrete si deciziuni*, tom XXVI, 1–30 June 1948, pp. 1527 – 1529).

fight for peace'[8]. One of the regional commissions (created to make a report on the situation of movable and immovable assets and subsequently to sell all this assets) even noticed that 'the activity of our commission is under the political control of the Jewish Democratic Committee'[9] The local Jewish organizations were obliged to sell the recovered goods and to hand over 80% of the profit to the Federation of Jewish Communities[10].

At the end of the 1940s several laws regarding the nationalization of Jewish properties were passed. They were directed especially at the institutional networks for social and medical assistance and the teaching establishments: 1948 – the schools; 1949 – the hospitals, the medical centres, the asylums, the canteens, etc. The education and the social assistance had to be the monopoly of the only existing party, noticed Liviu Rotman (Rotman 1996, 231). A key element of the communist strategy aiming the control and the liquidation of the Jewish communal life, these nationalizations were portrayed by the official propaganda as part of the 'the achievements of the people's democratic regime in assuring religious freedom'[11] and 'full equality with Romanian people and the other national minorities'[12]: 'The Romanian Labour Party is guided in his national policies by the Leninist directives, in accordance to which the majority nation has to reveal a particular concern and solicitude towards the national minorities'[13].

Once the Jewish schools were nationalized, the first schools in Yiddish (subsidized by the state) were founded in Bucharest, Iasi and Timisoara. The main tasks of these schools included educating the members of the Community in a 'healthy spirit'[14] and promoting Yiddish[15] language over Hebrew[16]. 'Instead of the Jewish schools

---

8   Open Society Archives (OSA), 300-60-1, Jews 1957 – 1959, no. 1272/ 28.02.1952 (Meeting of the Jewish Democratic Committee, in *Viata nouă*, 26.02.1952), pages 2–7.
9   Archives of the Federation of Jewish Communities, Bucharest, Fund X (Movable and immovable assets), File 9, 'Report on the activity of the regional commission for the goods of the Federation of Jewish Communities, based in Cluj' (October 1948 – May 1949), 2nd page.
10   See Archives of the Federation of Jewish Communities, Bucharest, Fund X (Movable and immovable assets), especially files 9–11 or Fund VII (Contemporary documents), especially files 15, 23 and 24.
11   OSA, 300-60-1, Jews 1957 – 1959, no. 1272/ 28.02.1952 (Meeting of the Jewish Democratic Committee, in *Viata nouă*, 26.02.1952), 7th page.
12   OSA, 300-60-1, Jews 1957 – 1959 (*Rumania. Freedom of religion acknowledged by Jewish official*), 1st page.
13   *Romania libera*, June 7, 1956, OSA, 300-60-1, Private property 1951 – 1969.
14   OSA, 300-60-1, Jews 1957 – 1959, no. 1272/ 28.02.1952 (Meeting of the Jewish Democratic Committee, in *Viata nouă*, 26.02.1952), 6th page.
15   The vernacular language of Jewish communities in Central and Eastern Europe. The status of modern Hebrew as the official language of Israel led to a decline in the use of Yiddish, bur also to the promotion of this language (considered to be a 'progressive language') by the communities that rejected Zionism.
16   For the promotion of the Yiddish language over Hebrew, see mainly Hary Kuller, 'Difuzarea idisului între cele doua războaie mondiale si după in Romania', *Buletinul Centrului, muzeului si*

existing during the previous political regimes, which educated the young people in the bourgeois and nationalist spirit, the Yiddish school offers the pupils a real education, rendering them dignified builders of the socialism'[17].

Not only the Communities and the Jewish organizations were forced to 'donate' their assets, but also the individuals. Despite the numerous hesitations in the Communist Party's politics on the question of emigration to Israel (Rotman, 1996, 232), more than 280 000 Jews emigrated between 1948 and 1989 (Ioanid, 2005, 203–204) and they were forced to leave their possessions behind. So did the Jews willing to emigrate in Europe or in the US: 'Only those whose family pay a ransom of about 3 – 4 000 USD can leave [the country]. Obviously, they have to leave behind all the things they own, the house, the furniture. [...] In the case of the Jews who have no relatives abroad willing to pay the ransom, there is only one way [...]: they are supposed to make a donation to the State – the house and all their belongings'[18].

The property rights of both the Jewish Community and its members were dramatically curtailed also in the 1980s, because of the aggressive 'systematization of the cities'. The communist regime tried to reshape the cities by means of an aesthetic – political plan. For instance, Dudesti-Vacaresti (a Jewish area in the historical centre of Bucharest, the capital of Romania), was demolished almost completely, because of the architectural ambition of the dictator Nicolae Ceausescu: he wanted to build a quarter dominated by the so-called 'House of the People' (nowadays the Palace of Parliament, the second largest building in the world after the Pentagon) and centred on the boulevard 'the Victory of Socialism'. More than half of the Jewish prayer houses in Bucharest were demolished between 1985 and 1988[19].

While examining the legal status of the ecclesiastic assets during the communist regime, one should emphasize the fact that, in most of Eastern and Central Europe, the synagogues, as the public space that the Jewish population could still enjoy as a community, tend to become a centre for propaganda of the communist regimes that surfaced after 1945 (for instance a strong *anti-alya*, anti-emigration propaganda), doubled by the tightest political control (Rotman, 2004, 39)[20]. 'The *Securitate* [secret police] had plenty of informers present when the celebration took place in

arhivei istorice a evreilor din Romania, no. 12/ 2006, 47 – 62.

17   OSA, 300-60-1, Jews 1957 – 1959 (D. Rubin, 'The second class of the pedagogical school in Yiddish', in *Romania libera*, 9 July 1954).

18   OSA, 300 – 60 – 2, Confidential Reports, Radio Free Europe (RFE), 1974 (*Concerning the situation of the Jews in Romania*, 11 February 1974, 5th page).

19   V. The chronological table of synagogues in Bucharest, published by architects Neculai – Ionescu Ghinea and Dan D. Ionescu in 1999 (consisting of some 110 temples/ synagogues/ places of worship built in Bucharest before 1985, of which 65 were demolished between 1985 and 1988), in *The Jews of Romania. History, culture, civilization* (CD edited by the Federation of Jewish Communities in Romania. The Centre for the History of Romanian Jews, Bucharest, 2004).

20   For a history of Jewish communities in other Central European states, see Horel 2002.

the synagogue. [...] everybody in the community knew that it was common practice. On each High Holiday, some unknown people, usually men, came to the synagogue, people we knew weren't part of the community and were there for one purpose alone: to find out if we were talking against the system'.[21]

But in Romania, as opposed to other Eastern and Central European states, the places of worship are affected more by the systematization of the cities in the 1980s than by the nationalization. Generally, the most important synagogues remain the property of the Federation of Jewish Communities (it is the case of the Choral Temple in Bucharest, which functioned both as the centre of religious life and as community headquarters, or that of the 'Holy Union' temple in Bucharest, which was transformed in the Museum of Jewish History in 1977), while the 'donation' to the government of the places of worship occurs mainly in the small cities or in rural areas.

The religious role of the Jewish community wad thus (apparently) maintained, even though the archives show 'the falsity of the communist politics of 'freedom of the religious cults' ' (Rotman, 1996, 235): 'The Jewish religious communities [are] the most dangerous. There are spies there. [...] They have about 603 temples, houses for prayers, synagogues. The houses for prayers are capitalist enterprises for espionage. [...] The synagogues reduction may be done and there won't be any complaint from the Jewish working population', considered the members of the political bureau of the party – state in 1953 (The meeting of the Political Bureau of the Central Committee of the Romanian Working Party from January 14, 1953, Rotman, 1996, 239–241).

'Restitution as a Reconstitution of National Identity'[22]

Like most of the Central and Eastern European countries, Romania put in place restitution policies after the collapse of the communist regime. However, the legislation concerning the restoration of private property at the beginning of the 1990s in the Central and Eastern European countries privileged certain victims (those of the majority population), while excluding the compensation of minorities (notably two important East European ethnic minorities, the Germans and the Jews), the non-citizens (emigrants who had lost or renounced their citizenship) and the non-residents (citizens of a state who reside abroad). 'The underlying moral economy framed a region-wide rhetoric of restitution as a reconstitution of national identity' (Barkan 2000, 122). 'The minorities, such as the expatriates, were often part of the agenda to keep all types of 'others' out' (Barkan, 2000, 128).

---

21 Centropa, Interview with Edita Adler, Romania (2003), Interviewer Andreea Laptes, <http://www.centropa.org/archive.asp?mode=bio&DB=HIST&fn=Edita&ln=Adler&country=Romania>, accessed 23 June 2006.
22 Barkan, 2000, 128.

By analyzing these policies in post-communist Romania, I aim to give an answer to the second question that I had asked at the outset – regarding the possibility / the impossibility of adding an 'ethnic' interpretation to the restitution laws (in terms of 'citizenship' and in terms of the '(re)construction of the nation' by the post-socialist authorities).

In Romania, the process of restitution for the Jewish communitarian properties 'Romanianized' during the Antonescu regime or nationalized by the communist regime was set in place after 1997, the date when the first normative acts (four emergency ordinances and a decision) of restitution appeared[23]. These normative acts allowed the restitution of a very limited number of communal and organizational Jewish assets (such as the Jewish Theatre, some of the former hospitals, etc).

The first important law pertaining to the restitution of communal property was approved by the parliament in June 2002[24]. The law concerns buildings that belonged to the religious denominations (such as schools and hospitals), which were nationalized between March, 1945 and December, 1989. This legal cut-off is considered by the members of Jewish Community prejudicial and exclusionary[25], because it excludes the period between 1940 and 1945, when a considerable number of property was seized. Moreover, the legal framework enacted separate statutes for different categories of property (religious vs. nonreligious, movable vs. immovable, etc).

If/ when the communal properties were restituted to the communities, they constituted 'mixed blessings', as Ruth Gruber notices (Gruber, 2002, 115). For instance, even though the Jewish Theatre was among the first buildings to be restituted to the Community (in 1997), even today[26] they didn't regain the possession of the building simply because the restoration and the maintenance represent major costs.

Three main types of actors are involved in this process of restitution of the communitarian assets, both in the elaboration and in the implementation of the restitution policies in Central and Eastern Europe:

• the local communities (in Romania, the Federation of Jewish Communities, based in Bucharest and different local representatives of this Federation) ;

---

23   The restitution of Jewish communitarian assets is regulated especially through the Emergency Ordinance (EO) no. 21/1997, modified by EO no. 101/2000; EO no. 112/1998; EO no. 83/1999; the Governmental Decision no. 1334/2000, the Laws no. 501/2002 and no. 66/2004.

24   For a short overview of the property restitution legislation in Central and Eastern European Countries, especially the restitution concerning the religious and communal assets, see Randolph Bell, 'Summary of Property Restitution in CEE', submitted to the U.S. Commission on Security and Cooperation in Europe (September, 2003), http://www.state.gov/p/eur/rls/or/2003/31415.htm

25   Interview with G.R., jurisconsult of the Jewish Community, May 2005, Bucharest.

26   In May 2005, when an interview with R., one of the employees of the 'Caritatea' Foundation took place.

- the international Jewish agencies, among which the most important is the World Jewish Restitution Organization (WJRO), based in New York and Jerusalem, created in 1992 by the World Jewish Congress and the government of Israel in order to represent the interests of Jews worldwide in the recovery of the Jewish assets after the fall of communism;
- and the foundations and associations constituted after 1989 at the regional or local level in order to defend the rights of the Jewish owners (the WJRO created an entire network of local and regional organizations, often in collaboration with the local Jewish communities).

In an autobiographical writing, Stuart Eizenstat, former 'extraordinary ambassador of the American State Department to Eastern Europe on a mission to encourage the restitution of assets confiscated from the religious communities by the Nazis and then nationalized by the communist governments' between 1995 and 2001 (Eizenstat, 2004), speaks about the relationships established between these three types of actors which vary greatly from one country to the next – going from collaboration to confrontation. The conflict, if it exists al all, turns around two questions: who might be the legitimate heirs of the decimated Jewish communities – only the narrow group of survivors or the WJRO, which claims to represent the interests of Jews worldwide? And which organization should manage the restituted goods? (see especially 42, 53). I won't address in this chapter the complex issue of the relationship between the local/ national/ regional/ and international actors and their participation in the decision-making process or in the implementation of the restitution laws. I would only mention the fact that in the case of Romania it is the 'Caritatea' foundation ('Charity'), created by the WJRO in 1997, which has exclusive rights to the communitarian assets that were restituted after 1997 (although – never forsaking its right to ownership – the Foundation conceded the right to use to the Federation of the Jewish Communities). In fact, the right of ownership belongs to the local antenna of the WJRO for very practical reasons – according to the representatives of the Jewish Community and of the Foundation (the local community, very limited as it is[27], could not afford to take in charge the expenses for the restoration of the assets affected by restitution).

As for the property belonging to individual members of the Jewish community, Romania, like most of the CEECs, restricted initially restitution to current citizens. Because many of the former owners emigrated during the communist regime, they became ineligible to receive property, unless they regained the Romanian citizenship.

The President of Romania promulgated in 1995 the first important law for (quasi)restitution: the Law no. 112 for the regulation of the situation of certain immovable goods that became state property. This law met strong critiques. Even if it recognized the former owner's right of reclaiming his or her property, the law stipu-

---

27   6 057 members, according to the 2002 census data.

lated that an owner could claim only one building, and this upon the double condi-tion that he had formerly lived there or the building was not occupied at the moment (thus, the number of possible property reconstructions was lowered). The Law no. 112 dealt more with 'the protection of the current inhabitants', who had the right to buy the buildings they had lived in at very low prices (Zerilli, 1998, 166). The leader of The Tenants of the Nationalized Buildings' Association thus considers the two laws in question to be 'an act of benevolence from the State's leaders [...] because the prices of those flats were reduced to almost nothing by the increasing inflation, after which the value of a house became, in a few years, comparable with the one of a TV.'[28] Apart from recreating the presocialist property, this law created new rights / new owners (the former tenants living in nationalized buildings) and excluded from restitution the non-citizens and the non-residents.

A close examination of the legislative framework (from the first 'restitution law' until the most recent one, initiated by the 'Justice and Truth' polical coalition and built around the principle of *restitutio in integrum* – restoration to original condition –, L247/2005), allows us to observe that the laws that have been drafted in the field of restitution, as well as the associated jurisprudence, lack consistency and often con-stitute the object of dispute and negotiations both among and within the various political parties.

The rhetoric of the 'people' and the 'nation' was particularly approached during these political negotiations. While generally the members of the National Peasant Christian Democratic Party or of the Liberal Party have tried to put the restitution (in-cluding the properties belonging to religious and ethnic communities) on the politi-cal agenda, the most vigorous opponents were the members of the ultranationalist Greater Romania Party (Otoiu, 2004; Stan, 2006). They argue that this retroactive, re-paratory justice (giving back the properties to the former owners) will in fact institute injustice, because of the displacement of the tenants living in nationalized houses. As a consequence, only a general 'redistribution' of land and housing would really 'deliver justice'. Their arguments are also built around the idea of 'Romanianess': they claim that the government should have implemented in Romania an 'ethnos'-based (Priban, 2004) restitution policy. 'A country is a living organism. If we cut it into pieces, in concert with the foreigners, we will offend God... We already have offended God...' (says Leonida Lari, member of the Greater Romania Party, during the parliamentary debates around the restitution laws, 24th of June 1997). But also the representatives of the Social Democrats favour greatly the idea of a 'redistributive' justice and of a limited restitution: 'It is worth despoiling those who are today living in poverty?', asks Ion Iliescu, former Romanian president[29]; and he concludes that, due to the country's

---

28   E.P., interview, April 26th, 2004, Bucharest.
29   Interview with Ion Iliescu, in 'Ha'aretz', 25th of July 2003, <http://www.haaretz.com/>.

bad economic situation, 'the Jewish property restoration requests should be either postponed or rejected'. Not only the prohibitive cost of restitution could explain, in Social Democrat's view, the 'necessity' of 'postponing' the restitution belonging to ethnic and religious communities, but also what they consider to be 'the possible dangerous consequences on inter-confessional and inter-ethnic relationships in Transylvania'.[30]

Conclusions

The literature on the restoration of the private property in Central and Eastern Europe proposes a double interpretation of the changes that occurred within the property regime. The first account stresses the features of continuity with pre-communist period and observes the fact that the events of 1980s were often experienced as a return to 'normality', as a *nachholende Revolution* (to use Habermas' terms). Like other countries of Central and Eastern Europe, post-communist Romania considered the interwar period as an essential point of reference: ideological or simply historical, this perspective forces the post-communist Romania, to a certain extent, to give itself a definition which bypasses the interwar period (Preda, 2002, 570). This rectifying revolution could also express itself in the elaboration of the 'public policies of past' (e.g. the restoration of the properties). In the various analyses dedicated to the way in which the post-communist countries 'broke loose' from the communist past through legislation intended to condemn its abuses, what dominates this field is an approach called 'transitional justice'. This perspective uses concepts and theories which were elaborated by the political and historic sciences in Germany (*Vergangenheitspolitik*) and in the Anglo-Saxon universities (Transitional Justice) (e.g. Kritz, 1995). It underlines the fact that the political ideas, combined with the notions of 'justice' and 'injustice', guide the elaboration and the implementation of 'the policies of the past' (e.g. *East European Politics and Societies*, 19: 3/2005).

The second possible interpretation underlines the continuity between both regimes (communist and post-communist) of property and conceives the process of (re)creation of private property as being marked by 'the collectivist inheritance'. The post-communist regime of property would only be 'the completion of a process of appropriation opened in the communist period by the members of nomenklatura' (CeFRes, 1997, 16), which would mark the creation of 'capitalism with a comrade's face' (Frydman *et al*, 1996, 5–11).

I aim neither to confirm nor to counter the hypothesis of a transmutation of the cultural and political capital into economic capital through the process of

---

30 Censure motion, initiated by the members of the Social Democratic Party, 16th of June 2005, Romanian Parliament, <www.cdep.ro>

(re)emergence of the private property in Romania after 1989 (Chelcea, 2000). Nevertheless, I have noticed that at the beginning of 1990s the constitution of property was privileged to the detriment of its reconstruction, and 'redistributive justice' was preferred to the retroactive, reparatory 'justice'.

A final remark regards the possibility of using the case study of the Jewish community holdings as a sort of 'privileged observatory', which would allow us to highlight the meaning of the notions of 'citizen' and 'nation' in the legislation of restoration. The legislation of 'quasi-restoration' elaborated upon at the beginning of 1990s (especially until 1997) gives us the image of a right of property, which can be understood in an ethnic perspective. These 'Romanian people', whose civil rights, including the right of property, are re-defined, and whose heritage of the former Party State[31] is restored, 'represent [...] an organic nation, by the ethnic understanding of citizenship' (Barbu, 2001, 23).

The case of the Jewish community possessions could constitute a 'privileged observatory', but at the same time, this is not inevitably 'typical' for the problem of the minorities' ownership, or for the property of all ethnic or religious communities in post-communist Romania. If we refer to the restoration of ecclesiastical possessions, even today a controversial question is posed by the assets and specifically by the places of the worship of the Greek Roman Catholic Church (Romanian Church United with Rome) and of the Reformed Church[32]. Obviously, to understand these controversies, one must underline the fact that not all the 'religious minorities' have had a similar 'recent past'. During the communist regime, the Greek Catholic Church was forced to 'unite' with the Orthodox Church in 1948 (Ionescu-Gura, 2005, 411–420; Vasile, 2003) and, as a consequence of this 're-unification', its patrimony was nationalized and used by the Orthodox Church (Iordachi, 1999; Mahieu, 2004). After 1989, the re-establishment of the Greek Catholic Church led to open and endless controversies with representatives of the Orthodox Church over the restitution of the patrimony confiscated in 1948. Also in this case, the 'structure of property rights [...] had a long afterlife in the course of dismantling socialism' (Verdery, 2003, xiv)...

---

31   Decree no. 30/ 18 January 1990, M.O., No. 12/19 January 1990 (Art. 1 : 'All the patrimony of the former Romanian Communist Party will pass to the State, and will be considered goods belonging to the entire people ').

32   V. Doc. 7795 – the report of the Commission on Legal Issues and Human Rights (Parliamentary Assembly of the Council of Europe), rapporteur: Gunnar Jansson (above all chapters C and D, 'Goods belonging to the Minorities and Communities', and 'Ecclesiastical Goods', respectively) as well as Resolution 1123 (1997) on the respect of international obligations and commitments made by Romania (text adopted by the Assembly on the 24th of April, 1997).

References

Andrusz, G., Harloe, M. and Szelenyi, I. (1996), *Cities after Socialism* (Oxford: Blackwell Publishers).

Barbu, D. (2001), 'De l'ignorance invincible dans la démocratie. Réflexions sur la transformation post-communiste', *Studia Politica. Romanian Political Science Review*, 1:1.

—— (2005), *Politica pentru barbari* [Politics for barbarians] (Bucharest: Nemira).

Barkan, E. (2000), *The guilt of nations. Restitution and negotiating historical injustices* (New York and London: W.W. Norton and Co.).

Bönker, F., Offe, C. and Preuss, U. K. (1993), *Efficiency and justice of property restitution in East Europe*, ZERP Diskussionspapier 6/93, Papers on Constitution Building No. 5, Center for European Law and Policy, Bremen University.

Borneman, J. (1997), *Settling accounts: violence, justice and accountability in postsocialist Europe* (Princeton University Press).

CeFRes (1997), 'Anciens et nouveaux propriétaires. Stratégies d'appropriation en Europe centrale et orientale', *Cahiers du CeFRes*, No. 11f.

Chelcea, L. (2000), *Gentrification, Property Rights and Post-socialist Private Accumulation (Bucharest, Romania)*, Institute for Human Sciences, Wien, SOCO Project Paper, No. 93/2000.

Dobry, Michel (2000), 'Les voies incertaines de la transitologie: choix stratégiques, séquences historiques, bifurcation et processus de path dependence', in: *Revue Française de Science Politique*, (vol. 50), No. 1, 585 – 614.

East European Politics and Societies (2005), 19:3 ('The role of ideas in post-communist politics: a reevaluation'), pp. 339–493.

Eizenstat, S. E. (2004), *Une justice tardive. Spoliations et travail forcé, un bilan final de la Seconde Guerre mondiale* [Imperfect Justice: Looted Assets, Slave Labor, and the Unfinished Business of World War II] (Paris: Seuil).

Federaţia Comunităţilor Evreieşti din România. Centrul pentru Studiul Istoriei Evreilor din România [The Federation of Romanian Jewish Communities. The Centre for the History of Romanian Jews] (1993), *Evreii din România între anii 1940 – 1944* [The Jews of Romania between 1940 – 1944], vol. I, *Legislaţia antievreiască* [Anti-Jewish Legislation] (Bucharest: Hasefer).

Frydman, R., Murphy, K. and Rapaczynski, A. (1996), 'Capitalism with a Comrade's Face', *Transition*, 2:2, pp. 5–11.

Gruber, R. E. (2002), *Virtually Jewish. Reinventing Jewish Culture in Europe* (Berkeley/ Los Angeles/ London: University of California Press).

Henry, M. (1997), *The restitution of Jewish property in Central and Eastern Europe*, New York, American Jewish Committee.

Horel, C. (2002), *La restitution des biens juifs et le renouveau juif en Europe centrale – Hongrie, Slovaquie, République Thèque* (Bern: Peter Lang).

Ioanid, R. (2005), *Răscumpărarea evreilor. Istoria acordurilor secrete dintre România si Israel* [The Ransom of Jews. The Story of the Extraordinary Secret Bargain between Romania and Israel], (Iasi: Polirom).

Ionescu-Gură, N. (2005), *Stalinizarea României. Republica Populară Română 1948 – 1950: transformări instituţionale* [The Stalinization of Romania. The Romanian Popular Republic 1948 – 1950: Institutional Transformations] (Bucharest: BIC ALL).

Iordachi, C (1999), 'Politics and Inter-Confessional Strife in post-1989 Romania: From Competition for Resources to the Redefinition of National Ideology', *Balkanologie*, 3:1, pp. 147–169.

Karn, A. (2000), *Restitution and Retrodiction. Talking Back to the Past in Postcommunist East – Central Europe* Working Paper, EU Center of California, 03/2000.

Kornai, J. (1990), *The Road to a Free Economy. Shifting from a Socialist System: The Example of Hungary* (New York: W. W. Norton and Budapest: HVG Kiadó).

Kozminski, Adrzej K. (1997), 'Restitution of Private Property and Reprivatisation in Central and East Europe', *Communist and Postcommunist Studies*, 30:1, pp. 5–22.

Kritz, N.J. (ed.) (1995), *Transitional Justice: How Emerging Democracies Reckon with Former Regimes*, Vol. I General Considerations, Vol.II Country Studies, Vol. III Laws, Rulings, and Reports (Washington: U.S. Intitute of Peace Press).

Linz, J. and Stepan, A. (1997), *Problems of Democratic Transition and Consolidation: Southern Europe, South America, and Postcommunist Europe* (Baltimore, University of Baltimore Press).

Mahieu, S. (2004), *Legal Recognition and Recovery of Property: Contested restitution of the Romanian Greek Catholic Church Patrimony*, Max Planck Institute for Social Anthropology Working Papers, no. 69/2004.

McAdams, J. A. (ed.) (1997), *Transitional Justice and the Rule of Law in New Democracies* (Notre Dame: Notre Dame University Press).

Offe, C. (1997), *Varieties of Transition: The East European and East German Experience*, (Cambridge, Massachusetts: MIT Press).

Otoiu, D. (2004), 'Mémoire du communisme, acteurs du postcommunisme. Les associations des propriétaires et des locataires des immeubles nationalisés', *Studia Politica. Romanian Political Science Review*, 4 :4, pp. 885–918

Preda, C. (2002), 'Système politique et familles partisanes en Roumanie postcommuniste', *Studia Politica. Romanian Political Science Review*, 2:2.

Priban, J. (2004), 'Reconstituting Paradise Lost: Temporality, Civility, and Ethnicity in Post-Communist Constitution-Making', *Law & Society Review*, 38:3, pp. 407–432.

Pogany, I.S. (1998 a), *Righting Wrongs in Eastern Europe* (Palgrave Macmillan).

—— (1998 b), 'The Restitution of Former Jewish Owned Property and Related Schemes of Compensation in Hungary', *European Public Law*, 4:2, pp. 211–232.

Rotman, L. (1996), 'The politics of the Communist regime concerning the Jews: Contradictions, ambivalence and misunderstanding (1945 – 1953)', in Stanciu, I., (ed.), *The Jews in the Romanian History. Papers from the International Symposium* (Bucharest, 1996), Institute of History 'N. Iorga', Romanian Academy & The Goldstein – Goren Center, Diaspora Research Institute, Tel Aviv University (Bucharest: Silex, f.a.), pp. 230 – 247.

—— (2004), *Evreii din România în perioada comunistă. 1944 – 1965* [The Romanian Jews during the Communist Era. 1944 – 1965] (Iaşi: Polirom).

Stan, L. (2006), 'The Roof over Our Head: Property Restitution in Romania', *Journal of Communist Studies and Transition Politics*, 22:4, pp. 1–26.

Vasile, C. (2003), *Între Vatican şi Kremlin. Biserica greco-catolică în timpul regimului comunist* [Between the Vatican and the Kremlin. The Greek Catholic Church during the Communist Regime] (Bucharest: Curtea Veche).

Verdery, K. (1996), *What was Socialism and what comes next?* (Princeton: Princeton University Press).

—— (2003), *The Vanishing Hectare, Property and Value in Postsocialist Transylvania*, (Ithaca and London: Cornell University Press).

Wasserstein, B. (2000), *Dispariţia diasporei. Evreii din Europa începând cu 1945* [Vanishing Diaspora. The Jews in Europe since 1945] (Iaşi: Polirom).

Zerilli, F. (1998), 'Identité et propriété en milieu urbain. Locataires et propriétaires dans la Roumanie contemporaine', *Yearbook of the Romanian Society of Cultural Anthropology*, vol. 1.

5. Reacting to Social Marginalisation

Aisalkyn Botoeva

The Institutionalisation of Novel Shopping Places in a Post-Soviet Country. The Case of Supermarkets in Bishkek, Kyrgyzstan

Introduction

The 24th of March 2005 will probably remain in Kyrgyzstan inhabitants' memories as one of the most shocking days in the history of the capital. According to various estimations, around 10. 000 people went to the main square to protest against the president of 15 years and against the results of the recently held parliamentary elections. The protest started with a peaceful demonstration, but rapidly took the form of an angry crowd breaking into the Government House. Right after the attack on the Government House, the president was reported to have disappeared from the building, and later from the country. He has not shown himself to the public since that day. Foreign and local journalists later reported that he settled in Moscow with his family. The opposition that came into power after the attack on the Government House demanded that he resign from the position of the presidency.

The night of March 24th was marked by unprecedented events, including the looting of the biggest supermarkets. Interestingly it was specifically supermarkets which became the main target of massive looting, along with the destruction and burning of some of the buildings.

The massive upheaval challenged people's minds and was food for gossip and various assumptions on political issues, the looting and their organisers.

Before starting my fieldwork, I had already been exposed to these talks through virtual forums and news on the Internet. Talks, reflections, and assumptions seemed to get tossed around from one extreme to the other. Some assumed that the looting was organised by the oppositional forces, while others claimed that it was Akaev's initiative in order to create bad publicity for the opposition. The looting made me look at the economic institution of supermarkets from another angle – their politicised essence.

This paper focuses on the discourses surrounding new shopping places in Bishkek. On the one hand, according to liberals and government officials, supermarkets represent the height of freedom, civilization and choice (Fleetwood, 2005). On the other side of the discourse are scholars, who argue that the 'fascination with consumption reinforces social inequalities and encourages social disappointment with political changes' (Zentai ND, 2). The empirical findings of my research exposed similar contentious debates regarding Bishkek supermarkets: 1) that they brought civilisation and modernisation into the infrastructure of the city, but 2) that they reveal growing social inequality. Supermarkets were depicted as advantageous and beneficial by mass media sources, politicians and later by Bishkek inhabitants. Along with their civilising mission, Bishkek supermarkets turned out to symbolise social inequality and also demonstrated to the general, poorer public that they are excluded from the circles of more affluent citizens through their shopping experiences. Bishkek supermarkets are indeed extensively politicised in nature; i.e. most of them are largely monopolised by the clique of politicians. And the economic success of politicians involved in the institutionalisation of supermarkets has provoked contentious public debate. The massive looting of supermarkets in the aftermath of the political upheaval in Bishkek in March 2005 became evidence of a widespread negative public perception of supermarkets. These incidents suggest that new economic institutions in the post-socialist world provoke fierce political disputes.

The fieldwork for this paper was conducted in April 2005, two weeks after the political upheaval and massive looting. The research was based on qualitative methods and included the collection of newspaper articles (1990–2005) and in-depth interviews with ten respondents.

Establishment of Supermarkets

It is important to clarify what kind of shopping places are considered to be supermarkets in Bishkek. Like the shopping malls discussed by Miller (1998), supermarkets can be distinguished from other kinds of trading places by several characteristics. First of all, supermarkets occupy separate buildings with various sections. Large supermarkets such as Beta, Goin, Dordoi Plaza and Silkway, which this work will discuss the most, are large, three- to four-storey buildings. Bishkek supermarkets represent a curiosity as they resemble Western department stores or malls, due to their division into sections that are rented by autonomous retailers. The supermarkets are owned by local entrepreneurs and are divided into many sections, so that each retailer has multiple roles crossing the whole prolific range of traders as described by Humphrey (as cited in Verdery 1999,7): that of supplier, manager, and seller. Another similarity with malls is that they function not only as shopping places, but also as places of entertainment. Thus, Plaza hosts a cafe and a playground for kids, while Silkway is a venue for billiard rooms, a cinema, and a restaurant. Another trait which Plaza and Silkway share with Western-style malls is in their circuit of ownership. When describing the work of malls in Britain, Miller *et al* claimed that the managerial circuit consisted of three main sets of actors. The first is the owners, usually property companies or institutional investors. The second set of actors is the managers, who are usually acting as agents of the owners. Then, finally there are the retailers leasing space in malls (1998, 42).

All four shopping centres were indeed novelties, as they presented commodities and services never experienced before by Soviet people. Fancy men's and women's clothes, advanced technical equipment, office and home furniture, beauty care products and food of all kinds were all in one place! Soviet shops never had such conveniences as security guards, public bathrooms, cafes and billiard and cinema rooms. These all seemed a wonderland for people who were used to a deficiency of goods and traditional long queues at Soviet shops. Regardless of their similarity to Western-style malls and department stores in their operation, peculiarly these shopping places continue to be called supermarkets by both, owners and Bishkek habitants. Following the general pattern of public reference, I shall use the word 'supermarket' in regard to these novel shopping places.

In line with Zentai's (ND, 3) remark about malls in Budapest, supermarkets in Bishkek became of 'primary importance in public policy agenda.' Thus, the opening ceremonies of supermarkets were usually accompanied by speeches from prominent political figures. The opening of Beta-Stores for instance was honoured by the visits of the well-known Kyrgyz writer and the ambassador of Kyrgyzstan in Belgium, Chingiz Aitmatov along with the President of Kyrgyzstan, Askar Akaev. *Vechernii Bishkek* described this pompous event as follows: 'Aitmatov noted the high significance of the supermarket and said: "Trade has always been an indicator of civilisation. Today we are adopting the new level of civilisation with the help of the owner of Beta-Stores and his faithful commitment to the development of trade in Kyrgyzstan"' (*Vechernii Bishkek* 2000, July 10, 3). While Aitmatov's words seem to be aimed at rationalising the state's cooperation with foreign entrepreneurs, President Akaev's words were too illusory. He called the owner of the supermarket a 'wizard, whose magic is revealed through this supermarket, which resembles a palace' (*Vechernii Bishkek*, 2000, July 10, 3).

The active participation of prominent politicians in the opening ceremonies does not only indicate the primary economic importance that was given to supermarkets. It also shows that supermarkets were not 'without political dimension' (Matejowsky, 2002).

Besides their ownership of most private enterprises, politicians have also become key figures in the whole process of the modernisation of cities. Humphrey's (2002) findings provide a good illustration of the key roles played by political figures in the economic sector. Politicians are involved in the reconstruction of cities through their regulation of market principles. While discussing the development of Moscow as a metropolitan city, Humphrey emphasises the crucial role of state officials in city planning. She describes the role of the city mayor Iurii Luzhkov as having the authority to make decisions on the transformation of the city, where much attention is paid to the development of expensive shops and vast malls. According to Humphrey, 'the showpiece shopping complexes are not banished to the outskirts but consciously constructed to make harmonious ensembles with potent architectural symbols of Russian history in the centre' (Humphrey 2002: 196). In line with Humphrey's observations on Moscow, Kyrgyz politicians became the key figures in the whole process of implementing a market economy – the number one issue in the public policy agenda. Those in power thus monopolised the newly emerging commercial sphere that played a crucial role in developing the country's economy.

The active participation of politicians in the establishment of supermarkets and wide mass media coverage should have played their role in the formation of public's attitude towards these economic institutions. But what are these attitudes? How do Kyrgyzstani citizens view supermarkets? These questions are to be addressed in the following sections.

Supermarkets and Their 'Civilising' Mission

The centre of Bishkek city has been transformed in its appearance in the last several years. The appearance of bigger supermarkets has made a significant contribution to these changes. Walking down the main avenue of Chui, one's eyes will involuntarily be drawn to the several storeys building of Dordoi Plaza shopping centre. The bright colours, big windows and modern façades of the building look attractive in front of greyish blocks of houses that remain from the Soviet era. At the entrance of the building flashy posters advertise the latest movies. The first floor of Dordoi Plaza is occupied by many small boutiques selling Bourgeois, Lancôme, Avon cosmetics, Levi's jeans and glitzy jewellery. Standing on the escalator that leads to the second floor, one can hear children's voices coming from the playground, which is usually packed, since parents from the neighbouring blocks bring their kids regardless of their shopping intentions. Thus, the playground that is meant to keep kids busy while their parents are shopping has in fact become a place of entertainment for young visitors. The second floor hosts many other boutiques with brand clothes, collections of French wine, furs, and coats. There is also a little café, the menu of which mostly includes 'European' cuisine. Music playing in the background and the well-thought-out design of Dordoi Plaza's interior adds to all the pleasures of consumers who decide to satisfy their exigent shopping desires here.

In the aftermath of the political upheaval in March and lootings of supermarkets, forums and chats were flourishing with hot issues. Members were expressing their concerns about looting and the destruction of the buildings, complaining that the city has become more like a 'big village now.' I find parallels between these concerns and Chodak's (1973, 256) idea that 'modernisation is a special, important instance of the development of societies, an instance where conscientious efforts are made to achieve higher chosen standards' (as cited in Sztompka 1993, 132). In one of his interviews former President Akaev blamed marauders for 'killing the motor engine of the capital city's economy through the destruction of small and medium businesses.'[1] This statement demonstrates that supermarkets became the main pillars in the sphere of developing private business that was believed to make the city more 'modern' and 'civilised.'

From my interviews, it is possible to see that the public in Bishkek generally considers supermarkets to be beneficial. According to the respondents, the budget of the government benefits from the supermarkets because of the taxes. The interviewees also recognized the contribution of supermarkets to the architectural design of the city. As customers, the respondents pointed out some practicalities, such as clean, comfortable and safe environments that guarantee high quality service, a large variety and control over commodities and the chance to return deficient goods. These were the main criteria upon which they based their judgments. Judgments have perhaps been based on the comparison with local bazaars, which definitely defy all notions of 'civilised consumption.'

The respondents often referred to 'Western standards' and 'the West' while talking about civilisation and modernisation processes. Often, the respondents pointed at specific material objects sold in supermarkets, which in their understanding were 'Western.' Melis, a 42 year-old government employee notes that: 'In the 1980's one of our colleagues travelled to some capitalist country. And guess what he brought to every one of us at work as small gifts – disposable plastic cups! I still remember those red, plastic cups that we perceived as items of luxury. And now, I can buy tons of such disposable cups at any supermarket here!'

Melis's comments are indicative of Fehervary's (2002, 369) discussion of post-socialist Hungarian citizens' perception of Western goods, '[They] became displaced metonyms of another world, as the opposition between the state-socialist system and the capitalist system became embodied in their products.' Gradually, all the products that were novel to Bishkek shoppers came to be associated with the West. The availability of such commodities in local supermarkets was the indicator of Westernisation, i.e. civilisation and modernisation. As Sztompka (1993, 132) states, historical definitions of modernisation are synonymous with Westernisation or Americanisation. As an example he quotes Shmuel Eisenstadt: 'Historically, modernisation is the process of change towards those types of social, economic and political systems that have developed in Western Europe and North America...' (1966, 1 as cited in Sztompka, 1993, 132). Thus, client-oriented supermarkets as products of the market economy and capitalism have been largely accepted as carriers of the modernisation process.

---

1   Source: http://www.gazeta.kg/view.php?i=11515, retrieved April 2, 2005

However, the 'civilising mission' of supermarkets turned out not to be the end of the story. The respondent's appreciation of supermarkets was only one side of the coin. Bishkek supermarkets are a good case for illustrating how new shopping places, when introduced into a post-Soviet milieu, may raise contentious debates. I further suggest that the contentious nature of supermarkets has been largely influenced by their politicisation. My findings show that the association of supermarkets with the wealthy West and civilisation has other associations, such as social inequality.

Western Splendour in the Middle of Glaring Poverty

It turns out that only a small percentage of the population can enjoy the fruits of capitalism represented by 'civilised' and 'modern' supermarkets. Despite the general consensus among the respondents about the advantages of supermarkets, not all of them considered these stores to be within reach. The results of my interviews show that Bishkek supermarkets still have a long way to go before making the transition from serving luxury, high-end niches to being mass merchandisers. In this way, they become, as Aisulu notes, an 'inducement of a beautiful life.'

According to the National Statistics Committee's data, the average wage of a person in the republic for the year 2005 equalled 2569 soms per month (approximately 62 USD). It should be noted that the average salaries provided by the National Statistics Committee represent the range of wages in governmental organisations. In the business sector, and also in international non-profit organisations workers may earn much more, starting from 100 USD and going up to 1500 USD and more. But the percentage of workers in these sectors is very small, approximately 15% of the population. According to the report of Governmental Committee on Migration and Labour in Kyrgyzstan, in February 2006 there were 101,000 unemployed people registered in the country. At the same time, the average price for a pair of jeans in local supermarkets is 1500 soms (~36 USD), the average price for a pair of shoes is 2000 soms (~48 USD), whereas at the bazaar, a pair of Chinese (considered lower quality and lower status) manufactured jeans is available at the price of 500 soms (~12 USD). While supermarket prices may be affordable for those who earn several hundred dollars per month, for 45.9% (which includes the 13.4% who live under the line of poverty) of the population, such shoes and jeans can only remain an unreachable dream.

As Zentai (ND, 18) claimed in reference to Budapest malls, these new shopping places 'actually generate and reinforce social inequalities, many times dividing society into the binary haves and have-nots.' Bishkek supermarkets, similar to Budapest malls, cause the bifurcation of consumers. The continued unaffordability of commodities in supermarkets is doubly negative due to the display of inaccessible things to the poor. Surely, increasing social inequality is not a direct cause of mushrooming supermarkets. However, I believe that supermarkets do explicate and demonstrate what is unreachable by many. Such a situation fuels contentious discourses around these economic institutions. In post-Soviet Bishkek it was impossible to avoid contentious debates, in which 'Western splendour' and 'Western glamour'[2] increasingly confronted the poor with their glitzy appearances in the middle of glaring poverty.

Furthermore, supermarkets symbolise the unequal distribution of wealth that is generally believed to have developed after the collapse of the Soviet system. While in Soviet times social inequality was present, it was not as apparent as it is in the transition period, when a large portion of society remains in a disadvantaged situation in comparison to a small group of the elite, and is not promised any 'common wealth' as under the Socialist regime. Thus, it should not be surprising to see increasing public discontent with the new regime, which in fact gained power by establishing new economic institutions.

The Politicised Nature of Supermarkets

While discussing the emergence of shopping malls in Budapest, Zentai (ND, 2) claims that 'fascination with consumption reinforces social inequalities and encourages social disappointment with political changes.' Moreover, her claim supports my point that new economic institutions in the post-socialist world provoke large political disputes. Zentai's argument is indeed a good illustration of the contentious political discourses surrounding supermarkets: 'The dream world of consumption frequently turns into a political nightmare: political regimes legitimise themselves through erroneous promises of expanding consumption' (ND, 2). Politicisation here should be understood as the active involvement of political agents in the establishment of supermarkets.

One might wonder how the public receives information about the owners. Local newspapers have always been one of the main sources of getting information about the 'big fish' in the sea of private business. There were many articles, which provided evidence of the fact that most supermarkets were owned by local politicians, i.e. by the elite: 'One of the first supermarkets in Bishkek, "Eridan", which was opened by the deputy of the legislative assembly Usenov, was sold to his colleague Baibolov' (Vechernii Bishkek, 1999, January 5). And: 'Many people know Erkin Muratov, the former leader of the communist party of Kyrgyzstan, who further continued his career as the governor of Issyk-Kul region in the republic. The last year he stopped his work in the state, and became an entrepreneur and succeeded in founding a new trading complex. The owner claims that he was able to build this huge shopping place with the help of loans, which he is going to pay back in seven years' (Vechernii Bishkek, August 16th, 1999).

---

2   Thse expressions were borrowed from the interviewees.

When asked whether they know the owners of any particular supermarket, respondents showed their extensive 'knowledge' on this matter. Thus, Tatiana listed the names of supermarket owners: 'Well, I know that Plaza belongs to Salymbekov. He somehow managed to accumulate the capital for the construction of such a huge building. The chain of '*Narodnyï*' supermarkets belongs to Akaev, as does Silkway.' In addition, the owners themselves, from the very beginning of the establishment of supermarkets, did not seem to try to keep their businesses a secret. Furthermore, the small size of the city and its relatively small population with extensive kinship and friendship ties affect the immediate spread of such news. One might constantly hear people talking about the owner of a newly opened dance club or a casino. Thus, supermarkets send an explicit message about who the proprietors and beneficiaries are. Ironically, the owners of supermarkets are often negatively viewed by the public, even though they are the founders of economic institutions that are claimed to bring civilisation and modernity.

Interestingly, though the looting was widely acknowledged among local habitants to be a shocking, immoral, and unexpected event, few felt sorrow for the owners. I believe that public indifference to the owners' loss from the looting has been influenced by a durable discontent with the political regime, with the politicians, and their unrestrained intervention in private business. The respondents shared the idea that it is impossible to be involved in big private business without being a politician or at least having connections. As Melis noted, 'Of course, there are entrepreneurs who earned their money by hard work in commerce. But most of them do have access to the officials anyway.' Mariya comments that, 'a big business has to involve both big money and useful ties.' Kamilla further remarks: 'In Russian, there is such a word as *krysha* [literally translated as a 'roof', here meaning useful connections], so you gotta have a *krysha* if you want to rent a building in a better part of the city. For instance Salymbekov, the owner of Plaza, he had a lot of money and also good connections.'

The case of Bishkek supermarkets is indeed a good illustration of Eyal *et al* (1998) theory on newly created capitalisms in transitional countries. Supermarkets seem to exemplify his claim that former and new politicians are actively involved in building private businesses. As Szelenyi argued, a small group of politicians which possesses high social capital is in an advantageous situation: their social capital[3] enables them to become beneficiaries of unfair privatisation.

According to Borocz (2000, 351), in the early nineties, former state-socialist managers' informal social networks with the state authorities became 'such a crucial feature of the transformation' that the structure of their informal ties has determined the organisation of most economic institutions. Informality within the state system

---

3   That is, in this case, their social networks and ties.

in Kyrgyzstan could probably be identified as a 'bourgeois order' in Borocz's terms, where an 'essentially malign form of informality plagued the highest levels of government and big business' (2000, 348–349). The Kyrgyz state corresponds to Borocz's thesis: it is often described as over-corrupt, and people are not surprised when another supermarket is opened by a local politician or another public building is sold into the private hands of a deputy's relatives. Newly emerging entrepreneurs who opened a supermarket in Bishkek were mostly state officials, who possess prestige and profitable social connections. State officials can start businesses because they reconvert their social capital into economic capital. In this case, power is money.

As Szelenyi claims 'the main beneficiaries of market transition are the "direct producers" and a class of new entrepreneurs is emerging from among them' (1995, 3). Former communists and party leaders benefit from the market economy and the majority of the owners of today's companies had been involved in politics or had informal connections with politicians before and after the fall of socialism: 'On the highest levels of economic management there was substantial change in personnel – but most of the current key players of the economy were already in some decision making positions before the fall of communism' (Szelenyi 1995, 5).

Szelenyi claims that post-communist society can be best described as a unique social structure within which social capital is the main source of power, prestige, and privilege. He argues that the 'possession of economic capital places actors only in the middle of the social hierarchy, and the conversion of former social capital into private wealth is more the exception than the rule' (1998, 6). Thus, most of the newly opened supermarkets were owned by local entrepreneurs, namely by the 'elite,' people who either formerly worked in the state, or are currently working as deputies, ministers, etc. They privatise formerly state-owned buildings, purchase lands closer to the town centre and get long-term loans without interest rates. It is their informal ties that enable them to maximise profits.

Drawing from the results of the interviews, it can be seen that there is general agreement that the owners of supermarkets are either politicians, or those who have political connections and personal ties. Thus, supermarkets are viewed as the products of an unfair and corrupt political regime, and often seen with resentment. The exhibition of the beautiful life of the rich with physical objects, not surprisingly, provokes public anger and dissatisfaction with the political regime, which is seen as being responsible for growing social inequality.

Bishkek supermarkets suggest that in countries in transition that are characterised by their high social inequality and low living standards, the commercial sphere becomes a tool of enrichment for the upper niche. For this reason, supermarkets became an embodiment of the prosperity of the state officials, their unrestrained authority and power, unequal access to capital goods, and property, of which the political cliques turned out to be the large proprietors.

Conclusion

This study explored contentious discourses surrounding supermarkets that were viewed to be both carriers of modernisation and civilisation and at the same time an embodiment of social inequality. While conducting the fieldwork, and more generally from the very beginning of the establishment of supermarkets, I observed a general acceptance of these new shopping places. The respondents agreed that they are proud of having such modern buildings, which decorate the city and boost its image in the eyes of local dwellers and foreigners. These convenient facilities with all kinds of services have never been experienced by the local consumers in Soviet shops. Thus, not surprisingly, all of the respondents, regardless of their economic status and the regularity of their supermarket shopping, expressed their appreciation of the 'civilising mission' of supermarkets.

Despite the general appreciation of supermarkets, most of the respondents agreed that these are not conventional places to shop, but are rather representations of unreachable wealth, luxury, and a beautiful life. Those who shop at bazaars do not choose them out of mere preference, but rather out of economic necessity. The political symbolism of supermarkets lends a bitter flavour to people's perceptions of this economic institution. Bishkek supermarkets turned out to symbolise social inequality, and demonstrate to the general, poorer public that they are separated out from more affluent citizens through their shopping experiences. While supermarkets do not exactly cut the society in two, they still serve as a front between the relatively affluent group and the rest. I say front, because it is in supermarkets that the interests, abilities, and social status of the poor and the wealthy clash.

References

Bodnar, J. (2001), *Fin De Millenaire Budapest* (Minneapolis: University of Minnesota Press)

Borocz, J. (2000) 'Informality Rules', *East European Politics and Societies* 14:2, 348–380

Burawoy, M. and Verdery, K. (1999), *Uncertain Transition: Ethnographies of Change in the Postsocialist World* (United States of America: Rowman & Littlefield Publishers, Inc)

Eyal, G., Szeleniy, I. and Townsley E. (1998), *Making Capitalism without Capitalists: Class Formation and Elite Struggles in Post-Communist Central Europe* (London: Verso)

Fehervary, K. (2002), 'American Kitchens, Luxury Bathrooms, and the Search for a "Normal" Life' *Ethnos* 67:3, 369–400

Humphrey, C. (2002), *The Unmaking of Soviet Life: Everyday Economies After Socialism* (Ithaca: Cornell University Press)

Hannerz, U. (1996), *Transnational Connections: Culture, People, Places* (New York: Routledge)

Mandel, R. and Humphrey, C. (ed.) (2002), *Markets and Moralities: Ethnographies of Postsocialism* (Oxford, United Kingdom: Berg)

Matejowsky, T. (2002), Globalization, Privatization, and Public Space in the Provincial Philippines. *Economic Development: An Anthropological Approach.* Cohen, Jeffrey and Dannhaeuser (ed), USA: AltaMaria Press.

Miller, D. et al. (1998), *Shopping Place and Identity* (New York: Routledge)

Miller, D. (ed.) (2001), *Consumption: Critical Concepts in the Social Sciences* (London: Routledge)

National Statistics Committee (2006), 'Zanyatost' i bezrabotitsa: itogi integrirovaniya. Obsledovaniya domashnikh khozyaistv', *Godovoi Otchet po Social'no-Ékonomicheskim Voprosam* (Bishkek: Redaktsionno-izdatel'skiĭ otdel)

Pine, F. (2002), 'From Production to Consumption in Post-Socialism?' in Mandel, R. and Humphrey, C. (2002), *Markets and Moralities: Ethnographies of Postsocialism* (Oxford: Berg)

Szeleniy, I. (1995), 'The Rise of Managerialism: The 'New Class' after the fall of communism' in *Discussion paper for the Collegium* (Budapest: Institute for Advanced Study)

Sztompka, P. (1993), *The Sociology of Social Change* (Oxfordshire: Marston Lindsay Ross International)

Zentai, V. (Forthcoming), 'Encircling Cities and Encapsulating Fantasies: Social Debates on Shopping Mall Culture in Hungary' in Unpublished Manuscript

Newspaper articles

Anikin, A. (1999) 'Bez pomyvki ne vkhodit', *Vecherniĭ Bishkek* August 16

Benliyan, A.(1999) 'Dorogo i serdito', *Vecherniĭ Bishkek* May 17

Kuzmin, G. (1999) 'TSUM poluchil po zaslugam', *Vecherniĭ Bishkek* January 21

No author. 'Mnogoobeshayushee nazvanie 'supermarket' ne vsem po plechu', *AKIpress* [website],   <http://kg.akipress.org/_ru_arc.php?&find=супермаркет&page=1>, (published online 3 May 2000)

No author. (1999), 'Nardep Nardepu', *Vecherniĭ Bishkek* January 5

No author. (1998) 'Politékonomist goda', *AKIpress* June 18

Sorokina, Z. (1997) 'TSUM kak barometr torgovli', *Vecherniĭ Bishkek* November 28

Tuzov, A. (2000) 'Put' v Narodnyĭ supermarket', *Vecherniĭ Bishkek* July 10

E. Carina H. Keskitalo

Vulnerability in Forestry, Fishing and Reindeer Herding Systems in Northern Europe and Russia

Introduction: Understanding Change and Societies in Flux

'Change' and 'flux' are two of the concepts that best describe contemporary society and the environment. In the last generation, large structural transformations have taken place: Communism has fallen, market capitalism and democracy have spread and economies and corporations have internationalised. States have lost some of their sovereignty over economic and political changes to private actors and international organisations. However, there presently exists little work describing the specificity of change with the detail required for understanding how people conceive of their own situations, vulnerability and capacity to adapt to change. Globalisation – generally seen as the intensification, deepening and broadening of international ties and increased consciousness of the world as a whole (Keohane and Nye, 2000) – is interpreted and acted upon differently by people subjected to different economic, political or environmental factors, and they act on these depending on their local conditions. Changes and trends thus take effect not only through large, abstract driving mechanisms, but within local and regional contexts, decision-making processes and economies.

This work describes change through the eyes of local people as its point of departure. It utilises the concept of vulnerability, regularly used in the context of global environmental change, to describe the perceived vulnerability in natural resource use sectors in northern Europe and north-western Russia – areas which have been affected differently by the changes over the last generation. In northern Europe, which is largely primary production-oriented, low populated areas have become increasingly more focused on service production (such as tourism), as the numbers employed in industry have decreased with technological advances and rationalisation. Subsequently, migration from these areas towards employment in urban regions has increased. In Russia, the last 20 years have seen dramatic changes, including system changes from which the Russian population and economy have only started to recover in the last few years. The change from the Soviet system has entailed a devolution and subsequent partial retrieval of regional power, a severely limited support system for rural localities and a concentration of resource ownership among the wealthy elite (Hønneland, 2003).

As cases, the study views the renewable resource sectors of forestry, fishing and (mainly indigenous) reindeer herding. The study thereby takes its examples from areas and sectors where the impacts of change are especially clear and observable. Specific case study areas for each of the three sectors were chosen on the basis of their importance for the selected sectors (and, where possible, to also illustrate any interlinkage between sectors). Forestry is studied in northern Sweden, Finland and north-western Russia; fishing in northern Norway and north-western Russia; and reindeer herding in northern Norway, Sweden and Finland. Starting from several local level case studies and an open inquiry into the changes and actors of change as these are perceived among local people, the study includes a perspective on the processes not only on the local but also on the regional, national and international levels impacting the case study area. This was accomplished by asking the local respondents which actors, agencies or groups impact them and their daily work. Effects on the local level were thus found to result from various scale levels, including regional implementation, national regulation, the impact of international companies and international trade and even international norms and conventions that impact local practices and determine access and rights to resources. The study thereby shows the interlinkage of the local with the global while demonstrating that viable adaptation can only seldom be developed solely on the local level, as decision-making power often lies with the state or other bodies, shifting and in some cases removing the possibility for local communities to assure the continuation of their communities and livelihoods.

Theory and Methodology

Vulnerability as a concept has largely been used in global environmental change discourse and literature on risk. It has been broadly defined as the 'capacity to be wounded,' a measure of the sensitivity of systems to exposure to change and the extent to which this is decreased by the inability to adapt. The focus in this article will be placed on social vulnerability and how this contributes to an understanding of 'what amplifies or mitigates the impact of ... change' and 'channels it towards certain groups, institutions, and places' (Downing, 1991, 380, quoted in Rayner, S. and E. L. Malone, 1998, 240). Self-definition and prioritisation of risk comprise a large part of what transforms a situation into a vulnerable situation: The definition by the actors themselves of what they perceive as risks or threats determines what they may act upon. Vulnerability is seen as limited by the *adaptive capacity* within the systems to ameliorate change, which is largely determined by the resources available in the living situation as a whole. Adaptive capacity may thus be seen as the potential for adaptation overall, within which particular adaptations (potential or ongoing, actual adaptations) may take place (Keskitalo, 2004).

The focus in this work is on the definition of vulnerabilities, adaptive capacity and adaptations by the local stakeholders themselves; stakeholders are defined here as the groups with investment and direct interest in resource use and management within a specific sector and area. The study was mainly undertaken through semi-structured qualitative interviews utilising mainly open-ended questions to stakeholders about their situation, perceived trends of change, problems and possibilities, and ways to adapt to change. About 80 interviews in total (around 20 per case study area/country) were conducted in the areas with stakeholders within the different branches of the sectors over 2003–2005. Interviewees for the study were selected from the targeted sectors (including both practitioners and administrators) and formal decision-making bodies. An effort was made to select individuals who have worked within the sectors for a long time, who are thus able to describe changes over time. In addition, a total of eight stakeholder meetings or focus group interviews – comprising previous interviewees as well as additional stakeholders in the targeted stakeholder groups – were held in selected areas, mainly to provide feedback on and corroborate the interview results.

In order to structure the description of the local narratives of change and place them in an explanatory framework, a conceptual framework for organising actors' narratives was developed. It compares the changes described by the actors with those described for economic and political globalisation and outlines the decision-making (governance) networks and norms through which any changes take effect. The economic dimension of globalisation is taken here to refer to the process of change from a national to a global scale of integration of production and trade. In this study, the crucial factors to be assessed for *economic globalisation* include the internationalisation of production/trade networks in both multinational companies (MNCs) and small- and medium-sized enterprises (SMEs) and how these international networks and demands lead to a shift in the level to which the location of production is relevant, or the de-coupling of trade networks from the local level. Changes may be expected through social and economic effects in terms of place-based employment, and an important question is which possibilities for adaptation exist within the economic and socio-political structure (Scruggs and Lange, 2002).

Political globalisation, as the second aspect of globalisation to be investigated here, can be conceived of as an internationalisation and deepening of global political processes, making it relevant to assess the degree to which a local organisation is impacted in its degree of political decision-making, power and employment by actors outside the locality. At this juncture it is also germane to assess the existing network and organisation of local and other actors through which any adaptation may be effected. The concept of *governance* is employed to focus on the multi-level and multi-actor character of decision-making and to better define the political context of change. Governance is understood here as the decision-making network including (but broader than) governmental and economic as well as political components – i.e. decision-making undertaken in companies as well as in government. The definition of the network of governance will be based on the perceptions among local and regional actors of *which actors and mechanisms* influence their capacity to act and *on what levels*. The degree to which this network consists of international, national, regional and local actors, or by administrative-political, private, or interest group actors is also taken into consideration. These governance networks are seen to differing extents as being organised around norms that structure decision-making in governance, such as the environmental and indigenous peoples' rights norms that local actors see as impacting the regulatory framework under which they act (Held and McGrew, 2002).

The following sections will summarise the relationship of forestry, reindeer herding and fishing, respectively to the factors described above, indicating the vulnerability and adaptive capacity for each sector to change. The final section of the paper will describe the summary vulnerability and adaptive capacity of the areas with regard to the investigated sectors.

Changes in Forestry in Northern Sweden, Finland and North-Western Russia

In the areas of northern Sweden, Finland and north-western Russia, forestry units exist that are among the largest in their respective countries. A substantial small-scale forestry industry also exists, consisting of smaller sawmills, timber transport and some refinement industry (including house-building companies). Among the interviewees, forestry situation is generally perceived as one of increasing economic internationalisation and growing demands upon forestry, which largely correlates with the impacts described in globalisation literature. This is manifested in companies moving (or threatening to move) if conditions are not sufficient. The local situation, especially in northern Sweden and Finland, is seen as being threatened by the outside forces of imports and cheaper labour, and forestry, generally no longer being municipality-bound, is moving out of the community (and taking employment with it). There are also higher demands upon larger-scale entrepreneurs (who have taken the place of permanently employed personnel) for efficiency and the nature of the business is viewed as increasingly time-oriented. There is also a large flow of imports from Russia to Finland, with a growing focus on the conditions for timber production. Local actors are also becoming increasingly aware of the different growing conditions of forests in other countries as well as the need for continuous re-investment and the importance of developing export networks in order to improve competitiveness.

Regarding changes and capacity in political organisations and with respect to political globalisation, the legislative and organisational environment provides certain avenues for dealing with the changes, including some strategies to cushion the transition. However, according to the interviewees, there are relatively limited mechanisms of support in place for forestry at the local and regional levels. Forestry sees itself as impacted mainly by economic and political actors and frameworks: the EU, state administration and national legislation, state support organisations, state and non-state environmental protection agencies, environmental protection organisations, international timber buyers (such as SCA and Stora Enso), not to mention the international market, forest certification processes, state loan institutes, banks and general opinion. However, co-operation and interaction between local and regional actors, which could theoretically support the development of localised governance to protect resource use at the local level, is relatively limited. Interviewees perceive interaction with forestry administrators (possibly beyond forest use planning) to be both vertically and horizontally restricted. They also feel limited in their capacity to impact their own employment in globalising companies, and in north-western Russia, many interviewees see themselves as constrained in their capacity to at all impact their conditions of employment.

Additionally, interviewees in Sweden and Finland emphasise that external actors to a large degree unite around external norms. This especially regards the demands for increased environmental protection, which are manifested in increased environmental awareness and the inclusion of environmental goals in forestry (including state forestry) bodies, in mounting market demands for environmentally-friendly production of wood and in more areas set aside for environmental protection (the latter stemming both from EU demands and domestic pressure). Local interviewees, primarily concerned about timber production and economic demands, perceive that some of the external environmental demands have not been adjusted to northern areas. For instance, regarding forest certification – a market-driven environmental initiative whereby environmental and social requirements on forestry need to be fulfilled in order to obtain the right to label wood products as certified – FSC (Forest Stewardship Council) certification in Sweden is particularly criticised. FSC is seen, to some extent, as duplicating and expanding the demands advanced in state environmental protection legislation. FSC certification is also developing in export-oriented forestry in north-western Russia; however, here FSC is perceived less as a threat and more as a possibility to improve the social responsibility of companies, even if interviewees are concerned that environmental concerns may limit logging outtake and thereby employment. Considerable differences can thus be seen here between the perceptions of the various certification programmes. PEFC (Programme for the Endorsement of Forest Certification), a somewhat less demanding standard often advocated by industry and dominating in Finland, provoked far less discussion by interviewees, mentioned only by a few actors.

On balance, local forestry networks have little decision-making capacity as well as very limited adaptive potential for responding to challenges on the local level without feedback from or integration with other levels (much of which does not exist today). Globalisation or trends similar to it can be seen as increasing local vulnerability as well as resulting in a de-coupling from the local level.

Changes in Reindeer Herding in Norway, Sweden and Finland

Reindeer herding is a small industry that competes with the financially much stronger forest industry and other sectors over forest resources. Reindeer herders also compete with meat producers from other countries, the sale of reindeer meat is their chief source of income. The reindeer herding sector constitutes only a fraction of the workforce in these areas, contributing relatively little to regional employment, which means that the sector is not able to advance arguments on the importance of the sector for regional employment similar to those of the forestry industry. As an occupation with long traditional standing and one particularly connected to the Saami (indigenous) identity existing predominantly in northern Norway, Sweden and Finland – the areas under discussion here – reindeer herding is often viewed as having special significance (even if only a minority of Saami are today dependent on reindeer herding). Herding is a nearly exclusive right for the Saami in Norway and Sweden, but can be performed by all citizens in Finland. However, there are concession areas in both Sweden and Norway where reindeer herding can be practised by non-Saami.

Reindeer herding practices have changed significantly over the last generation or some 20–30 years. To some extent, this is a reflection of the aging population in the areas, as well as of the increasing market pressures and competition from other sectors and of technological advances. The environment for reindeer herding has been shrinking through diminishing pastures and increases in other activities on pastures, increased mechanisation, stabilised meat production and increased costs for the livelihood. Reindeer herding today exists within a complex where grazing resource limitations, increased economic efficiency requirements and technological possibilities make for economic adaptation towards larger-scale reindeer herding, sometimes with an increased focus on the supplementary feeding of the reindeer to increase meat yield. The issue of economic profitability and a functioning meat market is emphasised here as the main problem in all three areas. A recent fall in meat prices, for instance, was thought to be caused by multiple factors, including changes in the import-export situation between countries, a lower consumer demand for reindeer meat products and competition with other game meat (such as New Zealand deer). Through these demands, especially regarding profitability and competitiveness on the international market, economic globalisation is evidenced in the areas.

The decision-making network for reindeer herding is limited due to competing land uses and consists mainly of limited numbers of reindeer herders, governmental administrators from various levels and restricted numbers of meat buyers and refiners (sometimes seen as constituting a monopoly buyer situation). While reindeer herders may be organised regionally, they have relatively little power and may conflict over grazing grounds or reindeer numbers. Currently, however, conditions for reindeer herding have been largely impacted by ILO Convention No. 169, an international convention concerning the right of indigenous peoples to land and water, to which Norway was the first ratifying party in 1990. At present, the Convention is being considered for ratification in Sweden and Finland, due to some extent to the pressure exerted on these countries by the UN and the EU. Resultantly, the ILO convention and its possible impact on the areas are widely discussed by interviewees, especially in the Swedish case study area, where the Convention has been used as an argumentative base from which to demand expanded rights for reindeer herders, which is a cause for some concern, especially in forestry. Beyond the ILO, there also exist other international developments that may impact the reindeer herding-forestry relationship. The revision of the FSC forest certification may also add features that support reindeer herding.

On the whole, reindeer herding is a relatively small sector, impacted in its land use by many larger sectors and having few strong or well-developed production interest chains of its own. It is also impacted from many levels, predominantly by national state regulations and support. While requirements on reindeer herding are increasing, however, there is a thinning of the reindeer herding structure itself taking place, with fewer active reindeer herders and larger technological reliance, limiting its ability to organise and influence development.

Changes in Fishing in Northern Norway and North-Western Russia

Fishing has historically been one of the basic economic activities at the Barents Sea coast. Fishing is the second biggest national export industry after oil in Norway, constituting 5–10% (when fish farming is included) and a major industry in northernmost Russia. The fish resources in the Barents Sea have, however, shown large variations during the last decades, often as a result of a combination of overfishing and environmental conditions that affect the fish food chain and other conditions for the fish. When fish populations fluctuate due either to natural causes or overfishing, the communities along the coast who are dependent on stable income are directly affected. In these areas, fishing has seen large changes, especially since the institutionalisation of the quota system, limiting the access to fishing as an occupation. The preferred fish processing system for the market has also changed, with a major restructuring of the northern economies as a result. The areas, especially northern Norway, traditionally signified by relatively small-scale fishing and combination sustenance, are consequently evolving towards more large-scale practices and a rationalisation of fishing. Russian market interactions concerning fishing have increased during this period, with much fish from Russian trawlers being landed in northern Norway and fish refinement (such as filet production) moving to Russia from northern Norway on account of the lower employment costs there. Factors of economic globalisation can thus be rather clearly discerned in the areas over time, with fishing moving towards larger international competition, much of it being undertaken by larger companies who can afford to pay for quotas, and refinement largely becoming de-coupled from the immediate area where the fish is caught, with large implications for the coastal populations in both countries. In a situation where fish quantities are limited by quota allocation, many efforts are being made by individual fishermen (especially in Norway) to add value through new types of refinement, to earn a higher income per unit catch to increase profits and to engage in fish farming where conditions and access to fish can be controlled. The situation reflects upon the relatively large integration of fisheries in the global market, with global fish production and price competition resulting in a relatively high but differential local vulnerability to changes that take place beyond the locality and even the state. In north-western Russia, many small-scale fishers also turn to subsistence lifestyles for supplementing fishing, thereby making for instance multi-use forest resources such as mushrooms and berries – as well as competition over forest resources with forestry – increasingly important.

This situation of ongoing change in the fishing sector is reflected in changes and conflicts on the political and organisational levels, largely concerning the quota distribution system. The political organisation of fishing on different scales, from the local to the international, can be seen as driving different policies, from support for small-scale fishing to a more large-scale fishing policy. In northern Norway and north-western Russia alike, small-scale local fishing is perceived to be disadvantaged by national interests – and fishermen are, e.g. in Norway, standing relatively united against what is regarded as a national policy driven by large-scale trawler interests. In response to this policy, indigenous organisations in particular have advanced arguments on resource rights for northern areas. The Saami Parliament (a Saami-elected advisory body to the state) in Norway thereby argues that the government does not have the right to remove fishing rights that have traditionally belonged to the local northern Norwegian population, a large part of which are Saami.

Such an argument is, however, easier to make in northern Norway, where the Saami are an acknowledged indigenous group and the ILO Convention No. 169 on indigenous peoples' rights to land and water (which some argue should also apply to sea resources) has been signed by the Norwegian government. For the areas under study in north-western Russia, however, no indigenous population has been officially acknowledged. Nonetheless, in support of resources for smaller communities and the rights of the coastal population to fish, many in the Archangelsk region back the movement towards setting up indigenous rights in north-western Russia on the basis of a Pomor identity, which is argued to be indigenous. The granting of indigenous status to the Pomor would result in larger resource rights to the region versus the state, based on Russian national legislation for indigenous peoples.

Generally, interviewees thus see fisheries as regulated to a large extent by state decisions and only somewhat impacted by local (and even regional or regional government) interests. International norms regarding indigenous rights are one of the authorities that interviewees refer to in their aim to secure rights to northern areas.

Conclusion: Vulnerability and Adaptive Capacity in the Sectors

In sum, the study sheds light upon the fact that vulnerability and the adaptive capacity to change are constrained by much of the decision-making regarding local resources undertaken by national or even international actors, including not only elected decision-makers but market actors, with little feedback from the localities on either of these. While no democratic means to influence the market exists, elected decision-makers' systems also have few mechanisms in place for bottom-up feedback (as opposed to mechanisms for the implementation of state regulations at the local level, which exist). As much of the adaptive capacity for the local level thus lies in decision-making at higher levels, it is difficult for local levels to communicate their needs for adaptation.

The adaptation strategies targeted by interviewees reflect this situation. On a general level, the economic adaptations discussed by stakeholders therefore mainly concern individual adaptations, which are often limited or facilitated by access to technology and other infrastructure and communication resources. These individual adaptations could be summarised as:

- Economic diversification, into, e.g., tourism or an increased reliance on subsistence (the latter in north-western Russia)
- Concentration on the most profitable practices (a trend contrary to that of individual diversification)
- Attempts to increase resource access
- Increased marketing and market orientation of production
- Increased control over dependence on natural conditions: increased de-linking of the system from natural conditions, such as in the case of supplementary feeding of reindeer and the increase in fish farming.

Political adaptations are restricted by the limited local support network, minimal possibilities for influence and low interconnectedness. Political adaptations would, however, include:

- Societal differentiation in employment, such as employment through state localisation of services in the area
- State subsidies and financing of investment: e.g. through state loan institutes
- Increased local/regional organisation: the development of organisation and support networks for increased influence, e.g. to exert control over external factors such as environmental protection measures. This may include the development of a leadership culture and capacitate the local level – although limited by restrained interconnections
- National-level changes in regulation, such as indigenous policy or the recognition of indigenous peoples, or the de-localisation of management to lower levels of government or co-operation bodies.

On balance, the sectors in the diverse countries viewed are strongly impacted by external changes – often seen by interviewees as difficult or impossible to counteract – and by a limited interconnectedness between levels and means to communicate local concerns. The sectors therefore evidence limited democratic possibilities to affect development. The governance network demonstrates a considerable spread across levels, mainly led from national or international scales of decision-making. International norms may have some positive implications for the areas – such as for the Saami in the case of the ILO – but may also be conceived of as external, misconstruing factors that limit local agency.

References

Held, D. and A. McGrew (2002) 'Introduction' in: Held, D. and A. McGrew (eds): *Governing Globalization. Power, Authority and Global Governance.* (Cambridge, UK: Polity Press).

Hønneland, G. (2003) *Russia and the West. Environmental co-operation and conflict.* (London: Routledge).

Keohane, R. O. and J. S. Nye., Jr. (2000) 'Governance in a Globalizing World', in: J. S. Nye and J. D. Donahue (eds): *Governance in a Globalizing World.* (Washington: Brookings Institution Press).

Keskitalo, E. C. H. (2004) 'A Framework For Multi-Level Stakeholder Studies In Response To Global Change'. *Local Environment,* 2004 (Vol. 9), No. 5, pp. 425–435.

Rayner, S. and E. L. Malone (1998, eds) *Human choice and climate change. Volume three: The tools for policy analysis.* (Columbus Ohio: Battelle Press).

Scruggs, L. and P. Lange (2002) 'Where Have All the Members Gone? Globalization, Institutions, and Union Density'. *The Journal of Politics,* 2002 (Vol. 64), No. 1, pp. 126–153.

Anastasiya Ryabchuk

Nostalgia and Solidarity. Social Suffering in Post-Communist Societies

The Present, the Past and the Ridiculing of Nostalgia

> Discourses of 'transition' in east central Europe in some ways echo the 'end of work' de-
> bates: the focus on endings, the erasure of past practices and the ridiculing of nostalgia
> (Stenning, 2005a, 236)

After the break-up of the Soviet Union in 1991, Western conservative commentators, such as Fukuyama, Duignan and Gann, wrote of the victory of liberal democracy over communism (Hefferman, 1998, 225) and little was heard from the region apart from success stories of capitalism (Stennning 2005b, 978). However, by the mid-nineties, 'the negative social costs of transition became more visible and a more pessimistic reading saw it not as a positive triumph of liberal democracy, but rather as a nega-tive rejection of an unworkable and inefficient ideology' (Hefferman, 1998, 227). As Watson (2000, 200) argued, 'the abstractions of 'civil society' and 'freedom', the ac-companying ideas of 'empowerment' and 'control', were at odds with the concrete situations of increasing stress and loss of control that many post-communist citizens see themselves in'.

Many people began to perceive the negative consequences not as temporary – on the way to creating a new economic system, but as an element of this new sys-tem itself. Ramet (1991, 53) spoke of these people as 'betrayed by the revolution' and showed how such feelings of 'betrayal' appear after the lapse of a certain period of time – 'long enough to convince the discontented that the system has failed to live up to its promises'. As Watson (2000, 186) puts it:

> The transition to democracy in Eastern Europe has not at all conformed to expectations,
> East or West. For one thing, whatever the gains, democratisation has not been experi-
> enced as an unequivocal improvement of what went before. In a number of ways, the
> changes have brought about disappointment – even hopelessness – to many women
> and men living in new democracies.

She goes on to list some of the 'most obvious aspects of the downturn of transition': premature mortality (especially among men in the former USSR), unemployment, civil strife, rising crime rates and prostitution. Manning (1995, 201) also noted the growth of classical social problems during transition, such as infectious disease, alcoholism, prostitution and higher crime rates, and death rates exceeding birth rates. High levels of social suffering and dissatisfaction, revealed in social surveys, can therefore be explained by the gap between hopeful expectations of transition and its real negative consequences that the majority of population experienced.

The rise of nostalgia for the communist past was of great concern to both neo-liberal and neo-conservative politicians and social scientists, who viewed Eastern Europe and the former Soviet Union as a *tabula rasa* where a new society could easily be built. They ridiculed nostalgia for the communist past and presented it as dysfunctional for society. They viewed the return of the past system as impossible and focused 'on erasing and ignoring the institutions, practices and geographies of socialism, which were deemed to have failed, and building a new social, economic and political system 'from scratch' (Stenning 2005a, 236).

In this paper I will take a critical stance towards the dominant discourses of 'transitology' that view nostalgia as dysfunctional and as preventing people from adequately evaluating their present and from bringing any kind of change and development. I will try to analyse the meaning of nostalgia in expressing social suffering and in serving as a source of solidarity for those who feel dissatisfied with their current situation. Unlike the more individualistic expression of suffering based on distinctions ('I deserve to have a higher position than the manual workers, because I am better educated' or 'my work is more important and more difficult, therefore I should be making more money'), expression of suffering through nostalgia is based on a very inclusive, collective 'us' ('Everyone is going through the same difficulties' or 'We all felt more secure back then'):

> …the angry understood the meaning of us in a very inclusive way. Those who were targeted as 'them' were seen as a small 'economic other' (capitalists in the West, the communist bureaucracy known as 'nomenklatura' in the East) whose downfall would finally make possible real participation of all citizens (Ost, 2005, 1).

As part of my research on the social suffering of public sector workers in post-communist Ukraine, I carried out sixteen in-depth interviews, asking respondents to describe their present situation and the difficulties they are facing. I also asked them to explain where they think their social suffering comes from[1]. My findings show the major concerns of this social category: growing poverty due to under financing of the public sector, risk of unemployment due to the state abandoning a number of its previous social commitments, widening inequalities and increasing differentiation of incomes and assets, and feelings of instability, insecurity and of 'being at the receiving end of transition'. My respondents, like many other citizens, expressed some 'nostalgic' feelings for the communist past. However, as I will argue in this paper, their

---

1   In this essay I will indicate the community that each respondent came from in brackets after the interview extract. K stands for Kyiv – the capital of Ukraine, B for Baryshivka – a small town, 70 km South-East of Kyiv, and S for a small village in Sumy region, North-Eastern Ukraine. All names have been changed. Brief information about each respondent's gender (m-male, f-female), age and occupation is provided the first time that he/she is quoted.

nostalgia highlights their present suffering and expresses their hopes and concerns for the future rather than a desire to return to the past.

Those Who Have 'Failed to Adapt'

The overwhelming bulk of poor in Russia live in poverty not because they, like their fellow sufferers in Latin America or Asia, were born in poverty, not even because they failed to 'adapt themselves' to the new market conditions. They have adjusted quite successfully... In fact, they would have long since been, not poor, but dead, if not for the swift rise of the culture of survival and the resourcefulness, diligence, and solidarity they displayed. No, they are poor for a different reason. The contemporary Russian poor man is not he, who through his own or somebody else's fault, failed to become well-to-do, but he who has been deprived of everything (Kagarlitsky, 2005)

My interviews and statistics both show that the majority of public sector workers are poor (receiving salaries lower than average), feel poor and describe themselves as poor, and that this poverty causes social suffering and dissatisfaction. According to the State Statistics Committee of Ukraine, workers in the fields of education, health care and social protection have the lowest average salaries after agricultural workers, compared to other sectors of the economy (Hrek and Yukhnovskyj 2005). According to the World Bank (2005), work in the public sector during transition was less rewarding than work in the private sector, not only because salaries were lower, but also because work in the private sector offered more opportunities for upward mobility. Risk of long-term unemployment was also much higher (since jobs were created mainly in the private sector and destroyed in the public one). Furthermore, higher levels of education did not guarantee better pay, and in fact, in Ukraine there has been an increasing demand for low-skilled manual labour.

In these conditions, my respondents felt that it was getting more and more difficult to sustain an adequate level of life, both in absolute terms (since their salaries were not enough to buy even the most necessary goods) and in terms of relative deprivation:

Life is so difficult nowadays. Salaries are so low and prices are so high. It is very stressful having to think about what to buy, whether we have enough money or not. We're thinking of whether to buy some meat, or a pair of shoes for our son's physical education classes. So either we don't have any meat for a month, or our child has to wear these old shoes that are too small for him now. And these are decisions my wife and I have to make every day, when we go to the market, when we're thinking of visiting a friend in a different city – what is more important, what to buy now and what can wait? Sometimes the kid wants chocolate, but we only buy lollipops because they are cheaper. This is difficult, earlier we didn't have to make such decisions, why do we have to do it now? I am working hard, my wife is working: we should be able to provide for the family. We're not beggars, we're intelligentsia. (Serhiy, B, m54, Physics and Maths teacher)

You have to stay for dinner with us. Hold on, let's just move the table towards the sofa. You know one of our chairs broke a few days ago – my daughter was rocking on it, and the chair's leg broke. So now we only have three chairs, just for us three, no guest chairs. So when guests come, we have to move this table towards the sofa, and somebody can sit on the sofa. This is not so bad, but I feel bad about it – not even being able to buy a new chair now – I saw one for forty hryvnias[2], but this is the money we have for food for a week! And we barely have any savings. It's New Year's soon, all these presents, a Christmas tree, my daughter is going to a play with her class, all this costs money. And we're not poor, there are poorer people than us, we are average, everybody lives like this and this is what makes me angry – this humiliation! You know, before there was some dignity in the work you did, but now you're feeling like a beggar! Oh, why am I telling you this? Sit down, please! (Svitlana, B, f38, Ukrainian language and literature teacher)

Charlesworth (2000, 52) presents an insightful account of the social suffering of the poor, who are economically deprived of satisfying their needs. He argues, that 'for the poor their situation means that the smallest aspects of existence are constituted from amidst a primal encounter with hardship and the humiliation that it generally involves'. The humiliation of Svitlana when she had to explain why there are not enough chairs in her house, or of Serhiy, who could not afford chocolate for his child or had to postpone a visit to his friend, are very well explained by Bourdieu (1984, 178) in his argument about the 'culture of necessity':

> The taste of necessity can only be the basis of a life-style 'in itself', which is defined as such only negatively, by an absence, by the relationship of privation between itself and the other lifestyles.

One may argue whether the situation of my respondents is truly that of 'necessity' and whether their own comparison of themselves with 'beggars' (note that both respondents used the same comparison) is adequate. After all, it is chocolate and visits to a friend that Serhiy has to postpone, not bread and milk. Similarly, Svitlana has found the money for her daughter to attend a theatre performance and to buy a Christmas tree and holiday presents. Indeed, for them it is 'not so much a question of whether they will survive, as it is the quality of their experiences in surviving' (Senett and Cobb 1977, 104).

In post-communist Ukraine the number of respondents who define themselves as poor is twice as high as the number of those who are officially defined as such (World Bank 1996). The question is whether it is the official statistics that underreport poverty and suffering, or whether it is the respondents who underestimate their situation, describing themselves as poorer than they really are. As a result of their 'survival strategies' people are not as poor as they present themselves. They do several jobs, often in the informal sector, keep their own garden plots, share with relatives and neighbours, exchange goods and services. My respondents were able to afford a lot more than what they would normally have if they had only relied on their official salary. Serhiy gave private lessons to his students and with his wife they had a big garden, chickens and a pig. Svitlana also had a garden, and in the summertime

---

2   Hryvnia is the Ukrainian currency (1 Hryvnia = 0.2 USD)

travelled to Kyiv to sell apricots, while her retired mother had an informal job in Kyiv, contributing to the family budget. What they gave as examples of their difficult situation were rather descriptions of the sacrifices they have to make every day to provide an adequate level of life and of the injustice of a system where an official salary is not enough for the most necessary things.

I believe that poverty is only overestimated if by 'poverty' one means passivity and 'not adapting'. In this context, indeed, the majority of the population has been active, resourceful and entrepreneurial. However, if one speaks of the material hardships that lead the poor to undertake these 'survival strategies' in order to defend their situation from getting worse, then poverty is, on the contrary, underestimated. My respondents show this very well when they simultaneously define themselves as poor yet refuse to be called poor. The say they are poor in order to complain about the injustice of a hierarchically stratified society where 'the majority of the population can barely make ends meet while a minority enjoys all the benefits of modern civilization' (Vera, B, f50, statistician). Yet they refuse to be called poor as this is 'passive' and 'not adapting' and refuse to distinguish their less well-off friends and relatives as such. Those of my respondents who answered 'average' to questions like 'where would you place yourself on the social ladder?' (one being the lowest position and seven – the highest), specified that what they meant was that the majority of the population is in similar conditions ('everybody lives like this'), or that they 'have no right to complain' because there are people who are worse off:

> I guess I'm average; most people I know live like me. Let's say, I'm four, maybe I have some friends at three or five. But this four, it's not like a good four. I know I can't complain. On the one hand, I'm not unemployed, they're at one, and I'm not working as a night guard for miserable money like our neighbour – he would be two, I guess. I have a job, and get my pay regularly, but my salary is not enough for anything, and I have to do a second job, and give private lessons – and I get so exhausted. And everyone is like that; everyone is dissatisfied with life, and with this system! So I think its not about positions – we could all stay at the same positions, but if everyone's level of life got higher, if the ladder itself started at a higher level… (Lena, K, f49, University lecturer)

> I don't know where I would place myself, but definitely in the lower half. But I also think that this lower half is much bigger, because most people are poor. I don't even know if I have a right to complain: at least I have a job. I could be worse off. There are people who are worse off, many of the people that I personally know, many people here in this village. At least I'm a doctor, I have some respect in the village, but all these people who lost jobs when our collective farm and our sugar beet factory closed down – their lives are really tough. And then they start drinking. So, yes, I could be worse off, I guess (Sasha, S, m57, general practitioner)

Having many friends or relatives with whom my respondents shared a common past, but who now occupy either much higher or much lower positions, also means that feelings of injustice of inequality and resistance to the adaptation discourse are unavoidable. Nostalgia for the communist past is used to refer to a situation when 'we were all equal' and to resist the division into those who 'have adapted' and those who haven't. The 'pervasive and forceful legacies of socialism in the nature and form of work and economic activity, of solidarity, community, social networks and of property relations' (Stenning 2005a, 237) mean that public sector workers are suffering not only 'against others' but also 'with others'. Rather than 'having failed to adapt' my respondents see that they and many people around them were deprived of many of the benefits they had under socialism.

Orientation Towards the Future

> The task to be accomplished is not the conservation of the past, but the redemption of the hopes of the past (Adorno and Horkheimer 1972, XV).

Social optimism depends on the economic situation in the country and much of the suffering (as suggested earlier) comes from material deprivation, inequalities and a difficult economic situation in the country. Thus, we can see how social dissatisfaction and suffering increased in 1998–99, when the Ukrainian economy was in crisis, and how suffering decreased at the beginning of 2000, when the economy was expanding. However, it also depends on the political situation and its 'openness', on the availability of different options for development and on the opportunities for personal engagement in the political process. Whether people 'agree' to suffer depends on whether they have the hope that the situation will improve (Bauman 1997) and whether they feel it is possible to do something to bring about social change. The enthusiasm of Ukrainians in 1991, when the country gained its independence after the break-up of the Soviet Union, and in 2005 when the corrupt oligarchic regime was overthrown during the Orange Revolution, and their increasing disappointment after the revolutions can be explained with Hannah Arendt's (1963) parallel from Rene Char about the 'lost treasure':

> A history of revolutions could be told in parable form as the tale of an age-old treasure which, under most varied circumstances, appears abruptly, unexpectedly, and disappears again, as though it were a fata morgana.

Hannah Arendt describes revolutions as moments 'between past and future', where the things that people did not like seem to belong to the past, and what they hoped for is still possible in the future. One of my respondents noted that:

> Back in 1991 I felt like something good could happen. You know, like something really could change, like all these people on the hunger strike in Kyiv, and all the protests against Chornobyl… and the coal miners… Like they couldn't just be standing there for nothing; it had to work! We knew we'd had enough and we wanted changes, there was this song during perestroika 'Our hearts demand changes, our eyes demand changes'. I can't even describe the feelings I had then. It was something beautiful. But then we lost our savings, then the economy collapsed, then when it was all over and everyone returned to work, except nothing was working. The people were betrayed, that's what

I say. And it's the same now. We had this Orange revolution, and I was there, I seriously was wearing this orange sweater to work all the time, even though I could have been fired, but I took the risk because I felt I wanted this change, and I felt… and we all felt so good. And now, what did we get? Life is the same as it was… (Vera, B).

This statement is very interesting, especially in light of the current discussions about the 'disappointment with the Orange Revolution' in Ukrainian and Western media and also when one speaks of 'nostalgia' as disappointment with the consequences of transition. We see here the difficulty in explaining the precise feelings Vera experienced, the precise things she was hoping for. All she tells us is that 'it was something beautiful' and that somehow she knew she wanted changes and she was ready to take the risks. As Simone Weil (1952) argues 'We have fallen into the trap of totalitarian systems because we were not at the height of something beautiful that was being born in us'. To place this in the post-socialist context, I would like to use Ost's (2005) book 'The defeat of solidarity' as an example. In it he argues that the leaders of the 'Solidarity' movement in Poland have betrayed the workers, who hoped for a more just and a less alienating political and economic system. The leaders of the Solidarity trade union did not remain faithful to the workers' interests. The 'lost treasure' of 1989 in Poland caused economic frustration and anger among the workers, who became the 'losers' of transition and are now portrayed in Western media as some archaic remnants of socialism, as a condition in need of alleviation.

Similarly, my respondents said that they knew 'what was wrong' under state socialism and they initially supported transition. However, as Hennadiy (S, m59, schoolteacher and museum worker) puts it, 'what was wrong and what we wanted to change remained, and what was true and what we wanted to keep disappeared'. My respondents also spoke of a 'betrayal' of their hopes, usually by the 'oligarchs, who never cared about the people' or by political leaders who 'only fight and shout a lot, but don't do anything' (Hennadiy, S). Betrayal also came from the state abandoning a number of its social commitments, and leaving the public sector workers to compensate, 'without being given all the necessary means, for the most intolerable effects and deficiencies of the logic of the market' and leaving them 'abandoned, if not disowned outright, in their efforts to deal with the material and moral suffering' (Bourdieu et al. 1999, 183). Common experiences of relative equality and stability under state socialism present a basis for solidarity and resistance to a system where inequalities and instability are the norm. But do these common past experiences represent a desire to return to the communist past? Why are people 'nostalgic for a socialism which they did not like very much when they had it but now sorely miss' (Kotz and Weir 1997)? Does 'missing' mean wanting the return of the past? Does it mean that the past was 'better'? If so, why did Vera 'demand changes' and saw 'something beautiful' in the possibility of change? I believe that when one speaks of suffering in relation to social change, it is important to note that respondents give not an 'eternal' image of the past, but rather a 'unique experience with the past' (Benjamin 1968, 242).

When my respondents said that life before perestroika was better, it should be read not as an accurate representation of life twenty years ago compared to now, but as a re-evaluation of the past coming from a present position and re-evaluation of the present through the past. Respondents went on to specify what things were 'better then': greater security, equality, social guarantees from the state. They sometimes also listed things that were 'better now' – more freedom, higher living standards, excitement with new opportunities – and those that were not open before (travelling abroad, starting own business), etc. Simone Weil's remarks on the social suffering of workers are insightful. She argues that instead of reading in workers' demands and in their hopes 'the cure for their misfortune' they should be read as 'the sign and token of their sufferings'.

> If they want control of engagement and nationalization, it is because they are obsessed by the fear of total uprootedness – that is, of unemployment. If they want the abolition of private property, it is because they have had enough of being admitted into wherever it is they work as immigrants allowed to enter on sufferance (Weil 1952, 51).

Similarly, nostalgia for the communist past does not show the superiority of the past system, but the 'uprootedness' caused by the present structural injustice. An adequate understanding of nostalgia is therefore not to see it as a desire to return to the past, but rather as a sign and token of the present sufferings and of the hopes and concerns for the future. As Zizek argues:

> Is not the ultimate source of Ostalgie (nostalgia for the Communist past) among many intellectuals (and ordinary people) from the defunct German Democratic Republic also a longing not so much for the Communist past, but rather for what that past might have been, for the missed opportunity of creating an alternative Germany? (Zizek 2005)

For my respondents and for many post-communist citizens, dominant discourses of transition and adaptation to new realities present no alternatives to neo-liberal capitalism. Therefore, expressing their suffering with others around the 'better' (albeit imaginary) past is perhaps one of the few ways of creating more open accounts of economic change, which show 'not only conflicts but alternatives, in the spaces opened up by the uncertainties and promises of post-socialism' (Stenning 2005a, 237).

References

Arendt, H. (1963) *On revolution*. (London: Faber and Faber).

Bauman, Z. (1997) *Postmodernity and its discontents*. (Cambridge: Polity).

Charlesworth, S. (2000) Social Suffering and Working-class life. In: Fowler, B. (ed) *Reading Boudieu on Society and Culture*. (Oxford: Blackwell).

Benjamin,W. (1968*)* Theses on the philosophy of history. In: *Illuminations.* (New York: Schocken Books).

Bourdieu, P. (1984) *Distinction: A social critique of the Judgement of Taste.* (Cambridge, MA: Harvard University Press)

Bourdieu, P. et al. (1999) *The weight of the world: social suffering in contemporary society.* (Stanford: Stanford University Press).

Hefferman, M. (1998) The Meaning of Europe: Geography and Geopolitics. (London: Edward Arnold)

Horkheimer, M. and Adorno, T. (1972) *Dialectics of Enlightment.* New York: Continuum. 1972, p. XV.

Hrek, N. and Yukhnovskyi, I. (2005*)* Buty chy ne buty seredniomu klasu v Ukrajini? (To be or not to be for the middle class of Ukraine? – In Ukrainian) *Dzerkalo Tyzhnia,* 17 (544), 7 – 13 May 2005.

Kagarlitsky, B. (2005) *Revolt of the middle masses.* <http://www.tol.cz>, 4 February 2005.

Kotz, D. and Weir, F. (1997) *Revolution from above: the demise of the Soviet system.* (London and New York: Routledge).

Manning, N. (1995) Social policy and the welfare state. In: Lane, D. (ed). *Russia in transition: politics, privatization and society.* (London and New York: Longman).

Ost, D. (2005) The defeat of solidarity: anger and politics in postcommunist Europe. (Cornell University Press).

Ramet, S. (1991) *Social currents in Eastern Europe.* (Durham and London: Duke University Press).

Senett, R. and Cobb, J. (1977) *The hidden injuries of class.* (Cambridge: Cambridge University Press).

Stenning, A. (2005a) Re-placing work: economic transformations and the shape of a community in post-socialist Poland. *Work, Employment and Society,* 19:2, 235–59.

———— (2005b) Where is post-socialist working class? Working-class lives in the spaces of (post-) socialism. *Sociology,* 39:5, 983–99.

Watson, P. (2000) Rethinking transition: Globalism, gender and class. In: *International feminist journal of politics,* 2:2, 185–213.

Weil S. (1952) *The need for roots.* (London, Henley and Boston: Routledge and Kegan Paul).

World Bank (1996) *Poverty in Ukraine.* Report No. 15602-UA. (Washington, DC: World Bank).

World Bank (2005) *Ukraine Job Study.* <http://www.worldbank.org>

Zizek, S. (2005) What might have been: imaginary history from 12 leading historians ed. Andrew Roberts. *London Review of Books,* 27:16.

About the authors

Aisalkyn Botoeva is currently involved in the Academic Fellowship Programme, which aims to support higher education in post-Soviet and former socialist countries. Her educational background is sociology: She received a bachelor's degree from the American University of Central Asia (Bishkek, Kyrgyzstan) and a master's degree from the Central European University in Budapest, Hungary. Her research interests lie in economic sociology and include the issues of consumption and economic transformations in post-Soviet countries.

David Duncan received a BA (with honours) in philosophy from Queen's University, Canada, and a master's degree from the Queen's School of Policy Studies. In 2005, he was the Visiting Scholar in Residence at the National Europe Centre, Australian National University, Canberra, and is currently a PhD candidate at the Centre of International Studies, University of Cambridge.

Elke Fein is a lecturer at the University of Freiburg/Brsg. where she currently teaches East European history and political theory. Her research interests include cultural and symbolic dimensions of the transition processes in Eastern Europe, the politics of history and memory, theories of culture and cultural change, discourse analysis and other qualitative social sciences research methodologies.

Noémi Kakucs completed her MA at the Gender Studies Department of the Central European University in 2006. She graduated in Hungarian and English studies at Pecs University in 2005. Her research focuses on how Hungary has integrated gender mainstreaming in national policy-making and examines the possible impediments (structural or ideological) to effective implementation.

E. Carina H. Keskitalo is a senior lecturer at the Department of Political Science at Umeå University in Sweden. She received her PhD from the University of Lapland, Finland in 2002. The research project in which she took part was supported by the EU-funded *BALANCE* project and the Academy of Finland-funded *Governance of Natural Resources in North-West Russia* project.

Katerina Koleva, LLM.Eur., (Saarbrücken) is a PhD student at the University of Saarbrücken, Germany and a temporary lawyer at the European Court of Human Rights.

Csongor Kuti, LLM, completed his SJD in comparative constitutional law at Central European University, Budapest in 2006.

Oksana Morgunova is a PhD student at the University of Edinburgh.

Dmitry Morgunov is a student at the University of St Andrews, Scotland.

Damiana Gabriela Otoiu is an assistant professor of political science at Bucharest University (Faculty of Political Science) and a PhD researcher at the Université Libre de

Bruxelles, Center for the Study of Political Life (CEVIPOL). She holds a BA in political science (2004) from Bucharest University and an MA in social science, École Doctorale en Sciences Sociales, Europe Centrale et Orientale. Her PhD dissertation is entitled *The (Re)privatisation of the Cities: Politics and Urban Property in Romania after 1989*. In 2005, she set up the Junior Research Group on 'Property Relations in Central and Eastern Europe' at the Institute for Political Research, Bucharest University.

Anastasiya Ryabchuk obtained a BA in sociology (with a minor in political science) at the National University of Kyiv-Mohyla Academy, Ukraine, and an MPhil in modern society and global transformations at the University of Cambridge, UK. She is currently a PhD student in sociology at the Ecole des Hautes Etudes en Sciences Sociales (EHESS) in Paris. Her areas of interest include homelessness, social inequality, poverty and social suffering in post-communist societies (with a focus on Ukraine).

Alla M. Samoletova is a PhD student in political science at the European University of St Petersburg, Department of Political Science and Sociology.

Róbert Sata completed his PhD at the Department of Political Science of the Central European University in 2006. He also holds an MA in international relations from the International University of Japan (2002) and an MA in political science, CEU (1999). His research focuses on normative questions of societal justice and equality, forms of minority protection, and collective minority rights theory.

Susanne Schatral, MA, studied the cultural history of Eastern Europe, history and cultural studies at the University of Bremen. She is currently a PhD candidate at the Jean Monnet Centre for European Studies at the University of Bremen. Her dissertation topic is *Women's Human Rights and Combating Trafficking. The Co-operation of International Organisations and Non-Governmental Organisations in Germany and the Russian Federation* (working title).

Diana Schmidt is a research associate at the Research Centre for East European Studies at the University of Bremen, Germany. She has worked on questions related to efforts of introducing global anti-corruption, environmental and democratic principles into the Russian context and on transnational networking with Russian civil society actors through the introduction of new internet communication technologies and foreign financial assistance.

Aleksandra Wyrozumska holds an MA in sociology from the University of Silesia, Katowice and an MA in nationalism studies from the Central European University, Budapest. At present she is a PhD research fellow at the Jean Monnet Centre for European Studies, University of Bremen.

Series Subscription

Please enter my subscription to the series *Changing Europe*, ISSN 1863-8716, as follows:

starting with
- ❏ volume # 1
- ❏ volume # ___
  - ❏ please also include the following volumes: #___, ___, ___, ___, ___, ___,

- ❏ the next volume being published
  - ❏ please also include the following volumes: #___, ___, ___, ___, ___, ___,

- ❏ 1 copy per volume   OR   ❏ ___ copies per volume

Subscription within Germany:

You will receive every volume at 1st publication at the regular bookseller's price – incl. s & h and VAT.

Payment:
- ❏ Please bill me for every volume.
- ❏ Lastschriftverfahren: Ich/wir ermächtige(n) Sie hiermit widerruflich, den Rechnungsbetrag je Band von meinem/unserem folgendem Konto einzuziehen.

Kontoinhaber: _____ Kreditinstitut: _____

Kontonummer: _____ Bankleitzahl: _____

International Subscription:

Payment (incl. s & h and VAT) in advance for
- ❏ 10 volumes/copies (€ 319.80)   ❏ 20 volumes/copies (€ 599.80)
- ❏ 40 volumes/copies (€ 1,099.80)

Please send my books to:

NAME_____ DEPARTMENT_____
ADDRESS _____
POST/ZIP CODE_____ COUNTRY _____
TELEPHONE _____ EMAIL_____

date/signature_____

A hint for librarians in the former Soviet Union: Your academic library might be eligible to receive free-of-cost scholarly literature from Germany via the German Research Foundation. For Russian-language information on this program, see
http://www.dfg.de/forschungsfoerderung/formulare/download/12_54.pdf.

Please fax to: **0511 / 262 2201 (+49 511 262 2201)**
or mail to: *ibidem*-Verlag, Julius-Leber-Weg 11, D-30457 Hannover,Germany
or send an e-mail: ibidem@ibidem-verlag.de

ibidem-Verlag

Melchiorstr. 15

D-70439 Stuttgart

info@ibidem-verlag.de

www.ibidem-verlag.de
www.edition-noema.de
www.autorenbetreuung.de